The Corporate Financiers

Great Minds in Finance

Series editor: **Professor Colin Read**

This series explores the lives and times, theories and applications of those who have contributed most significantly to the formal study of finance. It aims to bring to life the theories that are the foundation of modern finance, by examining them within the context of the historical backdrop and the life stories and characters of the 'great minds' behind them.

Readers may be those interested in the fundamental underpinnings of our stock and bond markets; college students who want to delve into the significance behind the theories; or experts who constantly look for ways to more clearly understand what they do, so they can better relate to their clients and communities.

Titles include:

The Life Cyclists

The Portfolio Theorists

The Rise of the Quants

The Efficient Market Hypothesists

The Corporate Financiers

Great Minds in Finance
Series Standing Order ISBN: 978–0–230–27408–2
(*outside North America only*)

You can receive future titles in this series as they are published by placing a standing order. Please contact your bookseller or, in case of difficulty, write to us at the address below with your name and address, the title of the series and the ISBN quoted above.

Customer Services Department, Macmillan Distribution Ltd, Houndmills, Basingstoke, Hampshire RG21 6XS, England

---

The Corporate Financiers

Williams, Modigliani, Miller, Coase, Williamson, Alchian, Demsetz, Jensen and Meckling

Colin Read
Professor of Economics, SUNY College at Plattsburgh, USA

palgrave
macmillan

First published 2015 by
PALGRAVE MACMILLAN

Palgrave Macmillan in the UK is an imprint of Macmillan Publishers Limited, registered in England, company number 785998, of Houndmills, Basingstoke, Hampshire RG21 6XS.

Palgrave Macmillan in the US is a division of St Martin's Press LLC, 175 Fifth Avenue, New York, NY 10010.

Palgrave Macmillan is the global academic imprint of the above companies and has companies and representatives throughout the world.

Palgrave® and Macmillan® are registered trademarks in the United States, the United Kingdom, Europe and other countries.

ISBN 978–1–137–34127–3

This book is printed on paper suitable for recycling and made from fully managed and sustained forest sources. Logging, pulping and manufacturing processes are expected to conform to the environmental regulations of the country of origin.

A catalogue record for this book is available from the British Library.

A catalog record for this book is available from the Library of Congress.

Typeset by MPS Limited, Chennai, India.

Transferred to Digital Printing in 2015

Contents

List of Figures

Series Preface

When one mentions the word "finance" to an interested and engaged listener, there can be one of many different reactions. The word may elicit a yawn from those who think of finance as the mundane process of ensuring the family savings will allow them to maintain in retirement the quality of life to which they have become accustomed. Students of finance, at college or in life, think of the term as a mechanism for a battle of wits, with buyers and sellers of securities pitting themselves against each other to see who can profit best from the same information. A banker might think of the conservative practices one employs with shareholder and depositor money by lending it back out to trustworthy businesses in the region, hopefully to earn a profit. And tax accountants and lawyers may think of the myriad of ways a corporation can organize to maximize owners' profits and minimize risk. Most listeners would prefer to relegate the intricacies of finance to an expert, as they would their legal or medical affairs.

Most people use the terms economics and finance synonymously. This misconception is understandable. The formal discipline of economics defines the laws or principles that govern the choices we make in meeting our needs. The term economics is derived from the Greek word *oikos*, meaning environment but also referring to one's house or life. It is combined with "nomics" from the Greek word *nomos* or "law of", to label the social science that studies our decisions in furthering our own interests.

To most people, these "economic" decisions are primarily thought of as financial because they often involve money. Households attempt to manage their income and wealth to ensure they are able to consume, in the present and the future, in ways that allow them to thrive. Such careful financial decisions that will govern our consumption now and in retirement are so critical for our well-being that it is natural for most people to consider finance as economics even though, more correctly, finance is a branch of economics that has significant and increasing relevance in the day-to-day and livelihood-defining decisions of us all and in the very function of the economy.

The field of finance is not mundane or routine. The discipline explains how value is created or destroyed, how markets allow individuals and institutions alike to plan for the long term, and how entities can hedge the risk inherent in an uncertain world and over the business cycle.

This series describes the life, times, theories, and applications of the great minds who contributed to the modern formal study of finance. Their collective contributions address the various interpretations of finance not through dry exposition and even drier equations, but through intuition and context, and a few equations and diagrams. Readers may be those interested in the fundamental underpinnings of our stock and bond markets, college students who want to delve into the significance behind the theories, and the experts who constantly look for ways to more clearly understand what they do so they can better relate to their clients and communities. The series provides important insights of great minds in finance within a context of their life and times. In doing so, I hope to bring life to the theories that are the foundation of modern finance.

This series covers the gamut of the study of finance, typically through the lives and contributions of great minds upon whose shoulders the discipline stands. From the significance of financial decisions over time and through the cycle of one's life, to the ways in which investors balance reward and risk, from how the price of a security is determined to whether these prices properly reflect all available information, and to the ways a corporation can create value and a market can measure it, we will look at the fundamental questions and answers in finance. We will delve into theories that govern personal decision making, those that dictate the decisions of corporations and other similar entities, and the public finance of government.

Some of the theories we describe may appear abstract and narrow. Others may seem obvious, once they are presented. A successful theory must be sufficiently narrow to make strong conclusions but broad enough to be useful. A theory that is general to the extreme will draw weak conclusions of little utility. The best theories draw the strongest possible conclusions from the weakest set of assumptions. And, a successful "unifying" theory in finance can replace a large number of lesser theories and concepts, just as physicists hold out for a unifying theory that can draw together their isolated understandings from a variety of specialties.

By focusing on the great minds in finance, we draw together the concepts that have stood the test of time and have proven themselves to reveal something about the way humans make financial decisions. These principles that have flowed from individuals who are typically awarded the Nobel Memorial Prize in Economics for their insights, or perhaps shall be awarded someday, allow us to see the financial forest for the trees.

While one might assume that every financial expert would be well-versed in these fundamental theories of finance, such is not always the case. An investor can succeed through sheer intuition without having studied the insights of theorists over a century of financial discovery. Mathematicians and physicists are increasingly employed to develop techniques that recognize patterns in numbers with little regard or understanding of the underlying forces that explain these patterns. And, computer experts can design algorithms that allow great banks of servers to constantly poke and prod the market to induce, and then profit from, movements in prices of stocks or bonds. By capitalizing on such shifts in prices milliseconds before others take notice, these algorithms can garner pennies, or fractions of pennies, at a time, thousands of times an hour, to yield huge profits.

These practitioners do not depend, or even care about the fundamental principles that drive markets and govern decision-making in the long run. To them, the long run expires within a week or a day. Such "technical analysis" is decidedly transient and short term. In fact, a steady and predictable investment opportunity based on well-known and well-understood information is simply insufficiently volatile to yield quick profits.

Unfortunately, such technical analysis that depends only on price dynamics in the short term has emerged as the lucrative Holy Grail of modern finance. It allows the most skilled practitioners to make money when markets are rising or falling. However, it reveals nothing about how financial decisions should be made in the long run to satisfy an economy's need for capital, investment, reward, and reduced risk. Nor does it make our economy more efficient. Rather, technical analysts devote a great deal of talent, energy, and effort as they clamor for others' pieces of a fixed economic pie.

The giants who have produced the theories and concepts that drive financial fundamentals share one important characteristic. They have developed insights that explain how markets can be used or tailored to create a more efficient economy. They demonstrate how individuals can trade risk and reward in the same way that a supplier might trade with a consumer of a good. They explain the reason for corporations, and also show why corporations can become too big. Through this process of analysis, all sides win. Greater efficiency is a tide that lifts all boats. These pioneers of finance explain how tools can be used to create greater market efficiency and even suggest the creation of new tools to create efficiency enhancements that may have proven elusive otherwise.

From a strictly aesthetic perspective, one cannot entirely condemn the tug-of-war of profits created by the technicians, even if they do little to enhance, and may even detract from, efficiency. The mathematics and physics of price movements and the sophistication of computer algorithms is fascinating in its own right. Indeed, my university studies began with a Bachelor of Science degree in physics, followed immediately by a Ph.D. in economics. However, as I began to teach economics and finance, I realized that the analytic tools of physics that so pervaded modern economics has strayed too far from explaining this important dimension of human financial decision-making. To better understand the interplay between the scientific method, economics, human behavior, and public policy, I continued on in my studies toward a Master of Accountancy in taxation, an M.B.A., and a Juris Doctor of law.

As I taught the economics of intertemporal choice, the role of money and financial instruments, and the structure of the banking and financial intermediaries, I recognized that my students had become increasingly fascinated with investment banking and Wall Street. Meanwhile, the developed world experienced the most significant breakdown of financial markets in almost eight decades. I realized that this once-in-a-lifetime global financial meltdown arose because we had moved from an economy that produced stuff to one in which a third of all profits by 2006 in the U.S. were made in financial markets, with little to show but pieces of paper representing wealth that had value only if some were ever ready to buy them.

I decided to shift my research from academic research in esoteric fields of economics and finance and toward better understanding of markets by the educated public. I began to write a regular business column and a book that documented the unraveling of the Great Recession. The book, entitled *Global Financial Meltdown: How We Can Avoid the Next Economic Crisis*, described the events that gave rise to the most significant economic crisis in our lifetime. I followed that book with *The Fear Factor*, which explained the important role of fear as a sometimes constructive, and at other times destructive influence in our financial decision making. I then wrote a book on why many economies at first thrive, and then struggle to survive in *The Rise and Fall of an Economic Empire*. Throughout, I try to impart to you, the educated reader, the intuition and the understanding that would, at least, help you to make informed decisions in increasingly volatile global economies and financial markets.

As I do so, I also hope to impart to you how individuals born without great fanfare can be regarded as geniuses in their lifetime. The lives of each of the individuals treated in this series become extraordinary, not because they made an unfathomable leap in our understanding, but rather because they looked at something in a different way and caused us all to forever look at the problem in this new way. That is the test of genius.

Colin Read

Preamble

This book is the fifth in a series of discussions about the great minds in the history and theory of finance. While the series as a whole addresses the contributions of significant individuals to our understanding of financial decisions and markets, this volume explores something we all take for granted and assume we understand, but which is much more nuanced and complicated once we begin to peer into its black box – how corporations create value.

It is unlike previous volumes in the series, in which the great minds – often without strict adherence to complex mathematical formulas – describe how corporations create value through their decisions regarding capital structure, governance, compensation policies, and the myriad implicit contracts they negotiate and renegotiate. Instead, the great minds in this volume show through impeccable logic how we can measure corporate value, and when a corporation's capital structure may, or may not, matter in its strategic decisions for expansion. These great minds also show just how important it is to define implicit contracts for the entities within the firm that generate corporate value, and the problems that may arise if corporate governance is blissfully unaware of the tensions between the corporation and those charged with doing its work.

This volume describes the theories governing the creation and measurement of corporate value not in isolation, but rather in the context of the void in understanding which these great minds successfully filled. You will first discover the early lives of these great minds because I believe that their life experiences informed their great insights. I then describe the times in which they lived and their significant theories and insights into financial decisions, followed by the various ways their insights were applied to benefit others. I close each section with the reasons the Nobel Memorial Prize in Economics committee recognized many of their contributions and a discussion of their legacies in financial history.

1
Introduction

Corporations create value. Financial intermediation in the United States represented just 2 percent of Gross Domestic Product in 1870, but this had risen to almost 9 percent of GDP by 2010.[1] The addition of direct business investment brings this share to more than 18 percent of GDP, or about double the representation of finance markets in the size of the American economy. This mobilization of capital supported the rapid expansion of global trade over the period of the Industrial Revolution. But, the freezing of capital markets has plunged nations and the world into recessions and depressions on several different occasions, including the recent Global Financial Meltdown. Even the layperson now realizes that financial markets are essential for the smooth operation of the global economy. Yet, while most all this activity depends crucially on the correct valuation of the value corporations create, accurate models of corporate value have existed for only the last few generations.

In 1776, just as a new nation declared its independence from Great Britain, the global economic superpower of the day, Adam Smith, in his *An Inquiry into the Nature and Causes of the Wealth of Nations*, offered the first treatment of the creation of corporate value.[2] More than a century and a half later, Ronald Coase's *The Nature of the Firm*, treated below, began to formalize the foundations for our understanding of the role of the entrepreneurial manager in creating value within the firm. In that same era, Frank Hyneman Knight (November 7, 1885–April 15, 1972) described the nature of risk and the risk–reward trade-off.[3] And, at about the same time as Coase described the nature of a firm, a little known financial analyst in Boston, with the aristocratic name John Burr Williams, created the first thorough treatment of how rational markets ought to capitalize the value corporations create.

As we shall see, the contributions of both Williams and Coase went underappreciated for several decades. This oversight can be attributed to the compelling beauty of scholars' focus on an alternate, and more mathematical, but less helpful, description of the market system, known as the neoclassical model, in sharp contrast to the untidy, complex, and nuanced inner workings of the modern corporation.

This volume documents the rise of our understanding of the capital structure and value creation of the modern corporation since 1937. I begin by providing a brief description of what we thought we understood for so long, since the publication of Adam Smith's *Wealth of Nations*. I demonstrate that so much work was done to formalize Smith's depiction of markets, and with such fantastic economy and success, that finance and economics scholars proceeded to pat ourselves on the back and reveled in what we now call the neoclassical model. From its inception in 1969, the first few presentations of the Nobel Memorial Prize in Economic Sciences recognized those still living economists and financial theorists who contributed to our understanding of the modern market economy. Almost every prize over the last couple of decades has encouraged a different line of discovery. They have increasingly recognized those theorists that help explain when and why the neoclassical model does not work well, and how to correct these flaws. The Committee also began to recognize those individuals who help determine the nuanced and myriad ways value is created within the walls of the modern corporation.

In this book I tell a story of this process of our discovery of corporate value. I begin with a brief description of the neoclassical model. I do so in much less detail than is treated in the other volumes of this series that are devoted to the workings and mathematical detail of financial markets. Instead, I provide an overview of the reasons why such a compelling neoclassical model of markets captivated the majority of our attention for so long.

I then move on to describe the life, times, and contributions of John Burr Williams. Williams, trained as a chemical engineer at Harvard, became both fascinated and flummoxed by the gyrations of financial markets in the 1920s and 1930s. When Williams was young his father was a senior executive for a large American insurance company, so Williams understood that market fundamentals, based on his model of the discounted cash flow of corporate earnings, do not fluctuate to nearly the extent suggested by their stock prices. Williams set out to correct what he saw as a failure of financial markets to properly perceive value. In doing so, he developed the principal models of corporate earnings valuation that we now call *fundamentals analysis* and which is now taught in every 'introduction to corporate finance' class.

At the same time, but for very different reasons, a British scholar named Ronald Coase produced a classic treatise on the nature of value creation within the firm. He, too, was inspired by the events of the Great Depression. Around the time he completed his undergraduate studies at the London School of Economics, he was offered a scholarship to travel around Depression-era United States for a summer to study how great American companies create value with so much more efficiency than their British counterparts. These American businesses had increasingly pioneered a more scientific approach to corporate efficiency following the World War I. Coase visited both shop floors and executive offices and returned enamored with both American commerce and the United States itself. The result of his travels was a little appreciated paper that described how he saw corporate value created within the corporation. In doing so, he reinvented a *New Institutional Economics* that relies on arguments which more closely resemble the way law is studied rather than the increasingly mathematical approach that was, and remains, in vogue in finance and economics.

Coase's work went either unappreciated or underappreciated for decades. He had written during the height of the Great Depression at a time when desperate nations sought explanations of the failure of global markets. A year after John Maynard Keynes (June 5, 1883–April 21, 1946) produced his seminal 1936 contribution to the ways in which a modern economy functions,[4] Coase described the creation of corporate value in *The Nature of the Firm*. A generation later, Coase produced another seminal paper, *The Problem of Social Cost*,[5] which attracted much more attention. In his later paper, he applied his same logic about the importance of the reduction of transactions costs within the corporation to the implications of zero transactions costs on market transactions. His revolutionary approach caused scholars to take a second look at his earlier paper and over the course of the ensuing decade, there sprouted a new field, now called *New Institutional Economics*.

Coase was remarkable and unusual not only in the clarity of his intuition and observations, but also in his reliance not on the compactness and formality of mathematics but rather on logic and painstaking descriptions of previously inadequately described institutions. As a consequence, his analyses were very accessible and provocative to scholars and practitioners alike. However, he wrote at a level of generality that required more formal treatment if professors were to teach his concepts, business leaders were to incorporate them, and financial analysts were to be able to use his ideas to demonstrate the potential for corporations to create synergistic profits and an intangible asset value in excess of their book value. Often, courts had to mediate disputes over this *goodwill*, and they too needed a more meaningful explanation of how such intangible value is created. Coase, and his followers, provided that explanation.

In the next dozen years, three sets of scholars each elaborated upon the concepts created by Coase. First, Oliver Williamson offered a much more formal description of the nature of the transactions costs a firm can avoid by creating value in-house. Coase had presented the concept that a firm creates value by avoiding the costly exercise of contracting within the marketplace each time it needed to complete a process. According to his analysis it can economize instead by insourcing these processes with employees and entities with whom it can negotiate and renegotiate an implicit production contract as often and as inexpensively as possible. The economy of these implicit internal contracts offers the corporation an advantage over the more cumbersome, and necessarily more generic free market. Williamson described such a *nexus of contracts* as the primary advantage a corporation can exploit to create value. Contrary to conventional wisdom, he even argued that increased *vertical integration* of a corporation can enhance these opportunities. Rather than an economic threat, vertical integration can act as an efficiency enhancer and a value creator.

Coase and Williamson shared a quality that others would subsequently follow. Both scholars adopted a multidisciplinary approach to their explorations. In fact, their work was almost immediately embraced by corporate law scholars who would otherwise avoid more technical treatises in economics and finance. Indeed, both Williamson and Coase became closely associated with the law schools at their respective institutions, and each helped found and edit a new journal that combined the disciplines of law and economics.

Their work directed corporate leaders to ways in which value can be enhanced, sometimes by combining units, and, at other times, by breaking up units that have become so complex that the necessary implicit contracting within a firm became cumbersome and bureaucratic. However, Coase and Williamson would leave to others the identification of other related forms of corporate value, even though they hinted at additional avenues for research.

As Coase and Williamson were developing the *New Institutional Economics*, a pair of more mainstream scholars, eventual Nobel Prize laureates Franco Modigliani and Merton Miller, permanently established in the modern study of corporate finance what Williams intuited decades earlier – that corporations can expand using debt or equity with equal efficiency. Meanwhile, two other pairs of scholars offered these additional insights. Michael Jensen and William Meckling described a new vocabulary, called the *principal–agent problem*, or *agency theory*, that could be employed to more fully describe the nature of the relationship between a principal who wants to have a task performed to satisfy its goals, and an agent it hires to perform the task. Unless the understanding and the *quid pro quo* of the mutual relationship between the principal and the agent is well-specified and exceedingly well-designed, the differing preferences of the principal and the agent invariably create suboptimal results. Once the divergent goals of the principal and the agent are better described, a better implicit or explicit contract can be created.

Jensen and Meckling's approach proved to be a framework that not only described and helped correct the divergent goals of principals and agents on the shop floor, but also demonstrated potential misalignments between the goals of the shareholders and the corporation's executive officers. Jensen and Meckling's approach created an entire literature on the optimal design of compensation schemes that align the principal's goals with the agent's performance and compensation. This topic remains one of the most intuitive and discussed factors among corporate directors, and even for regulators intent on ensuring that our financial system does not again suffer the meltdown that was induced by poorly designed compensation schemes.

Finally, Armen Alchian and Harold Demsetz helped to insert two additional terms into the corporate vernacular. They described the concepts of *moral hazard* and *shirking*, which allow us to more fully understand some of the human forces that Jensen and Meckling sought to avoid. The term *moral hazard* has been used in recent decades to describe the dangers that loom when an individual or entity makes financial decisions not based on whether they contribute to overall corporate and economy-wide efficiency, but rather on the perverse incentives offered to the agent. For instance, banks too big to fail may take on greater than optimal risk based on their ability to capitalize on potentially large profits if the risk pans out, but with the knowledge that taxpayers may indemnify their costly mistakes if the risk instead causes a significant financial loss. This notion and the problems that arise when there are privatized gains and socialized losses is exactly the scenario envisaged by Alchian and Demsetz.

Like Coase and Williamson before them, both Alchian and Demsetz and Jensen and Meckling formed bridges across disciplines and were likewise embraced by both legal and financial scholars.

In this series, we have described how markets measure value and securities prices and how individuals plan accordingly and arrange their personal finances based on the functioning of markets. But, until the scholars discussed in this volume directed their attention to the inner workings of corporate value creation, it has remained difficult to quantify such creation of value. The scholars in this volume correct our oversight. In doing so, they created a renewed interest in New Institutional Economics that is much more useful conceptually to corporate leaders, directors, analysts, and managers alike. At the same time, they have spawned a series of elaborations that further describe the challenges corporations must overcome and the value they can create. In doing so, these scholars reshaped the theory of the firm and the intuition that is now broadly understood and applied by practitioners who live outside the Ivory Tower of academia.

The theories of these great minds also represent a departure of sorts from the other branches of finance contained in this series. Beyond the formal mathematical analytics of John Burr Williams, most of the great ideas described here can easily be described through words rather than equations. Some of the ideas presented here could also be represented in mathematical form, but the mathematics would provide no great insights into the problems recognized by these great minds. The New Institutional Economics created by these great minds in finance provides a plethora of important insights, but without the burden of advanced mathematics required for other areas of finance treated in this series. As a consequence, the concepts presented here remain both timely and accessible.

Section 1
From Art to Science

The study of the theory of the firm enjoyed a renaissance in the period between the two world wars, but also suffered a curse. Our scrutiny of markets relied on the bright light of a scientific method borrowed from an era of physics that discovered the theory of relativity and quantum mechanics. Many of the same principles were applied to our study of markets and of corporations. By adopting these highly mathematical tools, we had to make a Faustian choice. Because nature is most efficient, one of the primary tools of the analysis of optimization is calculus. To rely on this powerful tool, financial theorists must assume that individual market participants are rational, and profit opportunities are usurped through arbitrage, just as a gas seeks to fill a vacuum and water seeks its own level. By adopting to hastily these convenient and plausible analogies, we glossed over the art of describing the nuances that make every economic entity somewhat unique. We are instead left with what we now know, for better or worse, as the neoclassical model.

John Burr Williams, an engineer by training, took these analogies of arbitrage and optimization and applied them to measure corporate value. While we still use his discounted cash flow model today in our *fundamentals analysis* of corporations, we also still rely perhaps too readily and conveniently on the neoclassical model. Yet, the analysis of corporate value is, in some sense, at odds with a competitive neoclassical model that predicts firms cannot earn profits in excess of the risk-adjusted rate of return on their investment.

2
A Fly in the Ointment

In 1776, economics became a discipline and studies of the advantages of the corporate structure became its primary subject of analysis. Ever since Adam Smith's *An Inquiry into the Nature and Causes of the Wealth of Nations*, economics has rejoiced in and been hindered by what we now refer to as the neoclassical model.

The neoclassical model is somewhat of a paradox, however. In essence, it states that competitive forces ensure that there cannot in reality be any supernormal, or excessive profits. These same competitive forces require firms to strive constantly for greater efficiency. Profit is simply the fair return earned for the risk and sacrifice made by the capitalist. If these profits are excessive, greater capital will flow into similar enterprises until these profits become proportional to risk alone.

Such a competitive ideal embodies a number of assumptions. First, it assumes information is perfect and costless. Second, it assumes there are no barriers to entry or exit in an industry, and nor are there any barriers to exchanges and contracting. Third, there is no market power on either side of an exchange. Finally, all participants are fully rational. In essence, the competitive ideal states that, unless one possesses some ability or scarce factor in short supply, profits are fleeting, and imitation is rampant.

The model is somewhat paradoxical because it predicts that entrepreneurs can, at best, eke out a living in a competitive market. In the neoclassical world without significant barriers to entry, there can, in the long run, be no profitable firm within a competitive market. Yet entrepreneurs constantly attempt to form corporations to earn its owners profits above the risk-adjusted rate of return.

This neoclassical model describes one extreme, called the competitive ideal. The other extreme is that of a monopolist who has complete market power, who prices not based on costs but on what the market will bear, and who can consistently extract profits in perpetuity, at least until someone else invents a better mousetrap.

After almost a quarter of a millennium, both these extremes are incredibly thoroughly described in the economics and finance literature. Unfortunately, neither extreme well describes the regimes within which the vast majority of corporations operate. Indeed, if an entrepreneur were told that the most, and perhaps the least, one could expect for their greater intuition and insight was a fair return to their sweat and equity, there probably would be little incentive to innovate.

In fact, the common perception among financial academics and practitioners is that it is possible to create value by simply doing things better than the rest. The neoclassical model does not preclude such a possibility, but instead chalks up such an innovation as fleeting, or arising from the successful marketing of a scarce and unique resource that only the lucky entrepreneur can employ. Until a few great minds in corporate finance emerged, the literature instead devoted most all its energy to describing the ideals and proving the rule, even when all the financial energy was devoted to proving the exception. And, to analysts, every corporation is the exception to the rule.

The competitive ideal is compellingly beautiful, in terms of both its intuition and its mathematics. For much of the history of what we call neoclassical economics, in fact ever since Adam Smith described the economies of scale of a pin manufacturer who employs what were then modern manufacturing techniques, economists have displayed a faith that a competitive equilibrium exists. Indeed, the theoretical existence of such an ideal, in a world of perfect and frictionless markets and of perfect information employed by fully rational agents, was proven only as late as 1959 by the great mind Kenneth Arrow. He also gave us a number of related results that provided the basis of modern security pricing. Perhaps enamored by the elegance of the competitive ideal and Arrow's contingent securities pricing, little effort was devoted to explaining how individual corporations create value. But without this understanding of value creation, the financial analyst's role was an art rather than a science.

By the turn of the twentieth century, economics was quite settled on the neoclassical model and the competitive ideal. Over the ensuing century, much of the work has been devoted to firming up the mathematics and the intuition. Most research that attempted to relax the assumptions of the neoclassical model, or, worse, to call into question the appropriateness of the assumptions, was considered to be outside the mainstream. Some work, however, was devoted to the relaxation of the assumption of perfect information, and this effort constituted the bulk of the work within the neoclassical model. It had the advantage in that, if one could construct, or assume, metrics for the level or distribution of information, the approach could generate nicely quantifiable results that led, in the limit, to the competitive ideal as information became perfect.

Under this approach, information could be viewed as a scarce factor of production and hence should earn a reward. One could then view the corporation as an entity that attempts to capitalize on its superior information. However, while such an extension is interesting and intuitive, it provides little guidance to managers who seek to create value within their enterprises.

Less embraced were those who proposed an abandonment of the assumption of rationality. While a relaxation of the information requirement could be viewed as tinkering around the edge of the neoclassical model, a repeal of the assumption of perfect rationality was, and for many still remains, economic heresy.

The great minds described here had the courage first to create a science out of the art of corporate valuation, and then to offer a much more nuanced approach to the discussion of how a corporation creates value. Most of these great minds won Nobel Memorial Prizes for their work, but one remained in relative obscurity until the importance of his work was acknowledged more recently by the mainstream finance literature. While John Burr Williams' early work, and the related contributions by Franco Modigliani and Merton Miller, are recognized, and constitute the bulk of most every *Introduction to Corporate Finance* textbook, Williams' results are often attributed to others who were academics rather than practitioners, and who were perhaps more elegant in their mathematics or rhetoric.

Nonetheless, each of the contributors included in this volume has made a lasting contribution to the theory of corporate finance and has offered insights to managers and analysts alike. Their intuitions are compelling. They offer a lens through which one can view the corporation and can use to recognize excellence that does not go unrewarded by the market.

To its credit, the committee charged with determining the recipients of the Nobel Memorial Prize in the Economic Sciences now often eschews conventional wisdom and rewards those who have the courage to think about important topics in new and potentially fruitful ways. While the great minds discussed here are sometimes relegated to the bastions of *institutional economics*, their insights give meaning and understanding to the valuation of modern corporations.

The intensely mathematical nature of the neoclassical model unfortunately obscured what was most important about economics. Markets are a mechanism for trade, and yet the mathematical complexities of the neoclassical model obscure the fundamental nature of trade, the transaction itself. Without a good understanding of the nature of the transaction, and any impediments to a smooth exchange without unnecessary costs, it is an esoteric exercise to understand the ideal market assumed by the neoclassical model.

The contributors to this volume understand that these transactions costs are the very reason why the corporate form has an advantage in the marketplace. Markets are excellent institutions to exchange commodities at arm's length when there is little of importance but the price and the available quantity. However, most products require many steps to produce. And each of these steps may require multiple arrangements, transactions, and coordinations. These elements can be costly if they don't each embody a set of predetermined conditions and arrangements. A firm can streamline these understandings and create efficiencies where there may otherwise be market failures. The great minds in this volume explain those elements that give the firm a value greater than the sum of its tangible assets.

3
The Early Life of John Burr Williams

John Burr Williams was the founding father of a new field of corporate finance. This seems somehow appropriate since his ancestors founded a new nation, and he wore their names like a badge.

John Burr Williams' first name is a variation of a name of the first American patriarch, Jehu Burr, who encouraged his sons, Jehu, Daniel, and Benjamin, to travel to America as indentured servants on the Winthrop Fleet in 1630. The fleet was a group of 11 ships that sailed to Salem, Massachusetts from Yarmouth on the Isle of Wight in the spring of 1630. The ships, which left in two waves, arrived in the new colony in June and July. Funded by the Massachusetts Bay Company, many of those 500 settlers who survived to the end of 1630 (of the 700 who had started out on the voyage) were indentured to the Company.

The first of the Burr family to arrive in the new Massachusetts Colony on the Winthrop Fleet was Jehu Bhurr, or Burr. Named after his father, Jehu and his wife, Elizabeth Cable, were followed later by two of Jehu's brothers. Jehu's brother, Benjamin Burr (1602–1637), arrived soon thereafter, and settled in the Hartford Connecticut area. Another brother, Daniel, also came to the new colony.

Upon his arrival, Benjamin and his young wife, Anne Hanna, set out through dense and mature forests to make their way to found the town of Hartford, Connecticut. This Hartford clan of the Burr family represented a variety of occupations – merchants, loggers, sawyers, farmers, tradesmen. They also became landowners who were well respected, and soon acquired considerable wealth.

These rural Burrs had large families to help run their farms, but, unlike Benjamin's brother Jehu and his descendants, they eschewed politics and preferred the rural life. They were pioneers seeking frontiers that would provide them with privacy, and economic and religious freedom. They proved to be tenacious and bold.

On the other hand, Jehu's clan reveled in politics. He had first settled in the Roxbury, Massachusetts area, and earned his freedom on May 18, 1631. Soon thereafter, he was drawn into colony building under William Pynchon (October 11, 1590–October 29, 1662). Pynchon was one of the original patentees of the Massachusetts Bay Colony and amassed great wealth for himself and for the men who followed him. He also gained notoriety by writing a book deemed scandalous at that time because it argued that one could seek atonement through obedience to God rather than through punishment and repentance. His *The Meritorious Price of Our Redemption* was so scandalous that it was burned in Boston and attained infamy as the first book banned in the New World. The controversy forced him to return to England for fear of his own safety. There, he remained to his death. He was followed much later by a more celebrated American novelist, Thomas Pynchon (May 8, 1937–).

Jehu remained in the Springfield area Pynchon had created. There, he became the tax collector for the Connecticut Colony. Then, in April 1638, he was elected the Deputy for Springfield for the Connecticut Legislature. From there, he moved his family to Fairfield, Connecticut.

When the first and second generations of American settlers were born in the colonies, the descendants of Jehu, Benjamin, and Daniel were named for these first settlers. Jehu had a son he named Daniel (1642–95), who in turn named his own son Daniel (1670–1748). Meanwhile, Benjamin had a grandson named Jonathan Burr (1679–1735). These two second cousins continued on the political and industrious branches of the Connecticut Burrs, respectively.

The two branches continued in their ways. Of the political Burrs, Daniel's son and namesake, fathered Aaron Burr.

Aaron Burr became a renowned reverend, founded Princeton University, and fathered Aaron Burr, Jr., the vice president to the third president of the United States, Thomas Jefferson.

While Aaron Burr, Jr. reveled in politics, it could be suggested that politics may not have agreed with him. Early on, George Washington had said "By all that I have known and heard, Colonel Burr is a brave and able officer, but the question is whether he has not equal talents at intrigue."[1] Given the Aaron Burr legacy, Jefferson was unwilling to have Burr remain on the ticket for his re-election, so Burr ran, and lost spectacularly, for Governor of New York in 1804. In the run-up to the election, Alexander Hamilton, the United States' first Treasury Secretary,

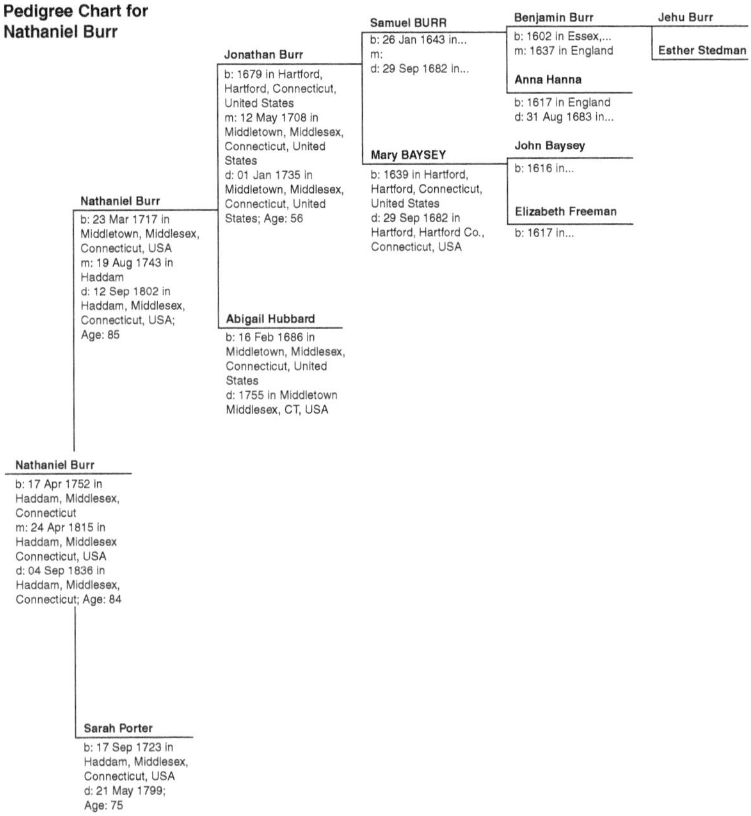

Figure 3.1 The Ancestors of John Burr Williams

was quoted as saying that Burr was "a dangerous man, and one who ought not be trusted with the reins of government".[2] Aaron Burr responded by challenging Hamilton to a duel in New Jersey. Hamilton's pistol discharged prematurely in that duel, which afforded Burr time and an opportunity to shoot Hamilton. Hamilton was brought to nearby Manhattan, in New York, where he died the following day. Because duels had recently been banned in New Jersey, Burr was tried, but was not convicted because Hamilton had died in New York. The duel was the end of Burr's political career, if not his aspirations.

Meanwhile, the direct ancestors of John Burr Williams, the Benjamin Burr branch of the family, continued to thrive in their rural existence. The son, Jonathan Burr, had a son, grandson (and fourth cousin to

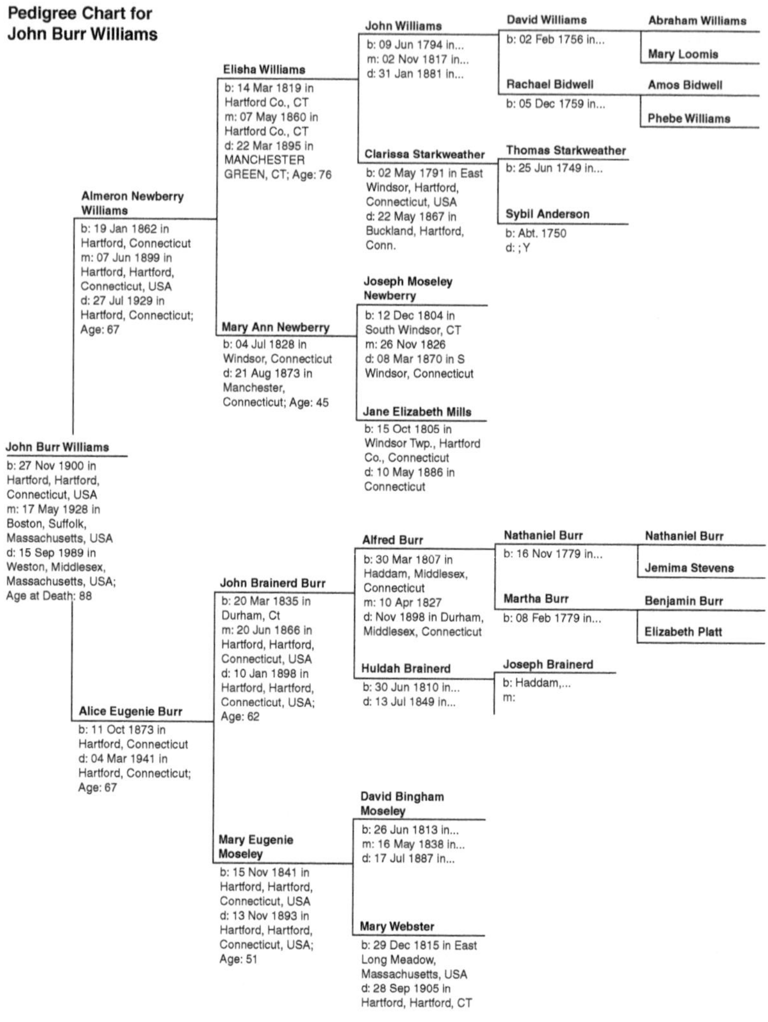

Figure 3.2 The Family Tree of John Burr Williams

Aaron Burr, Jr.), and great grandson, who were all given the name Nathaniel. The third of these Nathaniels was Nathaniel Burr (November 16, 1779–1860), the great great grandfather of John Burr Williams.

Nathaniel and Martha Burr (February 8, 1779–January 18, 1828) had a son, Alfred (March 30, 1807–November 1898). Alfred, in turn, had a son, John Brainerd Burr (March 20, 1835–January 10, 1898) with his wife, Huldah Brainerd (June 30, 1810–Jul 13, 1849). John and his wife, Mary Eugenie Moseley (November 15, 1841–November 13. 1893), then had a daughter, Alice Eugenie Burr (October 11. 1873–March 4, 1941), John Burr Williams' mother.

As the Burrs demonstrated, there is a strong tradition among early American pioneers of carrying forward family maiden names in the names of their offspring. John Burr Williams' name maintained this tradition by continuing on the Burr name as his middle given name. The Williams portion of his heritage, while perhaps less colorful, is no less pioneering.

Two English pioneers, William Williams (1623–December 17, 1689) and Jane Westover (1626–December 25, 1689), separately sailed from England to the colonies in the 1630s or 1640s, and met and married in Hartford, Connecticut on November 25, 1647. William Williams came to America as a cooper (or barrel maker). The pioneering couple raised a family, including a son, John Williams (1650–1713). William and Jane died within eight days of one another, in 1689.

The son John Williams also raised a son named John (May 22, 1687–September 15, 1723). These pioneers defined a lineage of Williams who resided in Hartford County, Connecticut for generations.

The younger John Williams and his wife Sarah (1699–1775) raised a boy, Abraham (1718–1807) who, with his wife Mary Loomis (1728–1809) parented David Williams (February 2, 1756–October 15, 1839). David and his wife Rachael Bidwell (December 5, 1759–December 24, 1828) raised John Williams (June 9, 1794–January 31, 1881), John Burr Williams' great grandfather and namesake.

John Williams and his wife, Clarissa Starkweather (May 2, 1791–May 22, 1867), had a large farming family of three girls and three boys. Their firstborn, a son named Elisha Williams (March 14, 1819–March 22, 1895), followed in the family footsteps and became a farmer and a grocer in Manchester, Connecticut, just north of Hartford. He and his wife, Mary Ann Newberry (July 4, 1828–August 21, 1873) of nearby Windsor, raised two sons.

The younger of these sons, Almeron Newberry Williams (January 19, 1862–July 27, 1929), began his life on the family farm in the Hartford area, then married Alice Eugenie Burr, of the Hartford-based Burr farming family. After attending public school, Almeron entered the insurance industry. He worked first as a stenographer in the Hartford office of the Phoenix Fire Insurance Company. He was transferred to the Rochester, New York office, and was subsequently beckoned back to Hartford to run its western New England region. In May of 1897, he

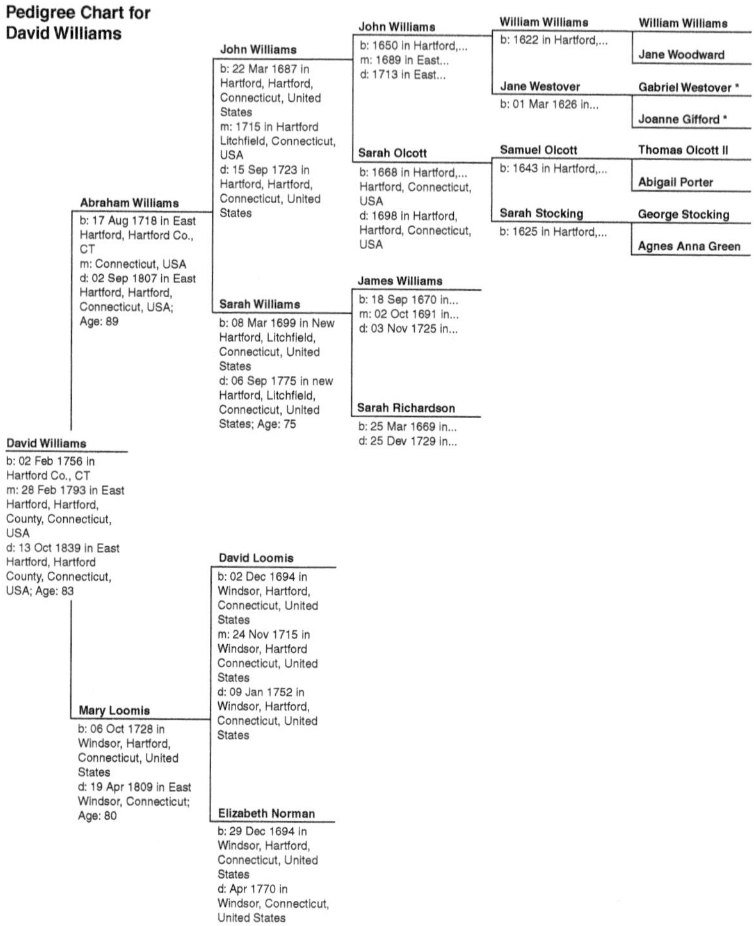

Figure 3.3 The Williams Side of John Burr Williams Family

joined the Aetna Insurance Company in Hartford, and rose first to its assistant corporate secretary, and then, in 1912, to its vice presidency.[3]

Almeron and Alice had married on June 7, 1899, and had a son, John Burr Williams, born November 27, 1900 in Hartford, Connecticut, followed by two girls, Pauline (September 29, 1903–January 3, 1935) and Eugenie (January 10, 1910–?). The family enjoyed an upper-middle-class lifestyle in an upper-middle-class neighborhood in West Hartford. The family home, at 34 Evergreen Avenue, was a nice Victorian home near the Hartford Theological School (now the University of Connecticut

School of Law) and within a couple of blocks of the Connecticut residence where humorist Mark Twain (November 30, 1835–April 21, 1910) raised his own family.

From this comfortable upper middle-class upbringing, John Burr Williams had opportunities that had never been granted to his farming ancestors. When it came time for him to attend school, all opportunities were available to him. Adept at science, he excelled in high school, and attended Harvard University with the aim of studying mathematics and chemistry. In 1923, at the age of 22 he graduated from Harvard with his bachelor's degree.

This was a period when the United States was still recovering from the strains of World War I and was also experiencing a dramatic reshaping of the economy. Manufacturing was growing rapidly at this time but without rampant inflation, in part because of the greater economies of scale and efficiency improvements occurring in industry but also because of the increased corporatization of farming and its intendant increases in efficiency. Rural areas were suffering from a collapse in commodity prices, and many rural savings and loans banks were to fold throughout the Roaring Twenties. As in many other periods of financial volatility, the insurance industry that employed John Burr Williams' father was growing rapidly and consolidating throughout this period. Williams' formative years throughout college and through the beginning of his career in finance occurred during one of the most dynamic periods of innovation and shifting global power.

The investing world of the 1920s was dramatically different from what we observe now, however. Williams' father, by this time was a senior executive of the Phoenix Insurance company. In an era before the Securities and Exchange Commission, he showed his son how a company's balance sheets could obscure its equity in subsidiaries in an attempt to keep the stock price down, yet still maintain the financial resources from these subsidiaries to pay handsome dividends. As a result, the dividend yield was higher for these companies that could conceal corporate earnings.

In that era of American tax policy, dividends were free from income tax, but capital gains were not. It was left for clever security analysts, then called statisticians, to ferret out these gems on balance sheets so that they could earn profits for the shrewdest of investors. Knowledge of this financial wizardry, often employed in the insurance industry, would eventually become an important element of young John Burr Williams' analytic toolbox, and would later motivate his subsequent academic work.

Williams was a mathematically precocious young man. With a degree from Harvard with specializations in mathematics and chemistry, and with his father's encouragement and influence, Williams continued on across the Charles River to the Harvard Business School. There he was immersed in the statistical methods of the day that were able to successfully remove 'noise' such as seasonal variations from financial data.

But, despite great inroads in statistical sophistication, or perhaps because of them, the statisticians of the day failed to predict the eventual collapse of financial markets at the end of the Roaring Twenties. Williams lamented that there remained much to be understood about the economy and the workings of financial markets. He set out to put financial markets on a firmer theoretical footing.

The subject of Williams' pet study at the time was the Travelers Insurance Company, a Hartford company that eventually evolved from his father's insurance firm. In his final year at graduate school in business, Williams wrote a long paper on how such a company could conceal large profits from statisticians' scrutiny, especially in the particularly competitive insurance industry. He realized they did so by reinvesting their profits into the expansion of their business. Certainly, this would mean that their asset base and earnings would grow, as would their share prices, as they internally funded the company's expansion. However, the analytic techniques of the day did not properly model and capture such growth as an explanation of the rising share value for such firms. Williams's curiosity and observations were leading him into a fresh approach to corporate valuation and the analysis of debt and equity financing.

Armed with his business degree, Williams's first job was with Hayden, Stone and Co. financial investment house in Boston. He had hoped initially to parlay his engineering background into the investigation of new and complex technology stock issues. Instead, he was told to immerse himself in straightforward statistical analyses of a number of stocks assigned to him, and to answer clients' letters seeking opinions on these stocks.

This was an era in which the market had an almost blind faith in the steadying power of the Federal Reserve. By then, even the Florida Real Estate scandal so fueled by fellow Bostonian Charles Ponzi had run its course. The average investor had perhaps wised to get-rich-quick schemes. Yet Williams himself was beginning to wonder whether the market remained overconfident in these final years of the Roaring Twenties. He began to study and practice hedging techniques that would protect his investments from downside risk. He was also gaining confidence in his insights and increasingly honed intuition after little more than two years out of business school.

In the winter of early 1928, Williams was ice skating alone at the Cambridge Skating Club when he was approached by a partner at Lee, Higginson & Co., Boston's most prestigious investment bank. The partners wanted Williams to join the firm as an investment analyst. At first he declined, but they persisted. They asked him what salary he would like to earn. When he responded, rather reluctantly, with a modest increase over what he was then earning, they explained to him no, that was far too little. Williams acquiesced, but when he announced his decision to his employer, he incurred their wrath. When a senior partner of Hayden, Stone told him it was unethical to hire a man away to a competitor, Williams immediately understood the monopsony model. While an employer may try to limit the choices of its employees to extract concessions or keep salaries down, Williams came to view such practices as immoral.

Williams jumped ship. The year 1928 found Williams with a new job, and also on a six-week honeymoon with his new bride, Edith May McCoy (February 17, 1902–September 10, 1997), whom he married on May 17 of that year. As soon as they returned from their trip to Europe, Williams thrust himself into the analysis of financial markets with every sense of an optimism that the market which continued to record new highs would maintain its upward trajectory.

The following year was a hard-earned lesson for Williams. As an analyst, he'd been following a few stocks that were flying high in the first half of 1929. One such stock was American and Foreign Power, a highly leveraged company that had grown its stock value to a price–earnings ratio in excess of 100. Its corporate finance strategy was so complex that it befuddled conventional financial analysis. Following the Great Crash, its stock value fell rapidly from almost $200 to $2, partly due to the collapse of some foreign exchange denominations.

As had an entire nation, Williams suffered a painful financial lesson in 1929. He concluded that sound financial investment requires an extensive training in economics. A few years later, when business was difficult, his family finances were sound, and his opportunity cost was low, Williams decided it was a good time to renew his studies. He entered the Ph.D. program at Harvard University, this time in the field of economics.

Williams' choice to enter the Ph.D. program was not entirely discretionary, though. By November of 1931, he had been transferred to the trust division of his company, which was then owned by the banking company that also funded Ivar Kreuger, a Swedish civil engineer who had built up a global match and financial instrument company. Krueger's business successes had earned him the label of 'the Match King'. As early as late 1931, rumors were circulating that Kreuger's financial empire was unravelling. He had once again borrowed from the Swedish bank Sveriges Riksbank, which today is perhaps best known as the sponsor of the Nobel Memorial Prize in the Economic Sciences, or the Nobel Prize for Economics in short. Krueger's borrowing by this time was so extensive that it constituted about half of the Swedish reserve currency. Threats of an impending downfall of his financial empire was driving down the value of the Swedish currency.

Kreuger was summoned to Germany to meet with his bankers. But, on the morning of the planned meeting, he was found in his hotel room dead of a self-inflicted gunshot wound. He left a suicide note explaining that he has "made such a mess of things that I believe this is to be the most satisfactory solution for everybody concerned."[4] His death precipitated a worldwide *Kreuger Crash* which gave rise to a whole series of Depression-era financial reforms meant to prevent the sort of frauds that had formed the foundation of his dubious financial empire.

Williams used this financial calamity as an opportunity to move on. He once again turned to study at his Harvard alma mater in September of 1932. Williams was well prepared for his studies. He was mathematically sophisticated, had a master's degree in business and a bachelor's qualification in chemical engineering and mathematics, and he also had years of real world financial experience, unlike most other students in his class. He had intended to make short work of his studies, and planned to graduate in two years.

There, Williams studied under and, as a consequence of his personal finance expertise and maturity, became close friends with two of his professors, the luminary Wassily Leontief (August 5, 1906–February 5, 1999) and Joseph Schumpeter (February 8, 1883–January 8, 1950), both giants in economics. During the course of his studies he also rubbed shoulders with John Kenneth Galbraith (October 15, 1908–April 26, 2006) and the future Nobel Memorial Prize winner, Paul Samuelson (May 15, 1915–December 13, 2009), both peers from more humble origins than Williams. At this time apparently he stood out at Harvard because of his polished shoes and matching suit, to the point that, as recalled in his memoirs, he was once heckled because he "looked like a capitalist."[5]

At Harvard, the hotbed of an emerging school of thought now associated with Keynesian macroeconomics, Williams had proposed to his supervisor, Schumpeter, a couple of potential thesis topics relating to the balance between aggregate supply and demand as a function of financial markets. Williams felt that the Great Crash and the Great Depression begged for a better understanding of this important issue. Schumpeter had other ideas, though.

Schumpeter instead proposed a problem that was right up Williams's intellectual alley. Williams therefore embarked on his thesis, *The Theory of Investment Value*, which explored the subject of the creation of intrinsic financial value for a corporate share. This topic capitalized on his extensive real world experience in corporate valuation. Even the Harvard faculty had to recognize Williams was already an expert in this new field that had, by that date, received only scant academic attention.

Williams completed his thesis in 1937 and began to seek a publisher for his results. Unfortunately, while the mathematics and chemical engineering literature was typically chock-full of equations that employed Greek symbols, finance treatises were still generally more art than hard science. His manuscript was declined first by the Macmillan publishing house and then McGraw Hill. An exasperated Williams took his thesis to the Harvard University Press, which agreed to publish it, but only if Williams helped offset the printing costs. The book came out in June 1938, two years before Williams was officially granted his Ph.D.

4
The Times

The 1930s saw a tremendous increase in skepticism about financial markets and corporate reporting, but also a dramatic growth in the appreciation for the application of more scientific methods to areas such as industry, economy, and finance. During the so-called *Roaring Twenties*, it seemed almost impossible not to succeed in investing on the financial markets. In the 1930s, those investors courageous enough to risk any of their remaining financial capital sought value like never before, and insisted in delving much more deeply into the sometimes arcane finances of publicly traded corporations. The discipline of finance was ripe for analysis based on greater scientific methodology.

The first to tap into this increased demand for better financial information, more sophisticated analysis, and the superior yields resulting from systematically investing in value was Benjamin Graham (1894–September 21, 1976). Born John Benjamin Grossbaum in London England on May 8, 1894, he moved with his family before his second birthday to New York City. Despite their relative poverty and the death of his father, the family prized education for their intellectually precocious son. They encouraged and supported his attendance to Columbia University at an early age, where he graduated as salutatorian of his class at the age of twenty.

Upon graduation, young Benjamin took a job as a runner on Wall Street, even though he was also offered employment teaching mathematics. Benjamin was attracted to high finance and, from his lowly perch, he saw some of what then constituted due diligence among Wall Street analysts over the Roaring Twenties.

Graham had discovered something Williams had already realized in Boston. Graham's big break came about from his willingness to delve into financial statements in greater depth than most who preceded him.

Graham had harbored a suspicion that a Standard Oil spinoff, Northern Pipe Line Co., was not fully revealing its assets in the cursory financial reports it issued. Graham indulged his curiosity and travelled from New York to Washington D.C. to inspect the full report the company was required to issue to the Interstate Commerce Commission. From his analysis he discovered that a stock trading at less than $70 per share actually held railroad bonds and other assets that were worth almost $100 per share. For a profitable company that could easily support expenses from its incoming revenue, the value of these assets on the books should be the foundation upon which earnings could augment further. Graham and his partner purchased upwards of 5% of the outstanding stock and then tried to induce the directors of Northern Pipe Line to release its assets to its shareholders. When the directors refused, Graham took his information to the shareholders. He made a brief speech from the floor of the 1927 annual meeting. His speech failed to have the effect he thought it deserved. He tried again the following year, but only after he garnered 40 percent of the vote in proxies. He finally succeeded in having the corporation distribute almost three-quarters of these assets to shareholders. His efforts as an activist shareholder earned him a princely profit, as the company's second largest owner by then. Only Rockefeller's own foundation controlled more of the stock than he did. Later Rockefeller became a shareholder activist advocate himself so that his foundation could expand their work.[1]

A few years later, in 1934, Graham and his collaborator, David Dodd, published what is now considered to be the first text in the discipline of value investing. In *Security Analysis*, and its successor, *The Intelligent Investor*, Graham distinguished between investment and its more disreputable cousin in 1934, speculation. Graham noted "An investment operation is one which, upon thorough analysis, promises safety of principal and an adequate return. Operations not meeting these requirements are speculative."[2] A couple of years later, after his own visits to Wall Street, John Maynard Keynes further espoused on the blight of the speculator.

Graham's pioneering work in value investing is now part of our standard financial intuition. His great idea, augmented by subsequent contributions from John Burr Williams and Ronald Coase, is to consider a share as part ownership of the firm's assets and its future cash flow. An active investor surmises these values and invests accordingly. This was in stark contrast to the approach of speculators, of whom John Maynard Keynes was a vociferous critic. In his widely read *The General Theory of Employment, Interest and Money,* Keynes had argued during the Great

Depression that American-style investing seemed to be driven more by animal spirits than by cool calculations. He believed that markets were usually driven by group psychology rather than rationality. He claimed,

> If I may be allowed to appropriate the term speculation for the activity of forecasting the psychology at the market, and the term enterprise for the activity of forecasting the prospective yield of assets over their whole life, it is by no means always the case that speculation predominates over enterprise. As the organization of investment markets improves, the risk of the predominance of speculation does, however, increase. In one of the greatest investment markets in the world, namely, New York, the influence of speculation (in the above sense) is enormous. Even outside the field of finance, Americans are apt to be unduly interested in discovering what average opinion believes average opinion to be; and this national weakness finds its nemesis in the stock market.[3]

Like Graham before him and John Burr Williams after him, Keynes condemned speculation because of the distortions and distraction it created with regard to the important match between savings and investment and their provision of a basis for economic growth. Unfortunately, when investment is transformed into gambling, investors who strive to expand the economic pie are replaced by speculators bent on merely dividing up the pie in ways that advantage them and disadvantage others. The market becomes a game not unlike judging in a beauty contest in which success is based not on objective criteria but rather on the subjective conjecture of how judges will vote. Keynes noted that:

> A more sophisticated contestant would take the analysis still further by imagining how each of the contestants forms their opinion of the prevailing public perception. Such layers of strategy upon strategy eventually divert attention from sheer beauty to a battle of strategy and wits... It is not a case of choosing those which, to the best of one's judgment, are really the prettiest, nor even those which average opinion genuinely thinks the prettiest. We have reached the third degree where we devote our intelligences to anticipating what average opinion expects the average opinion to be. And there are some, I believe, who practise the fourth, fifth and higher degrees.[4]

Graham agreed with Keynes' condemnation of the then present state of financial analysis. He advocated for more calculated and objective analysis rather than the subjective analysis that was practiced all too often. It should be facts and not opinions that dictate stock prices. He uses a similar analogy of a Mr. Market who shows up every day to make an offer for a stock. If the offer is ridiculous, the investor ignores it. If it is plausible, the investor considers it. Either way, Mr. Market shows up each day, but the true price of the stock is only the one prudent investors accept, not necessarily those Mr. Market quotes each day.

This approach to value investing is now widely practiced, perhaps most famously in the strategies developed by Warren Buffet. According to a book on Warren Buffet's value investing strategy, while Graham may have led a most successful investing life, his personal life was far more unconventional. Following the death of his son, he began an affair with his son's former girlfriend, Marie Louise Amingues, whose age was between his and that of his son. He travelled frequently to France to visit her and, when he proposed to his wife Estey that he spend half of the year in France and the other half in New York City, she divorced him.[5] Graham died in Aix-en-Provence, France, on September 21, 1976 at the age of 82.

While Graham may be considered the father of value investing, his approach can be likened to the mining of financial statements for hidden gems rather than the scientifically gleaning of the value of earnings based on the ability of a corporation to earn profits relative to the opportunity cost of capital in the broader economy. Williams would offer a much more formal and sophisticated approach. It is Williams's model we now teach in our corporate finance classes.

Beginnings of a theory

Williams agreed with Keynes's assessment and Graham's observation that the state of Depression-era investment was more speculative than substantive. However, while Keynes, Graham, and Williams had all studied mathematics as undergraduates, and all at top schools, Graham and Keynes relied much more on rhetoric honed from their respective studies in philosophy. By contrast, Williams was an engineer, and he strived to break things down to their essence to better understand what made them work.

As Williams observed the gyrations of the market from his perspective as an analyst through the late 1920s and the 1930s, he concluded that volatility ruled the day, even though dividends, and hence profits, fluctuated very little. He concluded that increased volatility arose because stocks were not accurately assessed and valued. His book, based on his dissertation, *The Theory of Investment Value*, explained how earnings were also somewhat volatile because they priced one-time events and incorporated various accounting conventions that were not always aligned with long-term profits. Finally, he noted that these profits must be compared with returns that can be earned elsewhere, and hence ought to be benchmarked against a broader risk-adjusted return. This is the basis of the modern Discounted Cash Flow and Discounted Dividend Models taught in business classes, and dividend investing strategies still practiced today by those who invest based on corporate fundamentals.

Williams's book was comparatively advanced, especially if one considers its audience at the time. In it, he described the formulas we still use to estimate the discounted value of future dividends based on various assumptions of dividend growth and on the appropriate prevailing interest rate. Williams also described a number of common sense prescriptions.

First, Williams argued that the intrinsic value of a corporation is calculated as the present value of its future dividends. Earnings do contribute to dividends, but they are not the same as dividends. He describes the difference in a poem:

> A cow for her milk
> A hen for her eggs,
> And a stock, by heck,
> For her dividends.
> An orchard for fruit,
> Bees for their honey,
> And stocks, besides,
> For their dividends.

Ben Graham agreed with Williams's emphasis on dividends and hoped it would offer an antidote to the speculative frenzy on Wall Street. He said "The emphasis on the primacy of dividends and the insistence that the value of reinvested earnings is to be found only in increased dividends sound a much-needed warning to Wall Streeters."[6]

While Williams's study was initially motivated to better understand how dividends affect a corporation's stock price, it occurred to Williams that there was also no reason his intuition could not also be applied to non-dividend-paying corporations. At some point in the maturity of the firm, retained earnings are reinvested at the appropriate return and will be returned to shareholders as dividends at some later point. If the money is lost, then the stock should never capitalize on that value. This intuition would turn out to be quite profound, and would earn two scholars treated later, Franco Modigliani and Merton Miller, a Nobel Memorial Prize a half century later.

Specifically, Williams observed:

> If earnings not paid out in dividends are all successfully reinvested, then these earnings should produce dividends later; if not, then they are money lost. In short, a stock is worth only what you can get out of it.

Williams honed our intuition to the very essence of corporate value. The stockholders and bondholders of a corporation lay claim to the earnings of the firm. These earnings can be paid out in the form of dividends, or can be reinvested into the firm, to pay out greater earnings in the future. The value of a stock is thus an objective measure based on cash flows, not the subjective beauty contest that Keynes feared drove markets.

Williams also advocated for more formal and quantitative corporate valuation based on the Discounted Cash Flow Model. He called this "algebraic budgeting." This concept was revisited in Myron J. Gordon's article "Dividends, Earnings, and Stock Prices" more than two decades later. Gordon wrote:

> The distinguished theoretical book on investment value by J.B. Williams contains several chapters devoted to the application of the theory, but his empirical work is in the tradition of the investment analyst's approach.

In fact, Williams's fundamentals and discounted dividend model approach is now used routinely to price stocks, bonds, or even the internal projects of firms. Jack Treynor used such a net present value approach to determine the level of internal project returns for a firm that eventually generated the formula we now use in the Capital Asset Pricing Model derived by Treynor, William Sharpe, and others in the 1960s.

The net present value Discounted Cash Flow (DCF) model is now the most frequently applied tool among analysts. A corporate finance course usually begins by quantifying the present value of future returns of bonds, based on the DCF model. Later in their studies, students of corporate finance are also taught how to quantify stock prices by Harry

Markowitz's Modern Portfolio Theory and William Sharpe's Capital Asset Pricing Model. Markowitz claimed that Williams's book inspired him to produce his model of the optimal diversified portfolio based on Williams's words about the importance of diversification.

While Williams shared a healthy skepticism with Keynes and Graham about market speculation, he still favored a market approach to overly oppressive government intervention. He preferred the profit motive to the lack of discipline of bureaucrats left to manage the economy. He also viewed taxes as discouraging savings, as had Franco Modigliani, who took Williams's conclusions still further. For instance, federal deficits offer a double jeopardy. Taxes will rise and hence detract from future dividends, and, as government competes for loanable funds, the prevailing interest rate rises and further depresses the net present value of future cash flows.

Williams's comments on how a market works do harken back to the words of Graham on Mr. Market and of Keynes' beauty contest. Williams noted that in identifying a stock's value:

> Concerning true worth, every man will cherish his own opinion; as to what price really is right, time only will tell. Time will not give its answer all at once, though, but only slowly, word by word, as the years go by; nor will the last word be spoken till the corporation shall have closed its books for ever and ever. Those who bought their stock long ago will know their answer in the main by now, but those who buy now will hear theirs only in the future.

5
The Theory – A New Finance Paradigm

Central to an emerging approach to asset pricing in the 1920s and 1930s was the principle of the time value of money. While Williams was not the first to originate the concept, he is the first to use it to such substantial analytic effect.

The time value of money has an interesting history that predates Williams by a couple of generations. This series documented the innovations of Eugen von Böhm-Bawerk (February 12, 1851–August 27, 1914) and Irving Fisher (February 27, 1867–April 29, 1947). These great minds described the reasons why humans discount the future and hence why there is a prevailing discount rate that is approximated by the market interest rate.

The Austrian School marginalist, Böhm-Bawerk, offered a number of reasons for this positive discount rate. First, he noted that humans are willing to pay a premium for the psychological enjoyment of consuming something now rather than waiting until the future arrives. Alternately, if we are asked to delay gratification, we expect some compensation. Part of this effect is an acknowledgement of our own mortality. We know we are here now, but the future is always uncertain.

A second reason is that we generally expect greater financial security and wealth in the future, as Franco Modigliani explained in his Life Cycle Model. With this increased income comes a reduced marginal utility of income. Hence, the transfer of a dollar today to a point of time in the future will translate into less future enjoyment, on the margin, when compared to today. An interest rate compensates us for the sacrificed utility, and a discount rate measures this effect.

Finally, Böhm-Bawerk recognized that production takes time to transform today's factors of production into a greater value for tomorrow's output. This transformation can be viewed as a premium for the time taken to produce goods. This transformation over time creates a return that corresponds to the interest rate.

Of course, the discount rate that converts future values to the present must also incorporate measures of risk and uncertainty. These complications arising from uncertainty were not fully described until the great minds that created Modern Portfolio Theory first incorporated uncertainty into measures of returns in the 1960s and 1970s. The father of Modern Portfolio Theory, Harry Markowitz (August 24, 1927–present), reported he was inspired by the work of John Burr Williams in describing how the discount rate affects securities prices. Markowitz attributes Williams as the first to effectively employ the discount rate in the valuation of the present value of future corporate earnings and hence the value of a security that gives the right to a share of these net earnings. By the early 1950s, the finance discipline was finally taking note of Williams's intuition and contributions.

This notion of valuation is in stark contrast to the backward-looking corporate valuation that had been employed by accountants for centuries, and is still in use today. Accountants calculate and quote the book value of a firm in the belief that the remaining value of physical and financial assets which constitutes the corporation should be the proxy for its valuation. This book value approach is perhaps valid for the valuation of a firm that is broken up and sold solely for its tangible assets. However, it is ineffective in measuring the synergies that a corporation can create in producing net cash flows that are more than proportional to the value of physical assets used to create the firm's product.

The first volume in the *Great Minds* series, *The Life Cycle Hypothesists*, described the theory of the father of modern finance, Irving Fisher (February 27, 1867–April 29, 1947). Before Fisher, the prevailing interest rate was whatever borrowers were willing to pay, and the discount rate was whatever equated the cost of capital to its discounted future earnings. If the prevailing interest rate was lower than the imputed discount rate, then a corporation should borrow and expand. If it was higher, then one cannot profitably borrow. This concept had not been applied any more broadly than that.

John Burr Williams first took discount theory into the realm of corporate valuation in his 1938 book, *The Theory of Investment Value*. His *discounted cash flow analysis* technique is now treated universally in textbooks that introduce students to the subject of Corporate Finance.

The treatment by engineer-cum-economist Williams is the now-familiar Discounted Cash Flow Model that translates future cash flows into a discounted present value today:

Discounted Present Value =

$$CF_0 + \frac{CF_1}{(1+r)^1} + \frac{CF_2}{(1+r)^2} + \ldots + \frac{CFn}{(1+r)^n} = \sum_{i=0}^{n} \frac{CF_i}{(1+r)^i}$$

where r is the appropriate risk-adjusted rate to discount future values, CF_0 is any flow of current income, and CF_i is the net cash flow generated in period i. If the analyst knows the present investment cost to generate these future cash flows, then the discount rate could be solved for to yield the *internal rate of return* of the project or entity.

If cash flows occur continuously over time, or if the time horizon is infinite, such that any period in time is infinitesimally short, the discrete time formula above can be converted to a continuous time integration:

$$\text{DPV} = \int_0^T CF(t)e^{-rt}dt.$$

If the future cash flows are constant, then both treatments can be easily calculated and yield similar expressions for the discounted present value of a constant future cash flow CF_0:

$$\text{DPV} = CF_0(1 - e^{-rT})/r$$

Williams also showed how one can incorporate cash flow growth assumptions into the analysis. The formula for growth can be most easily gleaned from the continuous time version of the methodology. Let us assume that cash flow is expected to grow at a constant rate of *g* per period. Then the discounted present value is described as:

$$\text{DPV} = \int_0^T CF_0 e^{gt} e^{-rt} dt = \int_0^T CF_0 e^{-(r-g)t} dt$$

If the future cash flows are constant, then both treatments can be easily calculated and yield similar expressions for the discounted present value:

$$DPV = \frac{CF_0(1 - e^{-(r-g)T})}{r-g} = \frac{CF_0\left(1 - \frac{e^{gT}}{e^{rT}}\right)}{r-g}$$

In the discrete time version, this expression is given by:

$$DPV = \frac{CF_0\left(1-\left(\frac{g}{r}\right)^T\right)}{r-g}$$

These expressions are valid for a growth rate g < r. The equation for net present value simplifies significantly if growth is expected to continue forever:

$$\text{DPV} = CF_0/(r-g)$$

This methodology is useful not only for the determination of the value of future cash flows garnered by a stock, but also in the determination of the value of a project within a firm, as discounted by its Weighted Average Cost of Capital (WACC). The WACC, adjusted for the risk of a given project, can be used to determine if the future cash flows of a project exceed the present investment costs. If this is the case, the project would add value to the firm compared to its average returns, and the security price would then benefit from the project. The methodology is also used to allow the analyst to calculate the firm's value based on its collection of projects and future cash flows.

This intuitive approach is rich with insights, extensions and complications. The insight is that the corporation can be valued as a sum that exceeds the value of its constituent assets. If this discounted cash flow approach yields a value that is greater than the value of its physical and financial assets, the accounting value is irrelevant. The corporation creates synergies that yield returns on their assets that exceed the value of the assets themselves.

On the other hand, if the accounting value of corporate assets exceeds the discounted cash flow from future operations, the firm is best broken up and sold for its asset value. We later treat the various reasons why such synergies can be created by a corporation.

Like his contemporary, the Value Investing guru Graham, Williams advocated for the payment of net earnings of a firm in the form of dividends, unless the firm can offer a superior return to the shareholder by reinvesting retained earnings into projects that offer a better return than the firm's working cost of capital. This WACC includes the firm's characteristic use of debt and equity to fund its growth and it is given by:

$$\text{WACC} = \omega_D r_D(1-T) + \omega_E r_E$$

where ω_D and ω_E are the relative outstanding debt and equity value of the firm and T is the tax rate. The formula presumes that expansion for the firm relies on the same mix of debt funding, at an after-tax cost of $r_D(1 - T)$ and equity financing as has been used in the recent past. One can also include funding from the issuance of preferred stock by adding the respective term $\omega_p r_p$ if necessary.

Elaborations

Williams was the first to develop a methodology of the corporate finance paradigm. The structure of corporate finance is designed to facilitate the corporation's creation of value. It employs its available capital, in the form of debt from lenders or bond purchasers, and equity from shareholders to create synergies and superior risk-adjusted returns. However, Williams's analysis begs a question. If a corporation wishes to expand, should it necessarily use the same pattern and weightings of debt and equity that it currently employs, or should it employ a different mix? Williams presaged this question and offered simple intuition to declare that, under certain circumstances, it does not matter. It would take another generation to show much more formally that Williams's intuition was correct, again, under certain circumstances.

Williams's argument of capital structure neutrality was particularly insightful. He noted:

> If the investment value of an enterprise as a whole is by definition the present worth of all its future distributions to security holders, whether on interest or dividend account, then this value in no wise depends on what the company's capitalization is. Clearly if a single individual or a single institutional investor owned all the bonds, stocks, and warrants issued by a corporation, it would not matter to this investor what the company's capitalization was. Any earnings collected as interest could not be collected as dividends. To such an individual it would be perfectly obvious that total interest- and dividend-paying power was in now wise dependent on the kind of securities issued to the company's owner. Furthermore, no *change* in the investment value of the enterprise as a whole would result from a *change* in its capitalization. Bonds could be retired with stock issues, or two classes of junior securities (i.e., common stock and warrants) cold be combined into one, without changing the investment value of the company as a whole. Such constancy of investment value is analogous to the indestructibility of matter or energy; it leads us to

> speak of the Law of Conservation of Investment Value, just as physicists speak of the Law of the Conservation of Matter, or the Law of Conservation of Energy.[1]

Notice that Williams correctly surmised that his neutrality of capital structure result is distorted if the forms of capital are treated differentially in tax legislation, either at the corporate or at the shareholder level. In doing so, he anticipated the significant literature that would qualify his result. In his next paragraph, he also correctly noted that his result of Conservation of Investment Value creates a benchmark toward which the market might grope, somewhat imperfectly. He stated:

> Since market value does not usually conform exactly to investment value, no "conservation of market value" is to be found in general. Only to a rough extent do total market values remain the same regardless of capitalization. The exceptions in practice are important enough to afford many opportunities for profit by promoters and investment bankers.[2]

Embedded within this statement is a profound observation. Williams had experienced the volatility of finance markets through the Roaring Twenties and the Dirty Thirties and knew what a firm was worth, based on the fundamentals of cash flows, often differed from how it was valued in the fickle market. He noted that these discrepancies create an opportunity more sophisticated market participants to secure profits. We now label this the process of *arbitrage*, a concept which now constitutes a foundational underpinning of much of modern finance. However, Williams did not develop his observation sufficiently. It was left to the great mind Eugene Fama (February 14, 1939–), who won a Nobel Memorial Prize based on his faith in arbitrage, and others to conclude in the 1960s that such arbitrage may force market values to converge to fundamental values. This conclusion, documented in *The Efficient Market Hypothesists* in the Great Minds in Finance series, remains controversial to this day. Williams's reluctance to fully embrace the theory of arbitrage may well have presaged this controversy in modern finance.

6
Legacy and Later Life

In a treatise that was published by an engineer turned economist and financier, who persevered and even had to pay for the publication of his great work, Williams established the field of *fundamentals analysis* and, for the first time, provided a scientifically-based methodology to value corporations and their securities. His methodology of securities pricing based on discounted present values formed the foundation of modern asset pricing and also formed the foundation for securities returns, which was later augmented by measures of risk and uncertainty.

Harry Markowitz, William Sharpe (June 16, 1934–), Robert C. Merton (July 31, 1944–), and Myron Scholes (July 1, 1941–) all earned Nobel Memorial Prizes by augmenting the concept of security returns with measures of risk. And while Merton and Scholes tip their hats to Sharpe, and Sharpe was inspired by Markowitz, Markowitz himself took the lead from the treatise by Williams that is growing in appreciation every decade.

In those pages, Williams also telegraphed the work by future Nobel Memorial Prize winners Franco Modigliani and Merton Miller for their subsequent work on the neutrality of corporate financial structures, and framed the issue of arbitrage that would lead Eugene Fama to earn a Nobel Memorial Prize for himself. These various formalizations of Williams's intuitions were developed over the course of many decades, but the buds of ideas that provided the foundations of more than half a dozen Nobel Memorial Prizes flowed from a single book published in 1938 by a relatively obscure academic and moderately successful financial analyst.

Williams's methodology should not be confined merely to the valuation of a stock, though, even if every corporate finance student is exposed to the Discounted Cash Flow approach, which is often now called the Discounted Dividend Model. In the 1960s, another Harvard Business School graduate applied Williams's methodology to project valuation under uncertainty and, in doing so, created a version of the now well-established Capital Asset Pricing Model.

Jack Lawrence Treynor (February 21, 1930–) began to work on project valuation while he was still a graduate student at the Harvard Business School in 1955 and 1956. He was interested in the appropriate discount rate to employ to discount the cash flow from an exceptionally long-lived investment project conducted by a corporation. As will be familiar to any bond investor, the resulting present value is highly sensitive to the choice of the discount rate. He also extended the work of his Harvard Business School predecessor by intuiting that the appropriate discount rate should reflect project uncertainties and riskiness, just as a bond discount rate will factor in the risk of inflation, reinvestment and maturity risk, price risk as prevailing interest rates fluctuate, and corporate bond default risk. In the subsequent years, Treynor augmented Williams's discount rate with his intuition about the importance of quantifying risk.

The pressures of life and his embarking on a career at the prestigious consulting firm Arthur D. Little, based in Cambridge, Massachusetts, afforded Treynor little time to continue the work he had begun at Harvard. In 1958, though, Treynor devoted a three-week vacation to a reading of Modigliani and Miller's 1958 paper on the Modigliani–Miller theorem, which will be more fully described later, and his own exploration of capital budgeting for a risky corporate project. Over the course of the next two years he followed this up with work conducted in his spare time. Finally, in 1961, he began to circulate a draft entitled *Market Value, Time, and Risk*.

While he was working in Cambridge, Treynor took his draft of the discounted cash flow project evaluation methodology to the only economist he knew from Harvard, a professor John Lintner (February 9, 1916–June 8, 1983), who went on to develop his own version of the Capital Asset Pricing Model years later. Lintner showed little interest in a paper by this young practitioner, perhaps because Treynor's paper did not have the academic *polish* that was becoming increasingly de rigueur. However, the paper was circulated to Merton Miller and then down Cambridge Avenue to Franco Modigliani at the Massachusetts Institute of Technology (MIT). Modigliani saw some promise in the concept and invited Treynor to lunch. Modigliani, who was renowned for his nurturing of young scholars, advised Treynor that he should study economics. Treynor took the advice seriously, was granted a sabbatical from ADL, and began a year of study of economics at MIT. There, he polished his idea of a risk-return tradeoff, broke the paper up into two papers, and completed *Toward a Theory of Market Value of Risky Assets* in 1963. Because Treynor was only dabbling in academia, he never actively worked to have his paper published. Finally, in 1999, it was published retrospectively. The second of his two papers had been published earlier, in 1976, in a collaboration with Fisher Black (January 11, 1938–August 30, 1995), of Black–Scholes options pricing formula fame.[1] They changed its title from *"Implications for the Theory of Finance" to* "Corporate Investment Decisions".

Treynor considered his academic pursuits a mere avocation, which did not distract him from his vocation: the practice of high finance. His lack of academic intensity perhaps cost him a Nobel Memorial Prize. He heard from Modigliani that William Sharpe was working on a concept similar to that Treynor had derived in his first paper – the exploration of how risk affects the return one must earn to justify the investment in a project. Treynor realized that this concept could, more generally, also apply to the valuation of a corporation. He reasoned that there was no point in publishing his paper if Sharpe had arrived at the same conclusion, and, given his lack of academic standing, Sharpe was far more likely to get his paper published. Had Treynor known that Sharpe's work was meeting with a great deal of resistance from the editor of the *Journal of Finance*, perhaps he would have persevered. Instead, he dropped his academic work. In 1990 William Sharpe's idea won him the 22nd Nobel Memorial Prize in Economic Sciences, which also simultaneously recognized other work on the risk–return tradeoff conducted by Robert Merton and Harry Markowitz.

Nonetheless, Treynor created a lucrative career in finance from his insights in project evaluation using the Discounted Cash Flow Model under conditions of uncertainty.

Others also draw on Williams's techniques. Commercial banks must ensure that a loan will create a net present value of future net cash flow that can justify a loan and substantiate the valuation of an income-earning physical asset such as an apartment building. The art of assessment of commercial properties points to some fundamental challenges of the net present value technique.

First, one must associate an appropriate discount rate to the analysis. This is typically a risk-adjusted interest rate. Usually, the current cost of capital is used as the benchmark discount rate. However, while the bank will hold the loan and the property as collateral for years, if not decades, prevailing interest rates will rise and fall over that time, while their payments, and hence returns on their loans, are locked in, unless, of course, interest rates fall and the borrower refinances.

In addition, while the bank may make assumptions about future cash flows, these flows are subject to the vagaries of the macro economy. More loans are made during booms than during busts. Both these tendencies create a risk that is not symmetric about the mean return. And, while a loan may have a known terminal value, analysts of projects internal to a firm only have an approximate termination date. The uncertain nature of the weighted average cost of capital, the terminal date, and even the cash flow themselves creates a great degree of uncertainty in what otherwise appears to be a sound and scientifically based analytic method. Nonetheless, one can construct reasonable estimates of net present values for appropriate circumstances, and can bound their results within a range determined by making plausible assumptions of the variables used to generate the results.

Williams admitted that his progress to the completion of his Ph.D. was a bit more pedestrian than that of his colleagues. For instance, while Williams attended Harvard, his contemporary and the great mind Paul Samuelson (May 15, 1915–December 13, 2009) began his studies at Harvard in 1934, completed his Ph.D. there in 1939, and went on to an illustrious academic career. However, unlike others in his class, Williams continued to invest in the stock market while he was still attending school. He was always searching for and purchasing undervalued firms, based on their price/earnings ratio, and selling them once their prices approached what he determined by his theory to be fair market value. In an age before personal computers and spreadsheets, his fascination with finance took time from his studies.

Finally, in 1940, Williams carved out sufficient time to defend his thesis. In a highly unusual move, he distributed copies of a manuscript that had already been in print for two years to Schumpeter, Leontief, and the department chair Alvin Hansen. The latter, in particular, took exception to his apparent impudence, and directed questions to Williams on Keynes' General Theory of Income, Interest and Unemployment. Williams vehemently challenged the work of both Keynes, and his disciple Hansen, by asserting that the Great Depression was caused by the stock market crash, the ensuing bank failures, and the fixed exchange rate regime. Hansen conceded, and Williams was awarded his Ph.D. in the spring of 1940.

Following his graduation, Williams continued to produce academic papers of publishable quality, but he was typically too busy making money in financial markets to shepherd his papers through the tedious stages of conditional acceptance, rewrite, and final acceptance. He also maintained a pragmatic mistrust of the conventional wisdom, a term John Kenneth Galbraith (October 15, 1908–April 29, 2006) had formulated, that kept a grip over Harvard economists like Joan Robinson (October 31, 1903–August 5, 1983) and Paul Samuelson. This school of thought posited that managers produce quantities to equate the marginal cost and the marginal revenue of production. Williams's vast experience with real corporations convinced him that managers have no such knowledge of the various theories and curves advocated by economists, and hence could not make decisions in the way proposed by economic theorists.

Instead, Williams labored to provide substitute theories based not on what he viewed as esoteric economic theories but instead based on the ways in which business managers match current production capacity to market demand. His theory culminated in an article entitled "The Path to Equilibrium" and published in the *Quarterly Journal of Economics*.[2] He also wrote a number of books and other papers as he tried to educate practitioners and theorists alike about the workings of real markets. These include two books, *The Theory of Flexible Exchange Rates*, and *Interest, Growth, and Inflation*.[3]

Throughout much of this career Williams remained a practitioner with a strong theoretical training; he was once honored with the opportunity to teach as a visiting professor, albeit teaching a course with a strong practitioner bent. Following some comments he made at a prominent meeting of economists, he was invited for a semester to the business school at the University of Wisconsin. There, he lectured on financial assets within the economics department. He considered that academic experience to be one of the biggest and most pleasant adventures of his career. Like other practitioners who have the opportunity to teach, he was honored by the recognition. Unaffected by the constant pressure placed upon tenure track faculty to research and write, and oblivious to the tedious departmental politics that are rampant in higher education, Williams felt it a privilege to teach at the university level. He repeated that experience a few years later, in 1968 for another half-year at the University of Wisconsin. Over the years, he also offered seminars at Berkeley, UCLA, the University of Utah, MIT, Harvard, NYU, Wellesley, the University of Indiana, and the University of Iowa.

John Burr Williams lived much of his life in Wellesley, Massachusetts, and died from the complications of a stroke on September 15, 1989 at the age of 88. He was survived by his wife, Edith, his sisters Pauline Williams Patton and Eugenie Grannis, his daughter Nancy (1931–2010), and his namesake, John Burr Williams, Jr. (1933–), who also enjoyed a productive career in securities investment, and two grandchildren.

Williams is appreciated more each year for his practical work in 1938 that formed the basis for corporate project valuation and for securities pricing. His work inspired many great minds to follow him, and added context and utility to the theories of his predecessor, Irving Fisher. He described why corporate valuation may mathematically exceed the sum of the value of the assets upon which the corporation relies. However, he left it to those that followed him to fill in the gaps in this theory and the exploration of the ways in which corporations create synergies that increase their value above the sum of its parts. Yet, while John Burr Williams remained in relative obscurity, Franco Modigliani and Merton Miller went on to win Nobel Memorial Prizes for a concept that he had largely pioneered.

Section 2
Is a Corporation's Capital Structure Irrelevant?

John Burr Williams produced an elaborate treatise that demonstrated how one might establish the value of a firm, based on its ability to generate cash over time. The obvious question might then be "What should one do with this cash?" Williams advocated for its distribution in the form of dividends. However, he recognized that these earnings could in fact be retained rather than being distributed. He posed the question: Should a corporation retain earnings to expand, or should it distribute earnings and then raise capital by selling more stock or by borrowing? Two great financial theorists bolstered Williams's intuition and earned their place in financial history and in every introductory textbook on corporate finance, usually immediately following the section devoted to Williams's discounted cash flow method of pricing a security.

7
The Early Years of Franco Modigliani

Some people achieve greatness for just a brilliant idea or two. Franco Modigliani is almost unique in that he had many big ideas, and his ideas spanned decades. His work encompassed many collaborations, and many sub disciplines. He was also legendary in his academic generosity. His legendary eclecticism is a product of his life and of his good fortune.

The Modigliani name alone portends greatness. It dates back to the expulsion of Sephardic (from the Hebrew word for Spain) Jews from Spain and Portugal in 1492, the year grade school students remember for the sailing of Christopher Columbus to the New World. Queen Isabella gave until August 3, 1492 for Jews to leave Spain, the same day that Columbus set sail from Palos. A third of those members on Columbus' ships, the *Nina*, the *Pinta*, and the *Santa Maria*, were Jews. Other Jews scattered across Europe following their expulsion.[1]

Two families, the Garsins and the Modiglianis, migrated to the Jewish communities of Italy that cultivated business across the Mediterranean Sea. The Garsins moved to Livorno, Italy and the Modiglianis ran businesses first from a small Jewish community named Modigliani, near Rome. Both families traded across the region, and both achieved considerable wealth. The Garsin family also conducted banking operations in Livorno, Marseille, France, Tunis, and London, England.[2]

The Modigliani family prospered under the family patriarch Mose Modigliani (1796–?). He passed his business on to his two sons, Cesare (1835–?) and Lazarro (1836–?). The elder son, Cesare, had three sons of his own, including Flaminio (about 1860–?), who was a successful engineer and who operated mines and forests under the family control.

Flaminio married Eugenia Garsin (abt 1860–?), who had grown up in Marseille but had met Flaminio while he worked in the port city of Livorno, about 40 miles west of Florence.

In 1883, the Modigliani family suffered financial calamity. The Modiglianis were bankrupted as the price of metals plummeted. As their family empire collapsed, Eugenia went into labor with her fourth child Amedeo (July12, 1884–January 24, 1920).

The family strived to protect some of the Modigliani assets in a most ingenious way as their business went into bankrupt. Eugenia was giving birth to a son as the bailiffs came to her home to seize their family's belongings. At that time, it was a provision of Italian law that a family was entitled to keep the bed of a pregnant woman. Thinking quickly, the family piled all their valuables onto her bed. Their ploy allowed them to retain these assets.[3] They were also left with a new son, Amedeo, who went on to fame as the modernist contemporary of Pablo Picasso, and who is remembered today for long faces in his paintings and sculptures. Amedeo is known as the founder of the Italian branch of the Impressionist Movement in modern art.

The younger brother of Cesare, Lazarro Modigliani (1836–?) was the father of Menachem Modigliani (1862–?) and the great uncle of Amedeo Modigliani. Menachem married Leone (1852–1922) and, in 1890, they had a child named Enrico (b.*c.*1890–?).

Enrico enjoyed the benefits of some of the family's hard-earned wealth. He was the first member of his family to go to college. There, he trained to be a doctor. Following his graduation, he remained in Rome and opened a successful pediatric practice.

In Rome, Enrico met Olga Flaschel. Enrico had a strong intellect and sense of social activism. In Olga he found a kindred spirit. Olga was well-educated and her family was also prosperous. Her parents dealt in pearls and coral and traded between the patriarch Emilio Flaschel's family home in Krakow and the matriarch Ernestina Cagli's family home in Florence. The center of their family business was an elegant jewelry shop in Rome. Their Rome home permitted Olga to attend the University of Rome. Already fluent in German, French, and Italian, Olga was an accomplished woman in her own right.

Enrico and Olga both shared an avenue for their sense of commitment to the community. As an extension of Enrico's pediatric practice and Olga's compassion, they became advocates for young unwed mothers. While they remained comfortably upper middle class, Enrico and Olga always remained committed and compassionate on behalf of those less fortunate. This is a value they also shared with their own family. At the same time, the family was full of life, laughter, and grace. They prized and appreciated education, and made a great deal of investment into the intellectual development of their child Franco, who was born on June 18, 1918, toward the end of World War I.

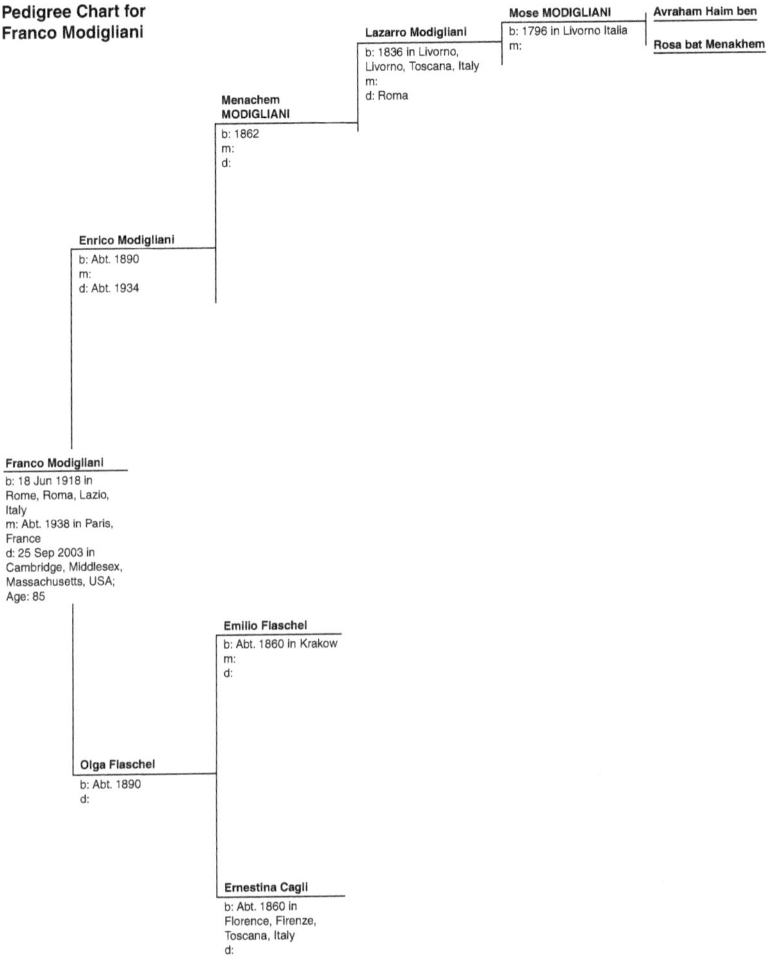

Figure 7.1 The Franco Modigliani Family Tree

Franco's mother was a substantial influence on his intellectual curiosity. Olga instilled in her son Franco the culture of a well-educated modern Renaissance woman. Franco learned a number of languages from her, but also added to the mix English, Greek, and Latin.

Franco Modigliani was intellectually precocious, academically spirited, and fascinated with finance. With his teenage cousins he had played a game of commodity exchange based on candies and peanuts with his teenage cousins. In his pretend group of academically precocious teens, Franco was appointed the finance minister to monitor and manipulate the relative price of these commodities. He set out a goal to prevent arbitrage between the commodities. Their adolescent antics fell under the scrutiny of the local Fascist committee at their seaside summer resort. The Fascists shut down their little experiment in global finance simulations, regarding it as subversive.[4]

But while he clearly was bright and inquisitive, Franco was also accused of not taking his studies sufficiently seriously. One of his teachers once responded to an essay he had written with the stern comment "They that sow the wind shall reap the storm."[5]

A traumatic event further hampered young Franco's academic progress. The young Franco had a great deal of respect and admiration for his father. However, when Modigliani was just 13 years old, his father died unexpectedly following a medical procedure. During this period of grieving, Franco was traumatized and his academic grades were rather inconsistent.

At this point his mother sensed that young Franco was in need of more intellectual challenge and so she arranged a transfer for him to the most elite high school in Rome. Franco did not stay there very long, however. He completed his graduation exams a year early, after only two years' study at the Liceo. He graduated from high school at a most dangerous time for Italian Jews, though. He began to attend college in 1935 just as the stirrings of war and anti-Semitic sentiment was beginning to percolate around Europe, and especially in Germany and Italy.

At the age of 17, Modigliani enrolled in the study of law at his mother's alma mater, the University of Rome. This was in an era before the widespread development of the literature in the areas of economics or finance. For a keen mind who was drawn to the human condition, law was a natural vocation. At the time, there was a growing interest in Italy in the Austrian School of economic and financial thought from journal articles written in German recasting the ideas of John Maynard Keynes (June 5, 1883–April 21, 1946), Karl Marx (May 5, 1818–March 14, 1883), Carl Menger (February 23, 1840–February 26, 1921) and Eugen von Böhm-Bawerk (February 12, 1851–August 27, 1914), the father of our understanding of the time value of money.

Modigliani's knowledge of German was employed by a local political movement, the Traders' Federation. He helped the Federation translate and incorporate writings in German in their opposition to the growing Fascist movement in the late 1930s Italy. At that time, Keynes was advocating for the introduction of price controls as a response to the rapid inflation arising from the war in Ethiopia. The Germans, too, were concerned about rising prices as nationalist demand for armaments was causing their economy to inflate. This pattern was being replicated in Italy, and Modigliani found himself right in the middle of the debate. In fact, he wrote an essay on price controls that earned him the top essay prize at his university. Ironically, this young Jewish scholar was awarded the prize by Benito Mussolini himself.[6]

Franco also discovered another prize at the University of Rome. He was reacquainted with the granddaughter of a friend of his maternal grandmother. He had met young Serena Calabi during his childhood, when he would spend summer in his mother's hometown of Florence, Italy. But, he had not seen her for years. When they met again, they fell in love quickly, and married soon thereafter.

Before their marriage, though, Modigliani endured a particularly tense period. Following the Italian war against Ethiopia and the Nazi and Fascist involvement in the Spanish Civil War, Modigliani became increasingly fearful of both the Fascist movement pervading Italy and the Nazi Movement sweeping Germany. Once Benito Mussolini had allied with Adolf Hitler and both nations began to institute anti-Semitic policies, Modigliani recognized the danger he might be in living in Italy. If he had been unable to complete college by 1939, it was becoming increasingly likely that he would not be able to complete at all. He and his newly engaged future wife followed the advice of her father, a staunch and vocal anti-Fascist, and moved first to Lausanne, Switzerland, and then to Paris. Modigliani satisfied his coursework while in Paris, and completed the requirement for his Juris Doctor degree in 1939. In the same year he and Selena also married at the Italian Consulate in the French capital. Then, at the age of 21, Franco took a big risk and travelled back to Italy in secret to accept his degree. They immediately began arrangement to move to the United States.

The couple left for the United States on August 23, 1939, on the very day that Hitler's Nazi Regime and the Stalin's regime in the Soviet Union signed their historic mutual non-aggression pact. This arrangement, officially known as the Molotov–Ribbentrop Pact, allowed Hitler a protected eastern flank so that he could concentrate his forces on Western Europe, for at least the next couple of years.

The Modiglianis arrived in New York five days after their departure from Europe and just four days before the outbreak of World War II.

By the time the Modiglianis had come to the United States Serena's family had already moved there and settled in the New York City area. As a result, when the Modiglianis arrived they were welcomed into a substantial community of Jewish exiles and family. Franco initially took up employment as an importer and seller of Italian books. Once Italy entered World War II in 1940, however, his supply of books dried up.

The same year, Franco earned a scholarship offered by Max Ascoli, himself an anti-Fascist refugee, who was building the New School for Social Research, sometimes called the University in Exile, which housed dozens of Jewish intellectuals who were fleeing an increasingly dangerous Europe. At the New School, Modigliani had the opportunity to pursue graduate studies in economics under one who would make a lifelong influence on him.

In this new setting, Modigliani came under the tutelage of Jacob Marschak (July 23, 1898–July 27, 1977). Marschak was a leading scholar in the quantification of economics and also in the nascent study of finance. He acted in the role of mentor to perhaps more subsequent Nobel Memorial Prize winners in finance than any other scholar. He would not only influence Modigliani's scholarship, but would also provide a role model for Modigliani in the art of mentorship and the sharing of his intellectual wealth.

While he worked on his New School thesis, Modigliani was also teaching at a women's college associated with Rutgers University in nearby Newark, New Jersey, and also at Bard College of Columbia University. He joined the faculty of the New School in 1944, upon completion of his thesis, and in the same year he also published his first landmark paper, on liquidity preference and interest rates in the prestigious *Econometrica* journal.[7] This work, "Liquidity Preference and the Theory of Interest and Money," established a theoretical argument that monetary policy had a neutral effect on aggregate demand. The theory substantiated an argument often advocated in the "Chicago School" that financial variables were ineffective policy tools. Combined with our expectations for inflation and the deleterious effect that inflation has on commerce, this approach supported an argument that steady and predictable financial markets offer the best support for broader economic goals. This line of research also initiated Modigliani's thinking about the independence of corporate expansion on debt or equity financing.

By 1942, Marschak had left the New School for Chicago. Five years later, Modigliani was also ready to move. While the Harvard economics faculty was keen to have him join them, the Department Chair, Professor Burbank, who was reputed to be an anti-Semite, persuaded Modigliani to decline the offer. He convinced Modigliani that he was no match for some of the other faculty there, and that he ought to "Be satisfied with being a big fish in a small pond."[8]

Modigliani found a more receptive and productive home, however. The next year, he was offered a $3,000 fellowship to pursue research at the University of Chicago and to rub shoulders with such finance luminaries as Milton Friedman. There, he would benefit from his first direct exposure to the "Chicago School." While at the faculty, he also began to teach at the crosstown University of Illinois. At that time, he could not have known that these years and academic explorations would eventually earn him the attribution of a founding thinker in a new study called finance.

Ironically enough, Chair Burbank's prophecy came to pass. At the University of Illinois, Modigliani made rapid progress, in terms of both research and his stature within the department. Within a couple of years of his arrival he had attained the rank of Full Professor, something that most faculty generally earn only after a dozen years or so. However, Modigliani's ambition, and the productivity of a number of other young professors, began to upset the old guard who had come, over the course of many years, to view the department as a sinecure. Soon, Modigliani was the only young faculty member left in the department. He saw the writing on the wall, and sought out a more productive academic environment. Following his departure, the local newspaper wrote the headline "Modigliani Leaves With A Blast – Now There Will Be Peace In The Department of Economics: The Peace Of Death."[9]

His University of Illinois years were nonetheless most productive for Modigliani. While based there, he focused on two particular themes. First, he explored the ways in which businesses create value and reduce risk. Second, he formulated, with the help of a graduate student, the way in which various agents develop their expectations for future income flows, and how these expectations affect current consumption. Both insights would revolutionize two different branches of finance. Modigliani was subsequently recognized with a Nobel Memorial Prize for contributions to both personal finance and corporate finance.

Modigliani was awarded a Nobel Memorial Prize for novel work he had conducted relatively early in his career, while still at Illinois. His ideas were quite ingenious. Up to this point there had been no real understanding of the economic mechanism that created sufficient investment capital to meet the needs of a growing economy. Irving Fisher had demonstrated over the first few decades of the 1900s how people may save in the wage-earning period of their lives to support consumption in their retirement. But, in the case of a growing economy, households have a tendency to over-save. Modigliani offered a deceptively simple explanation for this observed phenomenon. Since they do not predict with perfect foresight that their future income will be greater than their present income if the economy grows, households tend to over-save to be sure to cover their subsequent needs. This over-saving coincides with the additional investment needs for a growing economy.

Modigliani's simple *Life Cycle Model* helped establish the study of personal finance. In the life cycle model, the growing income of the young generates the income necessary to support both the young and the retired alike. His model explained why the overall rate of economic growth affects the savings rate, while he also provided the first model for the motivation behind the savings decisions of each individual household.

Not long after he had formulated his Life Cycle Model, Modigliani sought refuge from Illinois departmental politics by moving to the Carnegie Institute of Technology, now known as Carnegie Mellon University, in Pittsburgh, Pennsylvania. In his later years he recalled this time, from 1952 to 1960, as his most productive period. Whilst there, he collaborated with two brilliant faculty members, the school's dean G. L. Bach, and Herbert Simon (June 15, 1916–February 9, 2001), who were both engaged in creating a new and much more quantitative business school, along similar lines to the Cowles Foundation established by Alfred Cowles III at Chicago just a couple of years earlier under the leadership of Jacob Marschak. At the Carnegie Institute of Technology, he came to formulate two seminal ideas that led to a Nobel Memorial Prize he shared with Merton Miller – his Life Cycle Hypothesis, and the Modigliani–Miller Theorem.

8
The Early Years of Merton Miller

While Merton Howard Miller's namesake may denote he is the keeper of the mill, his contributions to finance are by no means run of the mill.

His namesake can be traced back to families that had shuttled between the commercial centers of London and Holland since the 1800s. In this era of burgeoning global trade, and following the defeat of Napoleon Bonaparte, England was the global naval superpower, while Amsterdam played important roles in the areas of banking and trade, especially the shipping of goods from Europe to England and abroad. London and Amsterdam were therefore two of the world's largest mutual trading partners, and many families and much cargo shuttled between these two world cities separated by only 200 nautical miles by ship.

The Millers were one such family. They worked in shoes, textiles, and cigar manufacturing within the Jewish communities on both sides of the English Channel.

The family patriarch, Henry Miller, was born in Rotterdam in 1811. He married Ellen Judah there, and they lived together in Amsterdam, where they had two boys – Judah, born in February of 1839 and Lewis, born in 1843. By this time, they were already moving the family between Amsterdam and London.

Ellen subsequently married again, to Joel Abrahams, a drafter who also divided time between the two communities across the channel. Joel and Ellen raised the two sons of Henry, and had a boy and two girls of their own. Each of them learned a trade, ranging from slipper making to shoemaking and cigar making.

The oldest boy, Judah Henry Miller married Caroline Jacob Stodel in London in October of 1862, and then moved his family to America in 1867 to pursue his cigar-making vocation.

This family, too, was equally mobile, but by then between London and New York City, a much wider gulf of water. Their three girls and five boys were born in London, except for the fifth child, Hannah, who was born in New York in 1870.

The sixth child, and fourth boy, Lewis, was born in London on October 25, 1871. Raised in London, he learned his family trade as a shoemaker. When he was 22 years of age, he married Esther Bollel (also originally from Amsterdam) on January 22, 1893 and moved his family to Massachusetts in 1902.

By the time the Miller family immigrated to the United States, it had grown through the birth of two children, Joel (February 2, 1895–June 27, 1955) and Hannah, named after an uncle and an aunt, respectively.

When he first arrived in America, Lewis supported his family by working as a sole cutter in a shoe factory. Lewis subsequently left factory work and became a city constable. The family was beginning to enjoy some of the advantages of middle-class life in America, and they placed a great faith in the value of education. His children attended Malden High School, from where Joel graduated at the age of 17, before moving on to study at Harvard.

Upon his graduation from college in 1916, Joel volunteered for selective service in the U.S. Army. By then, the United States was in the throes of World War I, and Joel Lewis was posted to a military university in France, where he taught the troops.

A few years after his return from service, Joel married Sylvia Francis Starr, a Yiddish Russian who had come with her family as they immigrated to the United States when she was just 13 years old. They had just one child, Merton Howard Miller, who was born in Boston on May 16, 1923.

Joel and Sylvia prized education, as many immigrant Jewish families likewise prized, but few could afford. Yet, Joel was not the first in his family to graduate from a prestigious Massachusetts university. By the early 1900s, a number of members of the Miller family were already residing in the Boston area. His uncle Joel, after whom he was named, had graduated from the Massachusetts Institute of Technology and had established a successful career as a research chemist. The younger Joel admired his uncle's ambition, and shared his uncle's commitment to sacrifice so that he may achieve a high quality education. Their work ethic paid dividends.

When Joel and Sylvia married, he was supplementing the family income by producing a newspaper in his hometown of Malden, Massachusetts. He published a wide range of stories, from the local

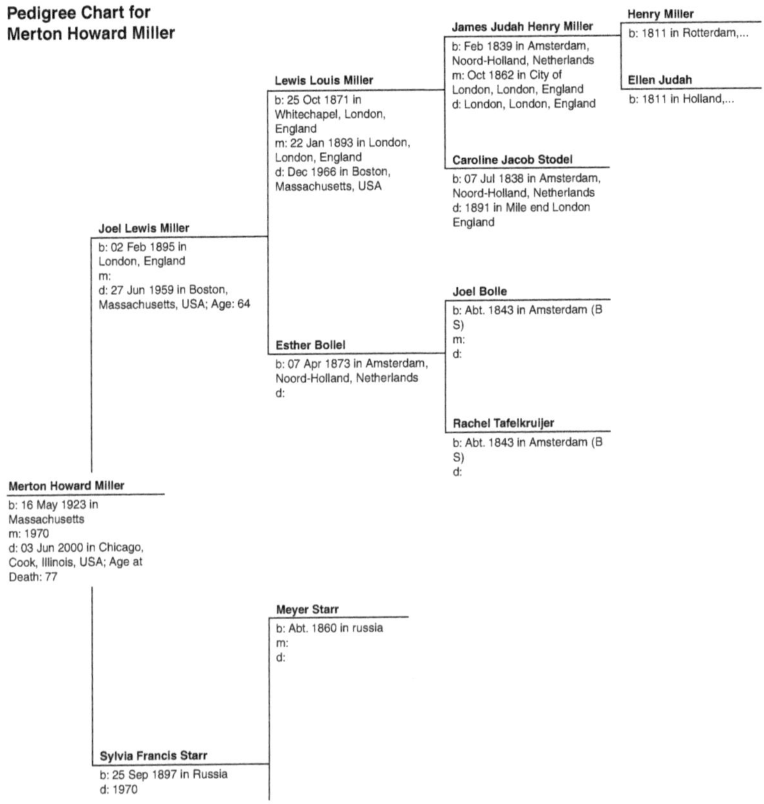

Figure 8.1 The Merton Howard Miller Family Tree

high school football games to the operation of Boston trolleys, and even had a scoop on the death of Pope Benedict in 1922. He was also a campaigning reporter ran a series of stories vigorously condemning a practice that allowed judges to appear in front of their own courts. This brush with the institutions of law no doubt piqued his interest in the law and his subsequent vocation. He began to put himself through school, first at Harvard, and then completing his law degree at Suffolk Law School, and established his own general practice upon graduation in 1929 at the age of 35.

Joel had a lifelong love of both Harvard and the law. He rose to serve as the Massachusetts Assistant Attorney General from 1945 to 1949. Throughout his career, he remained devoted to community service, on behalf of disabled veterans, the Salvation Army, the Boy Scouts, as campaign manager for a mayor, and on behalf of both the state Republican Committee and the Masons. Joel had represented his state at the Republican National Convention in Chicago in 1952 when the party nominated Dwight D. ('Ike') Eisenhower, who would go on to be elected as the nation's 34th president later that year.

Joel prized both education and public service, and his son and only child could hardly resist following in his footsteps, at least in the broadest sense.

While Joel and Sylvia's only child, Merton Howard Miller, was born in 1923 at the beginning of the Roaring Twenties, Merton's formative years occurred during the years of the Great Depression. His father graduated from law school and passed the bar before the Great Crash, but assembled his general practice just as the nation plunged into the depths of economic depression. Merton attended grammar and high school in most challenging times when one was grateful for any opportunity and would consider oneself fortunate simply to avoid poverty.

Miller was raised in Dorchester, a working-class area of Boston. He thrived in high school, graduated in 1940 just a month after his 17th birthday, and followed his father's path to Harvard. Miller clearly shared both his father's work ethic and his entrepreneurial spirit. Not only did he finish high school early, but he also graduated from Harvard with his Bachelor of Arts degree in Economics in 1943, well before the graduation of the rest of his class of 1944. While at Harvard, he was taught by some of the best economists in the country, including Robert Solow, who could go on to win the Nobel Memorial Prize in 1987.

On graduating from college in 1943, Miller married Eleanor Natalie Cohen (December 1922–August 28, 1969), the only child of Massachusetts-born Joseph G. Cohen, an insurance salesman, and Doris Paretzky. Eleanor had grown up on Evelyn Street in nearby Mattapan, a little over a mile from Merton's childhood home on Talbot Avenue in Dorchester and they had first met while she was attending Simmons College in Boston.

The year 1943 was not the best time to graduate from college. By then, conscription was in place to generate the troops necessary to fight World War II following the United States' entry into the war in late 1941. Merton was deaf in one ear, however, so he was instead asked to serve the national interest in the area of economic analysis.

Miller worked first for the Division of Tax Research of the United States Treasury Department in Washington, D.C., and then with the Division of Research and Statistics of the Board of Governors of the

Federal Reserve System and he continued to work in Washington after the ending of the war. While they were living in Washington, his wife, Eleanor, served with the Red Cross.

For six years after his graduation, two events delayed Miller's return to his academic studies. First World War II and then his economics work for the government intervened. While he had harbored hopes that the evening classes he was taking at nearby George Washington University in Washington could parlay into a Ph.D. degree at some point, by by 1949 Miller had realized that he would be unable to combine work and study with the rigor he desired. He felt he had to make an important decision, and, after much trepidation, shared his decision with his parents.

Miller had decided to attend the Ph.D. program full time at Johns Hopkins University in nearby Baltimore – in the new area of finance. He had been working in this particular area of expertise at the Federal Reserve for the last few years and he felt he had a good aptitude in this increasingly important field. He knew that his decision would be unpopular with his parents, given their love for and devotion to Harvard University. He readily admitted that Harvard may have been the better school, but he also felt different academic perspectives would enhance his intellectual development. What he did not share in his letter to his parents, however, was that he did feel troubled by the anti-Semitic tone that had developed at Harvard in the run up to World War II and the resentment of the Jewish intellectual refugees that were beginning to inundate American campuses.

It may appear somewhat ironic that Merton Miller took such a principled stand against the prevailing anti-Semitism at Harvard. He and Eleanor were raised in Jewish families, but they could hardly be regarded as orthodox. However, while in Washington, they were swept up in a new movement of followers of Felix Adler (August 13, 1851–April 24, 1933), the son of Samuel Adler, the rabbi of the Reform Jewish Temple Emanu-El in New York. Felix founded the "Ethical Culture Movement", commonly known as the Ethical Humanists.

Their beliefs included:

- The belief that morality is independent of theology;
- The affirmation that new moral problems have arisen in modern industrial society which have not been adequately dealt with by the world's religions;
- The duty to engage in philanthropy in the advancement of morality;
- The belief that self-reform should go in lock step with social reform;

- The establishment of republican rather than monarchical governance of Ethical societies
- The agreement that educating the young is the most important aim.[1]

This movement had developed in the late nineteenth century but had then stagnated until after World War II. In 1946, new societies for the movement formed in New Jersey and in Merton and Eleanor Miller's home of Washington, D.C. These societies often attracted individuals from academic communities and from a variety of faiths, not at all unlike the tradition of the Unitarian Universalists. To the Millers, the Ethical Humanists represented a moral philosophy they could practice. The group also attracted other intellectual notables such as Albert Einstein.

Merton Miller's choice of Johns Hopkins was not just a pragmatic one. Johns Hopkins at that time, as today, was known for its first-rate medical school. However, it was also developing a strong finance program. The university had offered him a teaching opportunity that would provide his family with a reasonable income, and that would also allow him to transfer some of his George Washington coursework.

Merton and Eleanor hardly took the decision lightly, and they knew his parents would not either. The young couple had delayed starting a family and had saved assiduously. In later life, Merton expressed gratitude to his parents who had instilled upon him such a determined sense of delayed financial gratification that he could make such an investment in education.

The young Miller family's move to Baltimore was also based on the belief that their new adopted city offered them support in ways beyond a decent paycheck. Eleanor had an uncle and aunt in Baltimore, and the city shared with Boston its urban sensibilities. Their decision proved to be a fortuitous one because Merton Miller went on to thrive at Johns Hopkins. He was especially excited about the opportunity to work with Fritz Machlup (December 15, 1902–January 30, 1983), an Austrian-American economist who was one of the first to emphasize the importance of knowledge and information on economic and financial variables. Prof. Machlup had arrived at Johns Hopkins just two years before Merton enrolled and he took Merton Miller under his tutelage.

The year 1949 also coincided with the establishment of the Graduate School of Industrial Administration at the Carnegie Institute. Herbert Simon had arrived from Chicago to work with G.L. Bach, William W. Cooper, and others who were attracted to the new school, which was devoted to creating the economic and behavioral science underpinnings of business studies. This was just at the cusp of an appreciation for new quantitative techniques and the computing technology pioneered at the Carnegie Institute that was intended to help with the new quantitative analyses. Herbert Simon, Charles Holt, John Muth, and Franco Modigliani collaborated in developing the new dynamic programming techniques that would revolutionize finance theory. They extended results from physics and pure mathematics to the analysis of economic and finance problems first under certainty and then under uncertain conditions. This was the academic hotbed into which Miller had entered.

The strength of Miller's experience at Johns Hopkins allowed him to be offered a visiting lectureship at the prestigious London School of Economics for a year upon completion of his Ph.D. in 1952. In that same year, their first child, Pamela, was born just as the family left for England.

Upon their return from London, Miller was offered a position at what was then the Carnegie Institute of Technology, but is now known as the Carnegie-Mellon, in Pittsburgh, Pennsylvania. Created by the "Gilded Era" American baron of business, Andrew Carnegie, in the heartland of America's heavy industry, the school had an excellent reputation for engineering. By this time, it was also developing a very strong reputation for a more analytic approach to finance and business. At his new institution he had the opportunity to work closely with the famous organizational theorist and behavioral economist, Herbert Simon (June 15, 1916–February 9, 2001), who went on to be awarded the Nobel Memorial Prize in 1978, and Franco Modigliani, his eventual co-author in their most famous joint work that helped establish the field of corporate finance. By the time they met, Modigliani had already completed his work that would earn him a Nobel Memorial Prize in 1985 for his development of the *Life Cycle* Model.

The collaboration

Modigliani had been pondering the nature of capital structure ever since he had begun to absorb the economic theories of investment that John Maynard Keynes had developed over the Great Depression. In his exploration of the reasons why a firm would invest in one project rather than another, Modigliani was constantly confronted with the conventional wisdom that the decision would depend on both the cost of investment funds for the firm and the way such funds were obtained, either through debt or an increase in equity. Modigliani remained unconvinced, however. He was increasingly sure that the method of financing expansion should not matter, especially if market arbitrage ensures value is based on what is produced, rather than how it was financed, as John Burr Williams had stated in relative obscurity decades earlier. In his collaboration with Merton Miller, Modigliani's intuition took the form of a postulate that the market value of liabilities could not depend on the capital structure. Their rationale was that shareholders could either replicate or reverse any corporate leverage through their own lending or borrowing. Of course, they can do so only if there are no asymmetries in tax treatment between lending and borrowing of the firm or the shareholder, and that each has identical access to financial capital. Despite these strong assumptions, the intuition is appealing.

Modigliani tested his postulate on one of his classes at the Carnegie Institute of Technology which Merton Miller happened to be auditing. The two soon-to-be collaborators both appreciated that their result defied conventional wisdom, so they worked laboriously on their analysis of the irrelevancy of an optimal capital structure, and applied significant mathematical rigor to their work.

9
The Times

The chief financial officer (CFO) of a corporation in bygone times was charged with determining the optimal capital structure of the firm. The CFO had to answer certain questions. Should the corporation borrow to expand, should it issue additional preferred or common stock, or should it expand out of retained earnings and perhaps forego a dividend? Until Modigliani and Miller provided clarity to these important questions, the choices were considered more of an art than a science, despite John Burr Williams's contribution in 1938. Franco Modigliani and Merton Miller showed that, under certain circumstances, the method of financing does not matter, at least with respect to shareholder value.

As noted earlier in the treatment of the contributions of John Burr Williams, the analysis which he had to pay Harvard University to publish, but which it is as timely today as it was then, offered an elegant and insightful proof of the independence of capital structure. Williams offered the "Law of the Conservation of Investment Value" in which he argued that the present worth of all future distributions of the firm are preserved regardless of whether they are distributed to debt holders, in the form of bond interest payments, preferred stockholders in the form of dividends, or common stockholders. A dividend delayed simply results in a larger dividend later as the funds are reinvested and receive, on average, the same risk-adjusted return as the equity as a whole. Hence, Williams argued, without formal proof, that the art of the determination of optimal capitalization is an esoteric exercise.

Williams's analysis is an important one for chief financial officers. How to best deploy retained earnings, or whether to issue debt or new stock to expand, is the first determination that must be made once a manager formulates a project that can generate for the company at least its average cost of capital. Williams's intuition was sound, even if it stood relatively unrecognized and unappreciated at the time:

> If the investment value of an enterprise as a whole is by definition the present worth of all its future distributions to security holders, whether on interest or dividend account, then this value in no wise depends on what the company's capitalization is. Clearly if a single individual or a single institutional investor owned all the bonds, stocks, and warrants issued by a corporation, it would not matter to this investor what the company's capitalization was. Any earnings collected as interest could not be collected as dividends. To such an individual it would be perfectly obvious that total interest- and dividend-paying power was in now wise dependent on the kind of securities issued to the company's owner. Furthermore, no change in the investment value of the enterprise as a whole would result from a change in its capitalization. Bonds could be retired with stock issues, or two classes of junior securities (i.e., common stock and warrants) cold be combined into one, without changing the investment value of the company as a whole. Such constancy of investment value is analogous to the indestructibility of matter or energy; it leads us to speak of the Law of Conservation of Investment Value, just as physicists speak of the Law of the Conservation of Matter, or the Law of Conservation of Energy.[1]

However, Williams recognized that this neutrality of the optimal capital structure was not without caveats. The treatment of various forms of corporate capital by tax authorities may affect a corporation's capital mix. In addition, the corporation's board of directors are charged with representing shareholder interests to the corporation, and often represents some of the corporation's largest shareholders. Tax ramifications, at both the corporate and shareholder levels, may then affect capitalization decisions. Accordingly, Williams qualified his conclusion:

> Since market value does not usually conform exactly to investment value, no "conservation of market value" is to be found in general. Only to a rough extent do total market values remain the same regardless of capitalization. The exceptions in practice are important enough to afford many opportunities for profit by promoters and investment bankers.[2]

Unfortunately, Williams's intuition and insights remained relatively unknown among mainstream financial academics. Not unlike the efforts of Paul Samuelson (May 15, 1915–December 13, 2009), Fischer Black (January 11, 1938–August 30, 1995), Myron Scholes (July 1, 1941–) and Robert Merton (July 4, 1910–February 23, 2003) in their 1960s reinvention of Louis Bachelier's (March 11, 1870–April 28, 1946) 1900 option pricing formula, Williams's result would have to be reinvented more than thirty years later by two academics trying to resolve among themselves the paradox of optimal capital structure.

10
The Great Idea

Andrew Carnegie (November 25, 1835–August 11, 1919) was a Scottish immigrant who epitomized the American Dream during its Gilded Age. He oversaw an immense expansion of both the transportation and steel industries in the United States which allowed a new America to overtake his former homeland of Great Britain as the world's largest economy. Carnegie achieved his remarkable success through the adoption of a new and distinctly American model of entrepreneurship and free markets. In turn, Andrew Carnegie went on to develop a philanthropic philosophy which he chronicled in his 1889 article that was later reprinted and commonly called *The Gospel of Wealth.*[1]

Carnegie's philosophy was that the rich ought to use the wealth they generate as a result of the free markets they enjoy to invest in society and enhance the economy. Carnegie's passion and insights came from his poor upbringing in Dunfermline, Scotland. His parents had sought opportunity in the United States in 1848 just as Carnegie was entering his teenage years. Carnegie had a lifelong bent toward engineering and entrepreneurship, from his beginnings as a telegrapher through to his investments in railroads, oil derricks, and bridges by the age of thirty.

Carnegie also dabbled in finance as a bond salesman in his efforts in Europe to raise money for American commerce. He used these proceeds to finance the building of the Carnegie Steel Company in Pittsburgh, Pennsylvania. In the year he republished his *Gospel of Wealth*, he sold his steel company to J. P. Morgan for $480 million, which is the equivalent to about $14 billion at present value. He used his handsome profit for this venture to set an example of philanthropy for the rest of his life. Among his endeavors were a string of local libraries, the Carnegie Hall for music performance in New York City, a number of museums and foundations, an endowment for international peace, and the Carnegie Institute of Technology in Pittsburgh.

Carnegie's vision was not confined to a narrow perspective, of finance, of industry, or of technology. He was a great believer in combining perspectives and creating synergies in the areas of society and in education. Consistent with his philanthropic philosophy to nurture the education of those who fueled economic consumption, he created the Carnegie Institute of Technology with the aim of educating the children of Pittsburgh's working class. The mission was broader than simply that of establishing a school of technology, though. His college also encouraged the study of business, economics, and other social and public policy studies. Cross-disciplinary research was particularly encouraged. In 1971, the College was merged with the Mellon Institute of Industrial Research to form Carnegie Mellon University.

In the 1960s, the Carnegie Institute of Technology worked to attract a series of great minds in economic and financial policy: for example, as mentioned earlier, Merton Miller and Franco Modigliani were colleagues there. Its express mission was to bolster the College's contribution in novel thought in finance and economics. This vision was promulgated by economist George Bach and political scientist Herbert A. Simon in an effort to improve American managerial expertise at the onset of the Cold War in the late 1940s. When William Larimer Mellon granted the school $6 million to found a school of industrial administration, Bach became its first dean.

The school was not only novel in its desire to attack managerial questions from a variety of perspectives. It was also an early adopter of computing technology in business simulations. The faculty Bach and Simon attracted were adept at theory, application, and technological innovation. Franco Modigliani was the perfect addition to that mix.

However, Modigliani was not the only high-profile faculty member to be attracted to such an innovative center in fomenting new ideas. Pioneers in behavioral finance, rational expectations, bounded rationality and quantitative decision making and cross-disciplinary research included subsequent Nobel Memorial Prize winners such as Robert Lucas, Jr., Herbert A. Simon, Oliver E. Williamson, Dale Mortensen (February 2, 1939–January 9, 2014), Edward Prescott (December 26, 1940–), Lars Peter Hansen (October 26, 1952–), Finn Kydland (December 1, 1943–), and the originators of the Modigliani–Miller Theorem, Franco Modigliani and Merton Miller.

Modigliani and Miller were asked to teach a course in corporate finance to the business students in the graduate program. However, neither of them had any experience in the nuances of the optimal capital structure of a firm, which was an issue at the core of corporate finance courses offered everywhere. They diligently read through the literature on the art of optimal capital structure, and they were left confused at the lack of a unified and accepted principle. With only cursory knowledge of John Burr Williams's pronouncement twenty years earlier, Modigliani and Miller pondered this seeming paradox and concluded that, no matter how they looked at the problem, they were drawn to the same conclusion: Capital structure should not matter. The paper they wrote was subsequently published in the *American Economic Review*, entitled "The Cost of Capital, Corporation Finance and the Theory of Investment"[2] has been known as the Modigliani–Miller (M&M) theorem ever since.

Specifically, they demonstrated that a firm's dividend strategy or its debt/equity ratio, its capital structure, should not affect the value of the firm or the stock, at least under certain assumptions that they further discuss at length in their paper. This result culminated in perhaps the most well-known theorem of corporate finance.

Recall Williams's agricultural analogy of corporate valuation in 1937. Williams's rather colorful intuition argued that the value of a corporation should depend only on the present value of its future dividends. While earnings contribute to dividends, they are not the same as dividends. He framed his intuition in the form of a poem:

- A cow for her milk
- A hen for her eggs,
- And a stock, by heck,
- For her dividends.
- An orchard for fruit,
- Bees for their honey,
- And stocks, besides,
- For their dividends.

In *Financial Innovations and Market Volatility*,[3] Merton Miller offered a strikingly similar analogy, perhaps unknowing of Williams' earlier metaphorical poem:

> "Think of the firm as a gigantic tub of whole milk.
>
> The farmer can sell the whole milk as is.
>
> Or he can separate out the cream and sell it at a considerably higher price than the whole milk would bring.

> (That's the analog of a firm selling low-yield and hence high-priced debt securities.)
>
> But, of course, what the farmer would have left would be skim milk with low butterfat content and that would sell for much less than whole milk.
>
> That corresponds to the levered equity.
>
> The M and M proposition says that if there were no costs of separation (and, of course, no government dairy-support programs), the cream plus the skim milk would bring the same price as the whole milk."

In 1958, Franco Modigliani and Merton Miller proved this intuition. They did so with a nod to Williams, even as they point out that Williams's analysis was insufficiently thorough:

> None of these writers [Williams and others] describe in any detail the mechanism which is supposed to keep the average cost of capital constant under changes in capital structure. They seem, however, to be visualizing the equilibrating mechanism in terms of switches by investors between stocks and bonds as the yields of each get out of line with their "riskiness." This is an argument quite different from the pure arbitrage mechanism underlying our proof, and the difference is crucial.[4]

They note that while Williams did not prove his "Law of Conservation of Investment Value," he nonetheless seemed to understand that arbitrage is the mechanism that provides for the discipline upon which Williams and Modigliani and Miller rely.

The M&M theorem

One way to demonstrate the result is to compare two firms that are the same in every way with the exception of their capital structure: One firm is financed entirely from equity, and the other firm is financed with a combination of equity and debt. In other words, the latter firm is leveraged because the equity owners will receive all earnings, net of interest paid to debt, but do not have to advance all the capital. The Modigliani–Miller theorem asserts that, under certain conditions, both firms have the same value. In other words, the weighted average cost of their invested capital, in the form of equity and debt, is irrelevant in the determination of corporate value.

To establish their results, it is necessary to make some qualifying assumptions that are relatively well-accepted in the finance literature. First, they assume that there exist perfect capital markets. This assumption requires that stocks and bonds are perfectly divisible, that there are no constraints on buying and selling securities, that information is perfect and costless for both sides of the market, that investors have the same unrestricted access to borrowing as does the firm, and that the market is fully rational.

Second, one must assume that full rationality and perfect information implies that all investors develop identical and unbiased expectations on the earnings of the firm, before interest and taxes, commonly called the EBIT.

Third, comparable firms with similar access to debt and equity are considered to be in a homogeneous risk class. In other words, within their class, these firms have the same risk and hence should offer the same expected earnings if perfect arbitrage exists.

Finally, all earnings are paid out in either interest or dividends.

To begin, we assume that there are no corporate taxes for the firm or personal taxes for investors. Under these assumptions, the value V_U of the firm with no debt, the unlevered firm, is identical to the value V_L of the levered firm:

$$V_U = V_L$$

The intuition of this result is relatively simple. Imagine an investor who is contemplating the purchase of shares in the two firms L and U. If the investor chooses to purchase the unlevered firm but borrows some of the money for this purchase in the same proportion and the same interest rate as does the levered firm, arbitrage ensures that the return to this investor, net of interest payments, must be the same as if shares in the levered firm were purchased.

This result immediately identifies the importance of one of the assumptions made by Modigliani and Miller. The investor's cost of borrowing must be the same as the cost facing the firm, and it must be able to attain the same level of leverage afforded the firm.

Their next proposition demonstrates that the weighted average cost of the firm's capital stays constant as the debt/equity ratio (D/E) increases. Let this weighted average cost of capital be given by r_0 while the required return to equity be given by r_e and the required return to debt by given by r_d. Then, the weighted average cost of capital r is a linear combination of the cost of debt and equity:

$$r_0 = \frac{D}{D+E} r_d + \frac{E}{D+E} r_e$$

where D and E are the respective share of debt and equity for the firm, r_0 is the unlevered cost of capital, r_D is the firm's cost of debt, and r_e is the required return to equity. Rearranging, we see that:

$$r_e = r_0 + \frac{D}{E}(r_0 - r_d)$$

A graph of these relationships is given by:

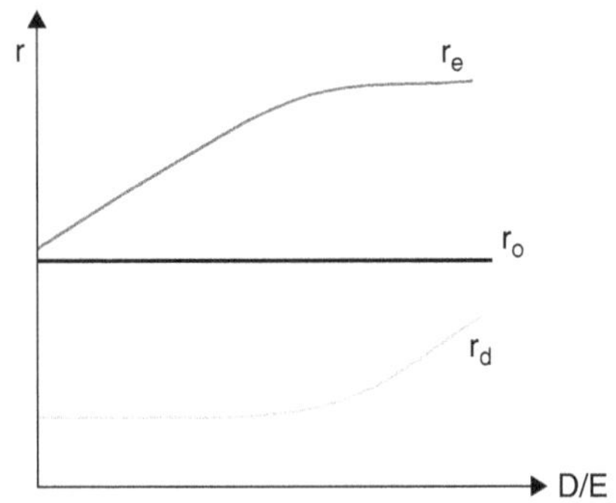

Figure 10.1 The Relative Cost of Equity and Debt

As the debt to equity ratio rises, the return on equity also rises commensurate with the greater concentration of the firm's risk on the smaller share of equity holders.

While they did not actually realize it at the time, their result also depends on the results of Ronald Coase, to be treated below. For the market to be efficient in the way on which Modigliani and Miller's theorem depends, there cannot be any transactions costs or similar barriers to the exchanges of debt and equity by the firm or by the respective financial markets.

The long-standing literature on the Weighted Average Cost of Capital is not naïve with respect to taxation, however. It is not difficult to extend Modigliani and Miller's results to include corporate taxes. Let these taxes be given by T_C. Then,

$$V_L = V_U + T_C D.$$

where V_U is the value of the unlevered firm (without debt) and V_L is the value of the levered firm. Without loss of generality, let us assume that debt interest rates are expected to remain constant and that the level of debt is in perpetuity, or can be constantly resolved at the same interest rate. Then, the term T_CD represents the tax rate times the total value of debt. Since the tax paid on interest is deductible for the firm, this term represents the savings to the firm that can then be capitalized into the value of the levered firm. Under this scenario with corporate taxes, the Modigliani–Miller theorem can be modified accordingly:

$$r_e = r_0 + \frac{D}{E}(r_0 - r_d)(1 - T_c)$$

where D and E are the respective share of debt and equity for the firm, D/E is the debt/equity ratio, r_0 is the unlevered cost of capital, r_D is the firm's cost of debt, r_e is the required return to equity, and T_C is the corporate tax rate.

This relationship does not change the qualitative aspect of the previous results and graphical relationship between the cost of capital and the debt/equity ratio. Increased leverage still concentrates risk on the equity holder and raises its commensurate return. However, we see that increased leverage provides for a tax benefit to the firm and hence the equity holder. The tax write-off acts as a subsidy that lowers the cost of debt to the firm and hence drops the weighted average cost of capital. This suggests that the value of the firm will rise with increased debt and leverage.

In their original 1958 article Modigliani and Miller actually failed to tease out the accurate expression under conditions involving corporate taxation. However, in 1963 they offered a correction that verified their qualitative conclusion but with the correct expression for the level of taxation for the corporation.[5]

11
Applications

There is probably no concept so widely taught in every introductory course in corporate finance that has garnered so much controversy and criticism. Often, the concept of the neutrality of capital structure is taught immediately after students have spent time mastering the calculation of the weighted average cost of capital. Then, students are taught that the choice of debt or equity financing does not matter.

Yet while one might view this seeming paradox with frustration, Modigliani and Miller offered their theory as an opportunity to engage in a richer discussion of precisely when capital structure does matter. This is the value of their contribution, especially as bolstered by their 1963 follow-up that elaborated, extended, and qualified some of their original conclusions.

This extension does not take into account whether or how individual investors are taxed, though. If individuals are not taxed on dividends and receive the same tax deduction from the debt they use to invest as does the corporation, the original formulation of the Modigliani–Miller theorem returns.

The essential element of what Modigliani and Miller established is that arbitrage makes the capital choice irrelevant, absent of tax and capital access asymmetries. This arbitrage result hinges crucially on the ability of a shareholder to gain the same access and terms for financial capital as can the corporation. Such perfect substitutability, which permits the leverage that can approximate or reverse the leverage of the firm, is likely violated in practice, but not in a consistent manner. A shareholder with a strong portfolio may have better access to capital than a firm with a low level of capitalization. While this assumption is analytically appealing, it is likely not practically appropriate.

Nonetheless, their intuition developed in the theory, and especially in its reliance on and elaboration of the principle of arbitrage, framed Modigliani and Miller's discussion in the late 1950s. A decade later, arbitrage formed the foundation of the great mind Eugene Fama's *Efficient Market Hypothesis*, in the great mind William Sharpe's *Capital Asset Pricing Model*, and in Fisher Black and Myron Scholes's *Option Pricing Theory*.

This notion of arbitrage is now a standard assumption in finance. For instance, when Fisher Black began to develop a theory by which an optimal investment portfolio could outperform the market, he proposed the use of stock options as a way to hedge risk at any time. Black began by assuming that an option price is a function of the underlying stock price and the remaining time until the option's settlement date. From this relationship one could determine how the option price must change to adjust for time. This rate must be proportional to the risk-adjusted time value of money. From that intuition, he developed a differential equation for the change in an option price over time as a function of risk, as measured by the stock's variance, the stock price, and the required rate of return.

Black's colleague, Myron Scholes, looked at the equation, listened to Black's intuition, and instead saw the problem as one of arbitrage. He wondered if options could instead be used to ensure a return for one who sold a stock short and purchased an option to cover the position. Because this hedge yields no risk to the investor, arbitrage should provide only the risk-free rate of return for the pair of transactions, if the option purchase and short were in the correct proportions. Such an application of arbitrage to *close a model* in finance is now a standard technique. It was not so thoroughly integrated into the finance theorist's toolbox, though, until Modigliani and Miller employed arbitrage in the first significant application to such great effect in their seminal 1958 contribution.

12
The Prize

The Nobel Memorial Prize is the only prize associated with Alfred Nobel that is awarded to the social sciences. Yet Nobel had not actually founded what is now formally called the *Sveriges Riksbank Prize in Economic Sciences in Memory of Alfred Nobel.* Nobel lamented his creation of dynamite, which had yielded numerous ways to contribute to the social good, but also produced some less benign applications. When Nobel determined he would create a legacy that would celebrate contributions by intellectuals to the social good, the disciplines of finance and economics had not yet entered the scientific realm. Only with the subsequent development of economics and finance as a social science which could inform and enhance the public good have these disciplines become candidates for recognition by the Nobel Committee.

The Nobel Memorial Prize is actually not administered by the Alfred Nobel Foundation. Rather, the Sveriges Riksbank Prize in Economic Sciences in Memory of Alfred Noble was created by Sweden's Central Bank and first awarded in 1969. Franco Modigliani and Robert Merton won the 17th awarding of the Nobel Memorial Prize.

Those who could be potential candidates for the Prize constitute a rather exclusive club. The various legitimate candidates for this club are aware of one another, even, at times, preoccupied by the possibility of being awarded the Prize. But, while the Nobel Memorial Prize Committee recognizes those who demonstrate the cleverness and utility of innovations in economics and finance, the committee also strives to signal important new paths in future research.

Kenneth Arrow (August 23, 1921–) had overlapped with Franco Modigliani briefly when both participated in the Cowles Foundation while it was still based at the University of Chicago. Their respective wives, Selma and Serena, had once shared stories of the events surrounding the awarding to Arrow of the fourth Nobel Memorial Prize in 1972.[1] Selma told Serena that, should the Nobel Memorial Prize Committee ever call early in the morning, which corresponds to midday in Sweden, one should immediately take a shower since there will be reporters on the doorstep within minutes.[2]

Modigliani learned of his own award of the prize early on the morning of October 15, 1985. According to his Nobel citation, Modigliani was being awarded the Sveriges Riksbank Prize in Economic Sciences in Memory of Alfred Nobel "for his pioneering analyses of saving and of financial markets". Modigliani actually received his award primarily for contributions other than the Modigliani–Miller Theorem. The committee noted that Modigliani's Life Cycle Model helped create the discipline of personal finance by demonstrating the mechanism through which people formulate their savings decision and by resolving how a growing economy typically mobilizes the increased savings necessary to fuel growth, while a declining economy will often end up spending beyond its means. His Life Cycle Model allowed us to understand, for the first time, some observations in econometric data that had previously defied explanation. It also had significant public policy implications because it provided theoretical reasons for why budget deficits can impinge upon personal and national savings.

13 The Later Years of Merton Miller

As mentioned earlier, Merton H. Miller, in collaboration with Franco Modigliani, developed the Modigliani–Miller theorem of corporate finance. With Harry M. Markowitz and William F. Sharpe, Miller was awarded the Nobel Memorial Prize in Economics in 1990.

According to the citation, Miller had received the Nobel Memorial Prize "for his fundamental contributions to the theory of corporate finance."[1] The Nobel Memorial Prize Committee made the award for his:

> ...pioneering contribution to financial economics [which] concerns the theory of corporate finance and the evaluation of firms on markets. The most important achievements in this field were made by Merton Miller, initially in collaboration with Franco Modigliani (who received the Alfred Nobel Memorial Prize in Economic Sciences in 1985 mainly for other contributions). This theory explains the relation (or lack of one) between firms' capital asset structure and dividend policy on one hand and their market value on the other.

Miller remained at Carnegie-Mellon until 1961. While they were still living in Pittsburgh, Merton and Eleanor had two more daughters, Margot in 1955 and Louise in 1958. In 1961, he left the Carnegie Institute to join the Graduate School of Business at the University of Chicago, where he remained for the rest of his life, apart from a one-year visiting professorship for the academic year 1966–67 which he spent at the University of Louvain in Belgium. At Chicago, he was appointed the Robert R. McCormick Distinguished Service Professor. Most of his work at this time remained concentrated on achieving a better understanding of corporate finance, except for a brief stint as a director of the Chicago Board of Trade. There, he became part of finance history.

At the end of the 1960s, commodity futures trading remained a sleepy business on the Chicago Board of Trade. At this time growing global competitive pressures induced its leadership to contemplate the creation of a new market for options trading. However, this was still a complicated financial transaction. Contracts were not standardized, and there was no prevailing theory of options pricing to help traders determine fair market values. In the 1970s, the Options Pricing Theory formulators Fisher Black and Myron Scholes and other University of Chicago colleagues contributed to the discovery of a solution to these roadblocks. Miller was asked to join the leadership team in Chicago the next decade at a point when the Exchange was beginning to grow dramatically.

The exposure Miller received in real financial markets shifted his research away from esoteric financial theory and toward the regulatory and economic problems in securities exchanges. He continued to serve as a director on the Chicago Mercantile Exchange, and chaired an academic panel there that was charged with the forensic investigation of the Crash of October in 1987.

In the tradition of Chicago and his fellow Chicago Nobel prize winners Milton Friedman (July 31, 1912–November 16, 2006), Theodore Schultz (April 30, 1902–February 26, 1998), and George Stigler (January 17, 1911–December 1, 1991), Miller became an avid and lifelong supporter of the notion of free markets. For instance, Miller remained a strong supporter of the use of financial derivatives, many of which were pioneered in those heady days of the Chicago Board of Options Exchange in the 1970s, with Miller's active participation. Indeed, Miller wrote a book, *Merton Miller on Derivatives*,[2] which argued government regulation in the derivatives markets would do little to contribute to market efficiency, and may, in the worst circumstances, create confusion and dysfunction in the market.

During this same period, from the end of the 1960s to the early 1970s, the Miller family suffered a personal loss, with the untimely death of Merton's wife, Eleanor. Merton Miller was left with three young daughters to raise. Sometime later, Miller remarried, and he continued to work at Chicago while the family lived both in nearby Hyde Park, and on a hobby farm in Woodstock, Illinois. His life was not confined to the academic and the domestic, however: Miller also remained a lifelong fan of the local American football team, the Chicago Bears, and held season tickets throughout much of his adult life in Chicago.

Miller contributed to the disciplines of finance and economics in other ways as well. In addition to his participation on the Board of

Chicago Board of Trade from 1983 to 1985, and his membership on the Board of the Chicago Mercantile Exchange from 1990 to 2000, he was also nominated to the American Academy of Arts and Sciences. He was also a member of the American Economic Association, the American Finance Association, and the Econometric Society.

Over his career, he wrote three books, *The Theory of Finance* in 1972 (with Eugene F. Fama), *Macroeconomics: A Neoclassical Introduction* in 1986 (with Charles W. Upton), and his 1997 *Merton Miller on Derivatives*. Toward the end of his illustrious career, Miller became regarded as one of the elder statesmen of the field of finance. He died on June 3, 2003 in Chicago and was survived by his daughters, Pamela, Margot, and Louise, as well as his two grandsons.

Upon his death, there was an outpouring of respect for Merton Miller's contributions. The great mind and fellow Nobel Memorial Prize winner Myron Scholes remarked that:

> He was a visionary, a man of intense curiosity, with a willingness to embrace ambiguity and use his brilliant intuition to overturn a multitude of long-held 'truths. His research exhibited a marvelous interconnectedness to once seemingly unrelated ideas. He has left us a research legacy that is unsurpassed in financial economics.[3]

Another great mind and Nobel Memorial Prize winner, Eugene Fama, expressed a similar academic affection:[4]

> Merton Miller epitomized the best of the University of Chicago Graduate School of Business. All who knew him at Chicago and elsewhere recognize him as a path-breaking, world-class scholar, a dedicated teacher who mentored many of the most famous contributors to finance and a graceful and insightful colleague who enhanced the research of all around him.

14
The Later Years of Franco Modigliani

Following his most productive years at the Carnegie Institute of Technology, Modigliani moved to one of the other two prestigious institutes of technology, the Massachusetts Institute of Technology (MIT), to which he moved in 1960. He was to remain there for the rest of his career. At MIT, he continued his work on the business cycle, rational expectations, personal finance, and the financial valuation of firms that he had first addressed with Merton Miller. There, Modigliani also remained very innovative and open to new research techniques. Early in the introduction of computational methods to finance, Modigliani helped develop some of the first large-scale econometric models of the United States economy. These tools were continued by the National Bureau of Economic Research and the United States Federal Reserve. Modigliani resided at MIT when he heard he had won the Nobel Prize in Economics Sciences.

After the awarding of the Nobel Memorial Prize, Modigliani remained active. He had an almost legendary reputation for his intellectual generosity toward his colleagues and graduate students. He was an early adopter of computational methods in economics and finance. Had computing technology existed a decade earlier, he and his graduate student, Richard Brumberg, would have been spared countless hours of tedious work as they together worked out how overlapping generations of consumers make their personal financial decisions. These two colleagues at the University of Illinois had tracked how the aggregate savings and spending of consecutive generations would track if these households realize an unexpected growth of income over their lifecycle. They discovered that households save more than they otherwise would as a hedge against later retirement had they known they would become increasingly comfortable financially. They carried out these comparisons not with the aid of computer spreadsheets, but, rather, through working on rows and columns of handwritten estimations. Shortly after their ground-breaking but tedious work together, Brumberg died suddenly of a brain tumor.

Modigliani immediately saw the advantages of computers that could take care of such human tedium. He became well known among colleagues as an early adopter of computer technology as early as the 1950s, and was an effective advocate for the utility of computing for his entire academic life.

Modigliani also entered into the political world during this period, drawing on conclusions he drew from his research. He had advocated for tax-sheltered pension plans, and argued that individuals should be permitted to borrow against the assets in these plans to smooth out lifetime consumption. He even applied for a patent based on this concept that is now routinely used as a personal financial planning tool.

By the time of the stagflation that affected industrialized economies in the mid to late 1970s, Modigliani also saw the danger of cost of living allowances on wages when the economy is subjected to external price shocks of the type the economy witnessed from rising oil prices following the OPEC oil cartel embargos. He correctly saw that such wage and price indexing could lead to an inflationary spiral that would wreak havoc on the financial markets and throw the economy into a recession from which it would be difficult to recover. He took this point to Washington, and even to his native home of Italy. Unfortunately, his advocacy in Italy, alongside his MIT colleague, Ezio Tarantelli, was ultimately to cost Tarantelli his life. The two colleagues proposed reforms to the Italian economy that caused Tarantelli to be murdered by Italy's Brigato Rosso (Red Brigade) just a few weeks before the successful national referendum in Italy that would eliminate wage indexing in labor contracts.[1]

When in Italy campaigning for their proposals in the winter of 1978 at the height of that country's economic and political turmoil and violence, his wife warned him not to turn around if someone should shout his name in the street, lest he might be shot. When he left his hotel room the morning after a televised debate in Italy, someone did indeed call out his name. As he picked up his pace, the supposed heckler caught him and grabbed his jacket. But, rather than being an assassin, the intruder proved to be a cobbler who wanted to tell him that Mr. Modigliani's comments on television the previous night were the only ones that were "anything comprehensible."[2]

Modigliani was also to nurture the intellectual development of his own family. His granddaughter, Leah, was a successful investment banker for Morgan Stanley and became an influential Wall Street voice in the 1990s. The two of them teamed up to develop what is now known as the Modigliani Risk-Adjusted Performance measure. Often known as the M-Squared, this was an extension of the Sharpe Ratio which analysts have often used in financial asset pricing. The M-squared measure is easier to interpret than the Sharpe index, however, because it can be expressed as a percentage that allows analysts to benchmark mutual fund returns against a broader portfolio.

On September 25, 2003 Franco Modigliani died in his sleep at the age of 85 in the home he shared with his wife Serena in Cambridge, Massachusetts. Perhaps appropriately just the previous evening they had been dining with the renowned Harvard economist John Kenneth Galbraith and his wife.[3] He was survived by his wife of 64 years, Serena, two sons, many nieces, nephews, and grandchildren.

Section 3
Transactions Costs and the Value of a Firm

While first John Burr Williams and then, more formally, Franco Modigliani and Merton Miller established that the capital structure of the corporation should not have any effect on its valuation, under certain circumstances, neither assertion explained precisely how a corporation can create value internally in a way that cannot be replicated simply through the outsourcing to subcontractors all the various processes necessary for its production.

Obviously, corporations capitalize on the specialization of labor, a process which was very well described by the Middle Eastern scholar Ibn Khaldun in the fourteenth century:

> The power of the individual human being is not sufficient for him to obtain (the food) he needs, and does not provide him with as much as he requires to live. Even if we assume an absolute minimum of food... that amount of food could be obtained only after much preparation... Thus, he cannot do without a combination of many powers from among his fellow beings, if he is to obtain food for himself and for them. Through cooperation, the needs of a number of persons, many times greater than their own number, can be satisfied.[1]

In his reference to what we now label under the category of economies of scale of a firm, Adam Smith described specialization of labor in his famous illustration of a pin manufacturer:

> To take an example, therefore, from a very trifling manufacture; but one in which the division of labour has been very often taken notice of, the trade of the pin-maker; a workman not educated to this business (which the division of labour has rendered a distinct trade), nor

> acquainted with the use of the machinery employed in it (to the invention of which the same division of labour has probably given occasion), could scarce, perhaps, with his utmost industry, make one pin in a day, and certainly could not make twenty. But in the way in which this business is now carried on, not only the whole work is a peculiar trade, but it is divided into a number of branches, of which the greater part are likewise peculiar trades. One man draws out the wire, another straights it, a third cuts it, a fourth points it, a fifth grinds it at the top for receiving the head; to make the head requires two or three distinct operations; to put it on, is a peculiar business, to whiten the pins is another; it is even a trade by itself to put them into the paper; and the important business of making a pin is, in this manner, divided into about eighteen distinct operations, which, in some manufactories, are all performed by distinct hands, though in others the same man will sometimes perform two or three of them. I have seen a small manufactory of this kind where ten men only were employed, and where some of them consequently performed two or three distinct operations. But though they were very poor, and therefore but indifferently accommodated with the necessary machinery, they could, when they exerted themselves, make among them about twelve pounds of pins in a day. There are in a pound upwards of four thousand pins of a middling size. Those ten persons, therefore, could make among them upwards of forty-eight thousand pins in a day. Each person, therefore, making a tenth part of forty-eight thousand pins, might be considered as making four thousand eight hundred pins in a day. But if they had all wrought separately and independently, and without any of them having been educated to this peculiar business, they certainly could not each of them have made twenty, perhaps not one pin in a day; that is, certainly, not the two hundred and fortieth, perhaps not the four thousand eight hundredth part of what they are at present capable of performing, in consequence of a proper division and combination of their different operations.[2]

The insights offered by both Ibn Khaldun and Adam Smith explain why long production runs and the specialization of labor give rise to economies of scale. However, these same advantages can be obtained by individual contractors that then sell their intermediate production to other downstream producers. This is particularly the case today, when the majority of corporate production is in the service industry, and these activities can often be done – and now are often done – at a distance through telecommuting, the prevailing mode that corporations continue to perform these processes in-house suggests that there are other reasons for the continuation of a mode of corporate value creation that has been robust for centuries.

The work of Ronald Coase and Oliver Williamson explain why in-house production by firms still prevails. Their arguments rest not only on the nature of production, as described by Adam Smith, but also on the nature of the management process and of limitations in the efficiency of the marketplace. While their observations and conclusions will seem rather self-evident once their arguments have been presented, these great minds described something we have all thought about in such a new light that their contributions go down as some of the most significant in the history of corporate finance.

15
The Early Life of Ronald Harold Coase

There are few Nobel Memorial Prize winners in finance or economics who are as unique in personality and academic character as Ronald Harold Coase (pronounced like "rose" or "chose"). Nor have there been many with as unassuming an upbringing, or as simple, but profound, a contribution to the literature. A single paper early in his career, entitled *"The Nature of the Firm,"* and another much later, have had a profound influence on our financial intuition. They have transformed how we think about our disciplines in ways as fundamental as the concept of free markets espoused by Adam Smith in 1776, or the not unrelated intuition of efficient markets, espoused first by John Burr Williams, and, three decades later, by Eugene Fama. In between these two dates, an unassuming individual of most modest means made a simple statement that revolutionized how we think both about organizations and also about property.

The Coase name is both vaguely and broadly familiar to most all readers of modern finance. His academic reputation is of a formulator of simple but profound concepts that relied more on common sense than academic or mathematical sophistication. That should not be surprising. He grew up within a family culture that, while literate and intelligent, were not college-bred over-achievers.

His family name dates back to well before the mid-1600s, being derived from Middle English 'Cosshe', which signified 'one who dwells at a small cottage'.[3] His ancestors, including Ronald Coase's great great great great grandparents, William Coase (1670–1734) and Ann Eady (1673–?), were residents of Devon, in the southwestern region of England. The Coase family resided there for generations, and had lived and died within a narrow radius, through William to his son Samuel (1715–?), his grandson James (Oct. 1763–June 5, 1825), great grandson Henry Hannaford Coase

(September 3, 1807–May 5, 1883), and, finally, Ronald Harry Coase's grandfather James Shapcott Coase (April 27, 1849–February 3, 1925).

James Coase, the son of Henry Hannaford Coase and Elizabeth Shapcott (November 8, 1811–October 1880), was born and raised in Devon. James' mother was a shirt maker by trade, while James was trained in his family's trade as a joiner, a carpenter-specialist. Joiners are artisans who join wood through elaborate mortises, tenons, and pegs, and construct the large posts and beams that form the skeletal structure of buildings, all without the use of nails. The exacting trade of post-and-beam construction was often passed down from father to son over a number of generations. Father Henry Hannaford Coase passed this trade on to both his sons, James, and also his older brothers John Coase (1835–1907) and Joseph Coase (1839–1907). Similarly, the family trade of shirt making was passed on to James' young bride Harriet Hodgson (July 1851–December 1924).

By 1871, three generations of the Coase family had moved to Stepney, London, and shared the same home. James and Harriet had their first son, Henry T. Coase (February 4, 1884–1970), when James was 20 years old and his wife just 18. Their first son did not reach his fifth birthday.

James and Harriet subsequently had two sons that survived childhood, Alfred James Hodgson Coase (December 1872–November 13, 1945) and Stanley Arthur Coase (March 1875–June 4, 1923), then a daughter, Eliza Selina Coase (March 18, 1878–June 1669). In 1884, when James was 34 years old and Harriet 32 years of age, Ronald Coase's father, Henry Joseph Coase (February 4, 1884–1870) was born, followed by another son Edgar George (January 1886–May 22, 1919) and, finally, a daughter Hilda, who died in infancy in 1906.

This generation was the first to diverge from the family joinery trade. Ronald's father, Henry Joseph, was a foreman at a tea warehouse, while his aunt, and Henry's sister was a clerk at a solicitor's office. Henry Joseph Coase did not continue school past the age of 12 but instead secured a job first as a commercial clerk. Along the way, Henry learned telegraphy, and this eventually proved formative for his son Harold.

The telegraph, from the Greek meaning 'long distance' and 'writing', and its written delivered message, the telegram, connotes the electrical dots and dashes that conveyed messages over the radio before the age of telephony. The system had some advantages in the early years of communications over long distances because it was simple, robust, and immediate. Telegraphy allowed the Titanic to reach out for help when it struck an iceberg, and it remained the most important means for an

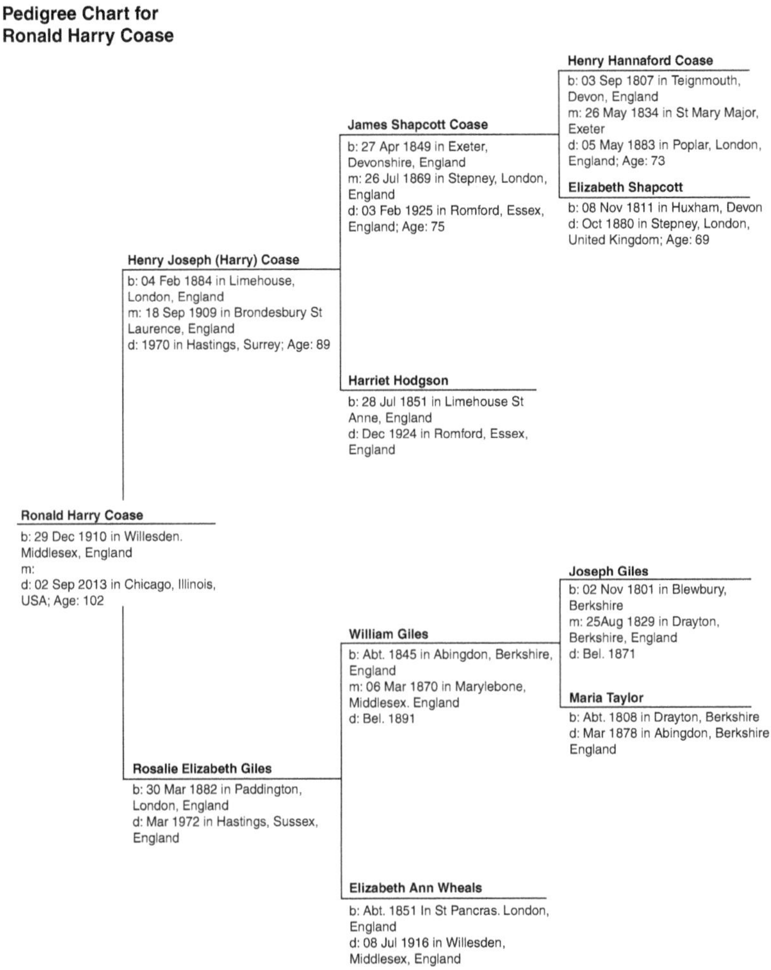

Figure 15.1 The Ronald Harold Coase Family Tree

army to communicate on the battlefield in World War I and even ship to ship in World War II.

While telegraphy seems arcane a century later when one can communicate via the Internet, immediately with almost anyone else in the world without the intervention of skilled technicians on either side, in the early 1900s the telegraph was considered high technology, and indispensable. Henry's Coase generation left the family trades of joinery and shirt making, and he found himself in a useful technological vocation that was then considered both novel and essential, even if relatively fleetingly so.

In its early days, the telegraph system in Britain was part of the postal system. The Royal Mail, was established in 1516 under Henry VIII. In 1969, the Post Office was moved to a Crown corporation and it continued to operate as a public monopoly until the government privatized it in 2011. Before this reorganization, it was run as a government department, and was granted a monopoly to move information.

Consistent with this charge to move information, the Post Office monopoly assumed control of telegraphy from railways and private telegraph companies in 1870. The delivery of telegrams became part of the government bureaucracy, and Henry Coase, the young telegraphist, became a worker in a government monopoly.

Government employment was considered to be secure and comfortable work for one able to endure a bureaucratic organizational structure. It also created an opportunity for Henry to meet his future bride, Rosalie Elizabeth Giles, who was also a postal worker.

Rosalie (March 30, 1882–March 1972) was born in Paddington, London to William Thomas Giles (1844–1891) and Elizabeth Ann Wheeles (1851–1916). Her father was a coachman and her mother a tailor. Their extended family lived as neighbors in a series of terraced houses occupied by other Giles family members. Within this extended family, Rosalie had a cousin who worked for the Post Office, where she too found employment, and her future husband.

Both Rosalie and Henry had started life with the expectation they would follow their parents' occupations – as tailors and joiners, respectively. Their families saw no need, and lacked the resources, to see either child past grammar school. Once employed as civil servants, though, both enjoyed a comfortable existence, with job and wage security, and both were left time to enjoy sports in their spare time, such as cricket, tennis, and football (known in the United States as soccer). The young couple married on September 18, 1909 when Henry was 25 years of age and Rosalie was 27 years old.

Both Henry and Rosalie were born to large families that lived in big households, often near many relatives. Household size helped smooth the vagaries of employment over the business cycle. With government employment, they had no need to have a large family of their own, or, for that matter, no reason for Rosalie to work, once Ronald Harry Coase was born, on December 29, 1910, in Willesden, Middlesex,

England, just a few miles west of London. Despite their lack of education, they were intelligent and literate, and they were able to provide for themselves and for Ronald a comfortable middle-class existence.

Just before his fifth birthday, Ronald's father enlisted in the Royal Engineers to help in the construction of the military telegraphic infrastructure in the British campaign of World War I. Over the course of the war, Henry Coase rose to the rank of Sergeant, and he won a General Services Medal, a Victory Medal, and a British War Medal for his service in Kurdistan.

England's entry into World War I may have prevented Ronald from having a sibling. Another factor may have been economic. Economists categorize decisions based on whether increased income causes an increase or a decrease in certain household decisions. When there is an increase in the level of income, we expect the purchase of luxury goods to increase more than proportionately. Alternately, other choices, labelled inferior goods, decrease in demand as incomes rise.

One such choice is family size. As affluence increases, a growing number of families choose to remain small. A reduced reliance on farming and on child labor means that children are not essential for family economic sustainability. Indeed, children become a financial burden rather than a capital asset. As a consequence, average family size decreases as income rises. The growing English middle class in the first couple of decades of the 1900s resulted in reduced family size.

Ronald Coase was a product of these times. While he grew up an only child, Coase reminisced that he did not grow up lonely. He loved to read and he enjoyed the library, although he also admitted that he was never too discerning in his literary adventures. However, despite his literary interests, he was not able to attend a good grammar school. He suffered from weak legs as a child to such an extent that the family doctor had him wear iron leg braces as a youngster. This limited his interactions with other children and perhaps even caused him to withdraw even further into books. Because of his disability, he was sent to a special school for the physically and mentally disabled that was run by the local county council. His education to the age of 12 was in no way proportionate to his intellectual aspirations.

In that era, it was customary for children, at the age of 11, to take exams that would determine their course of further study. Because of the delay in his education arising from his childhood health challenges, young Ronald missed the exam that year. This delay forced him to enter high school a year later than his peers.

Also at the age of 11, and on the cusp of high school, Ronald's father took him to a phrenologist with the hope of determining young Ronald's academic aptitude. Phrenology is a pseudo-science that attributes aptitudes and personality characteristics to various physical characteristics of the brain. The study of phrenology had been popular in the 1800s, and experienced renewed interest in London in the 1900s. Practitioners measure and feel the skull, which they divide up into 27 organs, to determine aptitude and intelligence. The London phrenologist who examined young Ronald concluded that Master Coase was "in possession of much intelligence... though you may be inclined to underrate your abilities." The phrenologist recommended Ronald take up horticulture and poultry-rearing as hobbies.

The diagnosis notwithstanding, once he was admitted to the Kilburn Grammar School, young Ronald began to thrive. He followed his period of study there with two additional years of preparation that would earn him a one year credit upon entering university. His first thought was to use those years to prepare for advanced university entry with the goal of studying history. However, because Coase had already entered the English equivalent of middle and high school a year later than other peers, at the age of 12 rather than 11, he was precluded from studying the requisite Latin and hence was barred from studying history at the University of London.

Coase next decided to pursue a science degree, with a major in chemistry. However, he soon found out that he did not really have an aptitude for mathematics. Once he had ruled out the arts because of the Latin requirement, and the sciences because of their mathematical intensity, only commerce remained. He later lamented that his decision to begin the study of business was one less made *by* him rather one made *for* him. He was not displeased by the prospects, though, as he had a socialist bent, in common with many young people of his age and times, and felt the requisite study of economics would be elucidating.

In October of 1929 Ronald Coase passed his A-level exams to allow him to attend the London School of Economics. This was also the month of the Great Crash which marked the beginning of the Great Depression.

At the age of 18, Coase arrived at the London School of Economics to study commerce. However, given his year advanced standing, he completed his studies before he met the university residency requirement. He decided to use the remaining time to study Industrial Law with a view to obtaining a Bachelor of Science in Economics.

On the completion of his studies, Coase was offered a Cassel Travelling Scholarship to the United States for the academic year 1931–2. The subject chosen for his scholarship was an exploration of U.S. factories. This academic exploration, and his resulting inspirations, would come to define the rest of his career and his legacy in finance.

In the summer of 1932, Coase had formed in his mind the unique advantage the corporate model offers. With his new-found intuition at hand, he returned from his travels in America and was hired to teach first at the Dundee School of Economics and Commerce for two years, followed by a year-long stint at the University of Liverpool, and then as a lecturer at his alma mater, the London School of Economics thereafter.

The heavy teaching load of a young faculty member prevented Coase from putting his newfound concepts down on paper, even if he did occasionally present them to his colleagues. In 1937 Coase finally published his paper "The Nature of a Firm" in the journal *Economica*,[4] one of the leading journals in economics, and published by his home institution, the London School of Economics. That year, in Middlesex, England, on August 7, he also married his life partner, Marian Ruth Hartung, of Chicago, Illinois.

Marian grew up in Chicago the eldest of two daughters of Henry and Elmira Hartung, and the sister of Margery. Her father was born in Ohio to German immigrants, while her mother was born in neighboring Wisconsin, also to German immigrants. Born November 23, 1912, she was two years his junior. Clearly, both the Coases and the Hartungs had longevity in their genes. She died a month before her 100th birthday, on October 17, 2012, while he died less than a year later at the age of 102.

16
The Times and the Theory

The modern corporation is exceedingly complex. The subtlety of its operations and the complexity of its systems has daunted all but the most academically courageous researchers. So many factors could weigh in on the creation of corporate value and the corresponding price of a corporate equity that, until the publication of John Burr Williams's treatise, financial analytics was regarded as an art rather than a science. Even the financing decisions a corporation could employ to expand was so varied that, until Modigliani and Miller produced their theorem, decisions as to the best capital structure were best left to intuition and business style. Only once a great mind comes along who can simplify the problem and hone our intuition could observers see the forest through the trees and begin to understand the important determinants of corporate value. Ronald Coase's seminal paper on the essential advantage of the corporate structure was one such high mark in our understanding of corporate finance.

Coase's first major article, "The Nature of a Firm," received little attention at first. In the preceding year, John Maynard Keynes had published his "The General Theory of Employment, Interest and Money," in response to the first global depression. It would take a war and almost another decade before stock markets returned to their pre-depression levels and economies began to grow and create value. While a better understanding of what creates corporate value may have secured some academic attention in the interim, the midst of the Great Depression was perhaps not the most receptive environment to explain how corporate value and goodwill is generated.

In addition, the late 1920s and the 1930s were a period of intense interest in the development of scientific models of corporate finance. John Burr Williams published his "Theory of Investment Value" in 1938, and, in 1930, Irving Fisher had published "The Theory of Interest," which represented a substantial reworking of some of his earlier work. Meanwhile, John von Neumann (December 28, 1903–February 8, 1957) was giving lectures on his expected value methodology that created the framework for the inclusion of uncertainty in finance theory. Coase's intuitions and concepts, in a paper that was barely twenty pages long, and with no equations, but within an increasingly mathematically laden literature, was going against the rising tide of mathematical rigor in economics and finance.

Also in the late 1940s, finance was emerging out of the shadow of economics. Scholars were increasingly setting the stage for more advanced and quantitative business studies, but few programs in business were prepared to move beyond a relatively simple narrative in business studies. Chicago was the exception. This was the formative age of the Chicago School, which would become incredibly influential in the creation of modern finance. Members of the Chicago School, including stalwarts such as Frank Knight and Milton Friedman, would at times challenge and eventually embrace Coase's ideas, but not without a fight.

Cowles and the Chicago School

It might be suggested that it is not clear whether Coase came to Chicago or Chicago came to Coase. Coase's mother and father had both worked for a monolithic government monopoly, the British Postal Service. Bureaucracies and monopolies were both anathemas for proponents of the Chicago School.

Coase, too, had developed a suspicion of public monopolies. At the London School of Economics, as a junior instructor, he was asked to teach a course on the economics of public utilities. Then, following the outbreak of war in Europe, he entered government service, first as a statistician for the Forestry Commission and then as Chief Statistician of the Central Statistical Office, and adviser to the War Cabinet. He saw bureaucracy first hand. Following the war, in 1945, he returned as Reader to the London School of Economics, where he continued with his research into public utilities while he taught courses on the principles of economics.

Then, in 1948, Coase had the opportunity to take a Rockefeller Fellowship to study the American broadcasting industry. This first-hand experience with a free market-oriented national broadcasting network, which was in stark contrast to the British model, resulted in his book *British Broadcasting: A Study in Monopoly*, published in 1950. Soon after its publication, he immigrated to the United States, first to join the University of Buffalo in 1951. Later in the decade, he moved on twice: in 1958, he moved to the Center for Advanced Study in the Behavioral Sciences, and then, just one year later, he joined the University of Virginia.

Founded in 1954, the Center for Advanced Study in the Behavioral Sciences is an influential body of researchers in the social sciences and humanities that was initially funded by the Ford Foundation to provide a forum for cross-disciplinary thought around important social policies. Throughout its life it has offered one-year visits to dozens of Nobel Laureates, Pulitzer Prize winners, and MacArthur genius award recipients.

When Henry Ford died in 1947, his legacy created the richest foundation in the world. The Ford Foundation had a number of elements in its mission, but Program V was both unusual and prescient. Its mission was "Through scientific work, (to) increase knowledge of factors which influence or determine human conduct, and extend such knowledge for the maximum benefit of individuals and society." Its mandate was to use the emerging behavioral sciences to help better understand human behavior.

While at the Center, Coase pursued his interest in broadcasting. He embarked on a study of the United States Federal Communications Commission, the principal regulator of U.S. broadcasting. At that time, there was much discussion on the optimal use of the airwaves, something that was increasingly regarded as a public resource. The allocation of the radio frequency spectrum would define how a rapidly growing and increasingly essential industry would develop, but the economics and finances of the airwaves was not yet well defined or understood. Coase wrote an article about how the pricing system might allocate this resource. His legacy took another brilliant turn.

Any student of free market economics would quickly conclude that all resources ought to go to their highest bidder. However, this is a simplistic conclusion. Just what rights go along with such a franchise as the airwaves?

The Chicago School recognized, and indeed evangelized, the importance of property rights within the free market system, and advocated for free markets with an almost proselytizing zeal. From that respect, Coase's interest in property rights and in the theory of the firm was within the crosshairs of Chicago sensibilities. The Chicago faculty interested in Coase's airwaves pricing issue included such notables as Milton Friedman and George Stigler, all evangelical proponents of free markets and the competitive price system. Coase had proposed that a public good could be successfully auctioned rather than be managed by a government agency. After some spirited discussions, Coase convinced his Chicago colleagues with his logic. They encouraged him to prepare a paper for publication in the *Journal of Law and Economics*. His 1960 article "The Problem of Social Cost"[1] became one of the most quoted and widely read articles in the history of modern economics.

While Coase is well known for an important proposition from that article, now commonly called *the Coase Theorem*, he had, a generation earlier, produced an equally momentous observation. His *The Nature of a Firm* had a title that was as equally compact, to the point, and profound as his later work, and was no less significant in its creation of a foundation for many subsequent explorations of what creates goodwill and synergy within a firm. With the celebrity that his *Problem of Social Cost* garnered, scholars began to take a second look at his earlier and equally profound discussion of transactions costs from the firm's perspective.

Coase's insights that defined the modern theory of the corporation began at an incredibly young age. They date back perhaps as far as a lecture he gave in 1932 as a young 21-year-old instructor at the London School of Economics, and culminated in his paper published in 1937.

Coase's innovation came in his courage to ask questions few others dared. In his time, the neoclassical theory of the firm treated a corporation as a black box. On one side input enter into the production process, and on the other side, outputs exit. Few scholars explored what happened between these two points, beyond some rudimentary but intuitive hand-waving. For instance, one can assert, from the principle of diminishing marginal returns, that a firm cannot produce an infinite amount of outputs, and, as one employs more of one input, without employing more of another, its contribution to output diminishes. When combined with free markets and the price system, economists predict the firm will discover that production in moderation may be more profitable than overproduction. Finally, firms in competitive markets have a greater incentive to produce at a rate that minimizes average costs, while a monopoly will instead balance its production decisions with its analysis of what the market will bear. Some subtleties aside, these rather basic conclusions almost completely painted the level of understanding of the corporate model. How decisions were actually made within the neoclassical black box were of less importance to the literature than the compellingly logical observations about what goes in and must come out of the box.

Coase's undergraduate scholarship which had allowed him to actually visit American firms was a transcendent experience for him. Only a decade or so earlier, the United States had displaced Britain at the pinnacle of global economic superiority. It did so based on a new and more scientific notion of industrial engineering and a striving for efficiency that was practiced on shop floors well before it was treated in academic journals. General Motors and Ford were rewriting the texts on industry, and young Coase was convinced that academics had completed missed that boat.

As Coase interviewed both shop and corporate managers, he came away amazed at their grasp of the problems and advantages of corporations. They were in the business of getting things done, and were adept at finding the path that would allow them to do so most cheaply, quickly, and efficiently.

These managers were inquisitive and pragmatic by nature. By eliminating the negotiations and contracting necessary for market purchases of intermediate factors of production, and by avoiding contract fulfillment monitoring costs by performing more tasks in-house, the manager can reduce its transactions costs and more easily coordinate each step in the dance of production. At the same time, the firm may also realize additional economies of scale.

Coase described these opportunities not through the use of dry equations, but by employing mind-expanding rhetoric. With his intuition at hand, it would not be a difficult exercise to augment his analysis with mathematics. Analytic compactness would result, even if intuition may not be enhanced under a more mathematical approach. However, Coase resided in a Faculty of Law, which relies on robust rhetoric rather than elegant equations. Coase and his law school colleagues believed there would be nothing to be gained in our understanding by simply peppering the analysis with mathematics. Indeed, from their perspective, such analytics would at best distract, and might in fact obfuscate. And the mathematics would do nothing to enlighten the line manager seeking a better understanding and a more efficient way to bring the product to market.

Since Adam Smith's *An Inquiry into the Wealth of Nations*, the economics discipline have been enamored with both the notion of economies of scale and the beauty of the competitive market. *The Wealth of Nations* was published at the time of the beginning of the Industrial Revolution, a period characterized by burgeoning trade and markets, and the end of the feudal system, a patriarchal royalty, and bureaucratic empires. Before the new economic era, markets were not well understood nor much contemplated. Now, we are indoctrinated and immersed in free markets. We take as a matter of faith that any product can be purchased at a competitive price in the marketplace. In the era of free markets, Coase had to mount a defense of larger firms and centralized production. Since the time Coase wrote "The Nature of a Firm" at the height of the Great Depression, the average size of firms has grown dramatically. At almost half a trillion dollars of income in 2014, for example, Walmart is the size of a top-25 nation. It has attained its size in part because of the efficiencies Coase delineated.

In Coase's world, firms avoid the transactions costs and the repeated renegotiation expenses by creating long-term contracts among the factor providers employed exclusively within the firm. These savings do not multiply forever, though. Eventually, as the firm grows, these economies of scale give rise to other inefficiencies and diseconomies of scale. A manager must constantly seek to balance the efficiencies of transactions costs saved with the inefficiencies that arise as an entity becomes too big, too centrally planned, too bureaucratic, and, ultimately, too sluggish.

In offering his explanation for how a firm can both garner efficiencies and generate accounting goodwill through synergies that allow the firm to generate value in excess of the sum of a corporation's parts, Coase created a movement. His followers pioneered a new, institutional explanation of corporate goodwill, but he remained vulnerable to criticism that such an approach, while intuitive, is not mathematically satisfying. Coase argued for corporate advantages and market failures, while traditional neoclassical economists, as espoused by the Chicago School, glorified markets and the very decentralization Coase claimed created inefficiencies. In a tip of his hat to his contemporaries and those who came before him, Coase noted:[2]

> Marshall introduces organization as a fourth factor of production; J. B. Clark gives the coordinating function to the entrepreneur; Professor Knight introduces managers who co-ordinate. As D. H. Robertson points out, we find "islands of conscious power in this ocean of unconscious co-operation like lumps of butter coagulating in a pail of buttermilk."[3] But in view of the fact that it is usually argued that co-ordination will be done by the price mechanism, why is such rganization necessary? Why are there these "islands of conscious power"? Outside the firm, price movements direct production, which is coordinated through a series of exchange transactions on the market. Within a firm, these market transactions are eliminated

> and in place of the complicated market structure with exchange transactions is substituted the entrepreneur-coordinator, who directs production. It is clear that these are alternative methods of coordinating production.[4]

Coase was trying to put a name to some vague force within a firm that creates value, not unlike the way physicists use dark matter as an explanation for the glue and mass that holds our physical universe together. Both concepts are difficult to describe and analyze, but, without them, it is difficult to understand what holds things together. Coase struck a nerve. It would be left to others to more fully flesh out this new Coasean institution that creates corporate value and gives rise to corporate valuation that is in excess of the sum of the value of its physical assets. We can call this value proposition *goodwill,* but we still have much work to do to understand its very nature.

17
Life and Legacy

Coase lobbed the first ball into the court. The neoclassical model assumes markets work without friction, much as the theory of gases assumes that molecules can move freely within a container. In fact, it was economists bent on creating a social science with the same mathematical foundation as that found in physics which gave rise to the perfect and *atomistic* neoclassical ideal of the competitive market in the first place. It should come as no surprise that frictionless markets formed the foundation of a market-oriented economics. It might be surprising, though, to imagine it took so long for the economics and finance profession to realize and acknowledge the legacy of such an oversimplification.

Product markets are certainly fast approaching the competitive ideal of minimal transactions costs. In this process the Internet has become the great leveler. The cost of locating any of millions of products has never been lower. As a consequence, there has been a substantial increase in the number of competitors vying to sell an identical product to a given consumer. This heightened competition has, with little doubt, made for much more competitive markets for those types of products that are amenable to sale over the Internet. For instance, the costs to research a product and choose a retailer, and then the cost to ship the product quickly to the end consumer is now relatively low.

At the same time, though, suppliers have amalgamated. Companies are bigger, more vertically and horizontally integrated, and command more market power than before the Internet age. Transactions costs in product markets have fallen, but the economies of scale and the savings in transactions costs and contracting within the various factor markets and stages of production increasingly offer an advantage to large corporations. Product markets may be approaching the competitive ideal.

But, within the corporation, the economies of scale arising from reduced transactions costs is moving in the other direction. For instance, a company like Amazon is able to effectively compete in the product market precisely because of the advantages it has created for itself in its vertically integrated supply chain system. The synergies such firms create are precisely the types of advantages Coase described.

Coase made another insight for which he is even more renowned. The notion that was labeled by his Chicago colleague and eminent price theorist George Stigler as *the Coase Theorem* arose from Coase's other notable work *The Problem of Social Cost*. There he explored the reverse: Could the decisions that are often made relatively and efficiently within an organization, a bureaucracy, or even a broad society also be decentralized and made by the market as a whole if it could do so without transactions costs? Coase showed that, even if there are surpluses which markets cannot capture fully, something economists call externalities, private negotiations can lead to a unique and optimal outcome, regardless of which side of the transaction had the initial allocation. In other words, even when there exist factors that were conventionally thought to frustrate a free market negotiation, the efficient competitive outcome can be attained so long as each side of the exchange is free to negotiate costlessly with the other.

This deduction has profound implications on the establishment of property rights. While government can perhaps affect the initial ownership rights, initial ownership is irrelevant to the determination of final ownership, except with regard to the wealth of each side following the transaction. Government can influence the wealth distribution but it will not affect trade, in the absence of transactions costs between the parties.

Coase's analysis is generally interpreted as meaning that government need not intervene to resolve allocation disputes because, under certain conditions, the parties are in the best position to negotiate a resolution, regardless of the initial allocation of rights. The conditions require zero transaction or bargaining costs. If these conditions are not met, government can play an important role in reducing transactions or negotiations costs, and in establishing well-understood property rights that will lead to the fewest and least costly disputes. Courts and agencies can then play an important economic role in creating an environment that can moderate the transactions that promote market efficiency.

While the motivation of Coase's most well-known paper may have initially been whether a public good like the frequency spectrum could be successfully and efficiently auctioned, his 1961 paper had implications far beyond the exchange of property rights. Indeed, *The Problem of Social Cost* is one of the most widely cited economics papers of all time, and is invoked in literatures well beyond economics and finance. And, unlike his earlier *The Nature of the Firm*, his 1961 paper was an almost instantaneous success. Its implications were widely understood, regarded, and perhaps extrapolated too broadly. His seminal paper also induced a number of readers to reread and more fully appreciate his earlier and no less influential work.

But while the intuition behind the important concept of internalizing of transactions costs within the corporation in *The Nature of the Firm* was wholly developed by Coase, he offered some credit to this future colleagues at the University of Chicago, with whom he defended his concept and, in the process, turned their skepticism into acceptance. Not only did Coase turn these skeptics into supporters, but he also forged a relationship with the University of Chicago economics and law faculty that eventually parlayed into an offer to join them, within the School of Law, edit the *Journal of Law and Economics*, and forge a new discipline in both economics and in law.

Coase's foray into the *Journal* was because of his paper on a proposal for Federal Communications Commission spectrum auctions. The discussions and debate which ensued resulted in a new and fledgling journal through the University of Chicago. Coase was still teaching at the University of Virginia when the illustrious Chicago economists invited, or perhaps even commanded, Coase to meet to debate his concepts with them. The room was full of future Nobel Laureates from the University of Chicago, including the ardent free-marketer Milton Friedman and famous price theorist George Stigler. They met at the home of Aaron Director with the express goal of pointing out to Coase the error of his analysis. Stigler later recollected that the count of the room went from 20 against Coase's theorem and 1 for, to 21 for. Coase convinced perhaps the most luminary assemblage of economists in the country that one can create and then transact property rights for such intangible public goods as radio frequencies. He may also have convinced his colleagues that the absence of such property rights creates a *Tragedy of the Commons,* as named by Garrett Harden in his influential 1968 *Science* paper of the same name,[1] where, if a resource belongs to nobody, it belongs to everybody and often becomes abused.

Coase may have convinced Director, but Aaron Director may have also impressed Coase. Director, who was also Milton Friedman's brother-in-law, and brother of Friedman's Ph.D. wife, Rose Director Friedman (December, 1910–August 18, 2009). Aaron Director was a fierce defender of free markets, in the Chicago tradition, and was also a legal expert on antitrust law. While the goals of antitrust law, to increase market competitiveness and hence reduce inefficiencies, are laudable, an explanation for the efficiency of the corporate model in avoiding transactions costs was perfectly consistent with Director's academic leanings. Coase's analyses could also be used to argue against government intervention in the marketplace and within firms potentially eyeing mergers.

Coase managed to influence many others too, from Oliver Williamson to Douglas North, and also other future Nobel Memorial Prize laureates. His insights into transactions costs was fundamental, but so was his ability to elucidate creative intuitions without the sometimes obfuscating effect of advanced mathematics. He inspired the foundation of the *Ronald Coase Institute,* which was a group of scholars Coase assembled beginning in 2000 to motivate transformational economic change. Its declared vision is "To better understand how real economic systems work, so that individuals and societies have greater opportunities to improve their well-being." His mentorship of these young scholars continues on in his memory at the Institute's home in St Louis, Missouri.

While Coase's curriculum vitae may not be as long as those of some of his Chicago colleagues, the papers he wrote were among the widest read and most influential in the areas of economics and finance. He followed his 1937 *The Nature of the Firm* in *Economica* with a 1938 essay entitled *Business Organization and the Accountant,* which was reprinted in 1973 in a collection of London School of Economics essays edited by James Buchanan and G.F. Thirlby and published by Weidenfeld & Nicolson in London. His 1959 foray into the *Journal of Law and Economics,* entitled *The Federal Communications Commission,* was published as the first paper in the journal's second volume, and was followed a year later by *The Problem Of Social Cost* as the first paper one year later, in 1960.

Coase then followed up these with two more papers in the *Journal of Law and Economics,* first with "Durability and Monopoly" in 1972[2] and then with "The Lighthouse in Economics" in 1974.[3] In 1990 he was awarded the Nobel Memorial Prize "for his discovery and clarification of the significance of transaction costs and property rights for the institutional structure and functioning of the economy",[4] followed by the publication of an essay in the *American Economic Review,* based on his Nobel Memorial Prize lecture, in 1992.[5] He also wrote two books which were published through the University of Chicago Press, *The Firm, the Market, and the Law,* in 1988, followed in 1994 by *Essays on Economics and Economists.*

Following his retirement from both the University of Chicago and the editorship of the *Journal of Law and Economics,* Coase continued academic pursuits until his death. He was somewhat reclusive in his old age and never learned to drive. But those who knew him remembered him for his brilliance, his uniqueness, and his invariably profound insights.

More than most academics, Coase was fortunate to strike upon brilliant intuitions as if by happenstance, but usually with profound implications. He claimed, in all modesty, that greatness was thrust upon him. But, while his writings were more rhetorical than mathematical, and perhaps appeared more practical than theoretical, his results remain both simple and profound.

18
The Early Life of Oliver Eaton Williamson

Ronald Howard Coase and Oliver Eaton Williamson shared an unassuming and humble nature, and both of them championed a completely original and unconventional approach to the valuation of the corporate form. However, while Ronald Coase also had a humble name, his contemporary, Oliver Eaton Williamson, had a name that had a distinguished heritage.

Oliver Eaton Williamson was born to humble parents in a region of the country renowned for its modest sensibilities. He was born September 27, 1932 to Scott Williamson and Sara Lucille (nee Dunn). Both taught high school in Superior, Wisconsin.

The Williamson side of the family had not lived for long in Wisconsin. Oliver's father, Scott Gilbert Williamson (July 8, 1898–March 24, 1971), was born and had grown up in North Hudson, Wisconsin. He was the son of a Scotsman, James Williamson (June 20, 1851–July 14, 1934), who was born and had immigrated from Dunrossness in the Shetland Isles of Scotland to farm and establish a family in Wisconsin.

The Shetland Isles, north and east of Scotland, in the direction of Norway, has been populated since the Mesolithic period more than ten thousand years ago. Until the discovery of oil relatively recently, the region relied primarily on agriculture. But, with long and cold winters, and short but cool summers, many of its residents were mariners. Some of the Williamson ancestors had circled the world, and at least one had died at sea. By James Williamson's birth, though, his parents were landlubbers. James was the grandson of Laurence Williamson (1775–1841), a mason, and the son of Laurence Williamson (July 27, 1823–May 20, 1863), a tailor, and Helen Marion Johnston (June 16, 1824–February 9, 1908) of Dunrossness, Shetland, Scotland.

At the age of 30, James Williamson and his young bride Jane Manson (June 13, 1856–March 2, 1915), whom he married just a couple of years

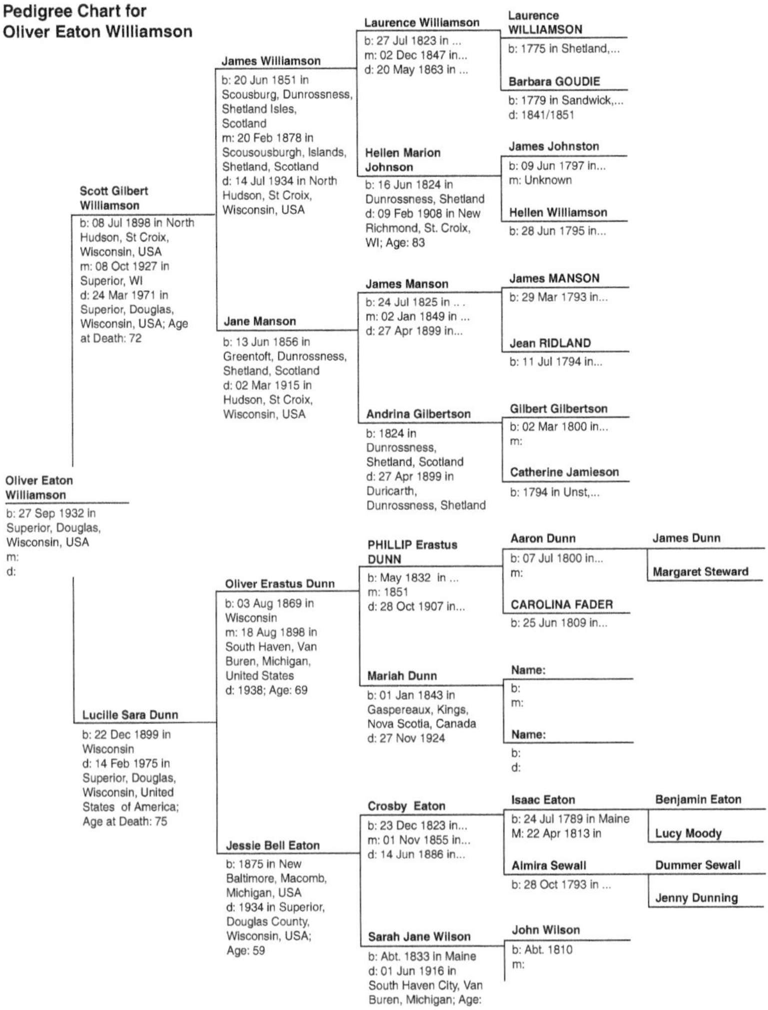

Figure 18.1 The Oliver Eaton Williamson Family Tree

earlier, left his parents, four sisters and three brothers to depart for America. They arrived across the ocean on May 15, 1881 with their newborn daughter Marion Anderina Williamson in their arms, and settled in the dairy region of North Hudson, Wisconsin, about 20 miles east of Minneapolis, to raise a family of another ten children.

James became a carpenter and passed his trade on to one of his children, while other boys learned the skill of blacksmith. The men of the family worked at the local railroad shop for the Chicago, St Paul, Minneapolis and Omaha Railroad, one of the largest employers in the town of Hudson. The youngest son, Scott Gilbert Williamson (July 8, 1989–March 24, 1971), parted with the family tradition of railroad work and followed one of his sisters to college, just as his mother Jane passed away.

Scott studied to become a high school teacher at Wisconsin's teacher college, the Superior Normal School, founded in 1893, and renamed Wisconsin State Teachers College in 1926. He graduated from college, took a summer trip to his father's homeland of Scotland in the summer of 1921, and returned to Superior to teach high school in the hometown of his future wife, Sara Lucille Dunn.

While Scott Gilbert Williamson came from a line of Scots who had worked the land and the sea, and worked with their hands, his future wife, also a high school teacher, had a distinctly American heritage. Their second child, Oliver Eaton Williamson, carried that heritage in both his given and his middle name.

Let us begin with the Eaton part of his name. In 1637 John Eaton, Sr. (December 26, 1595–October 29, 1668), the son of Richard Eaton (1565–January 14, 1616), the second in two generations of reverends from Warwickshire, England, came to Boston in the Massachusetts Colonies with his wife Ann Moses (1599–February 5, 1660). They had married in 1621, in the same year as Ann lost her first husband. Sixteen years later, they departed for the New World with their six children. Upon their arrival, they settled first in Salisbury, a little more than a day's trip north of Boston.

Some believe they travelled to Massachusetts Bay aboard the ship *Hector* that had departed from London, England on May 10, 1637. John's brother, Theophilus Eaton (1590–January 7, 1658), an agent for King Charles I, arrived on the *Hector* to serve as president of the Massachusetts Bay Company that sent administrators and indentured servants to the Massachusetts Colony in support of their corporation.[1] John and Theophilus' mother had also come over with them following the death of her husband.

The *Hector* arrived on June 26, 1637 under the religious leadership of John Davenport. At that time, John Winthrop, Governor of the Massachusetts Bay Colony and leader of the Winthrop Fleet, kept a very tight rein on his Boston colony. His control over the colony induces some new colonists, on occasion, to strike out to establish their own colonies under less oppressive leadership. Theophilus set out for New Haven, Connecticut, to the south, while John Eaton went north to Salisbury. Theophilus would found New Haven and become governor of the Connecticut Colony. Another brother, Nathaniel, went on to found Harvard University, but was subsequently forced out of his leadership position at the College by Governor Winthrop.

John Eaton was less interested in colony building, however. Instead, he concentrated on farming, barrel making, and real estate.[2] He was considered by his contemporaries to be a wise and practical man blessed great tolerance and a strong conscience. His eldest son, John (1619–November 1, 1682), remained in Salisbury at the family farm and continued in his father's real estate business. He and his wife Martha Rowlandson (1621–July 17, 1712) had one son, Joseph, who continued the family real estate business but also was a carpenter, a hunter, a trapper and adventurer in the backwoods of Maine, as well as serving as a captain in the militia.[3]

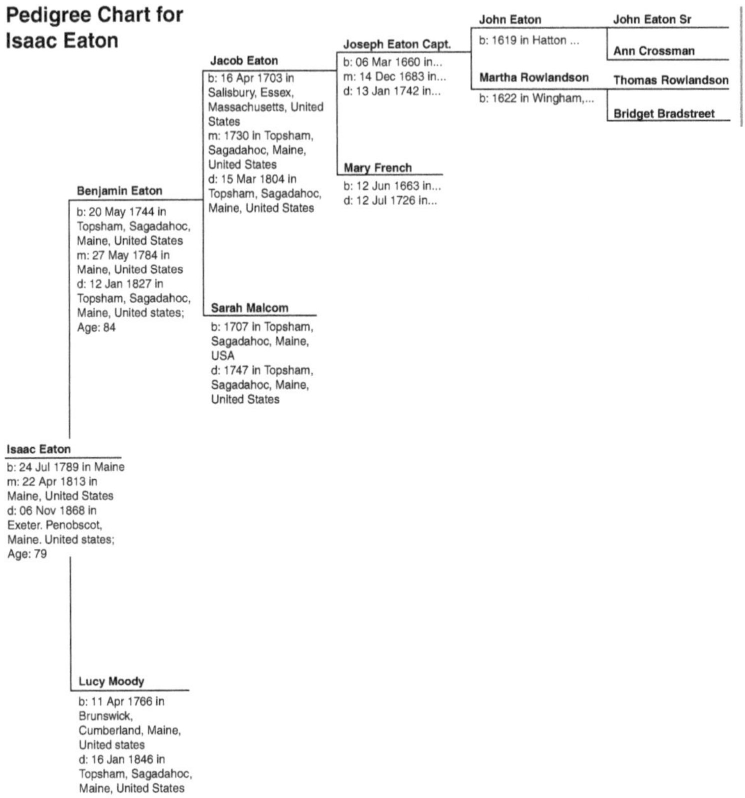

Figure 18.2 The Eaton Family Tree

John Rowlandson's wife Martha's family also had fascinating – and, at times, harrowing – roots. Martha, two brothers, the Reverend Thomas (1625–July 7, 1682) and Joseph (September 24, 1631–November 23, 1678), and a sister, Elizabeth (1627–December 29, 1679), had traveled to the Massachusetts colony in 1637. The elder brother, the Reverend Thomas, had married Bridgett Bradstreet, and they had a son, Joseph (December 18, 1663–November 23, 1678), who also became a reverend. He married Mary White (1637–January 5, 1711) and they settled down to live together in Lancaster, Massachusetts.

At first light on February 10, 1675, three tribes of Indians attacked the village of Joseph and Mary, killed 13 people, and took two dozen hostages, including Joseph, Mary, and their daughter, Sarah. Sarah died a week later from wounds suffered during the attack. The couple was then taken from village to village over the course of three months as the Indians attacked other settlements. Meanwhile, women in Boston raised £20 as a ransom, which was paid for their release.

Following the release, the family moved to Wethersfield, Connecticut, where Joseph became a pastor. When he died, in 1678, Mary moved to Boston with her children. She married Captain Samuel Talcott, and wrote an account of her harrowing ordeal. The book, *A Narrative of the Captivity and Restoration of Mrs. Mary Rowlandson*, became a bestseller and established Mary as one of the first recorders of colonial literature.

Mary's cousin, and John Eaton's son, Captain Joseph Eaton, had adventures in the forests of Maine that were certainly less harrowing, but his adventures nonetheless animated the generation he created. His wife, Mary French (June 12, 1663–July 12, 1726), made the decision to remove themselves from their comfortable home in Salisbury to Topsham, Sagadahoc County, Maine. There settled the two youngest of Joseph and Mary's six boys.

The youngest child, Jacob (April 16, 1703–March 15, 1804), became the patriarch of four generations of Eaton sons, Benjamin (May 20, 1744–January 12, 1827), Isaac (July 24, 1789–November 6, 1868), and Crosby (December 23, 1823–June 14, 1886), well away from most of the hostilities of the Revolutionary War, the War of 1812, and the Civil War.

Crosby Eaton began his life on the family farm, taught at the local school until he was 21 years old, and then moved to Massachusetts to run a cotton mill. At the age of 25, he moved his family to Casco, Michigan to operate an orchard there and grow grain. He became a stalwart of the local Republican Party and held a number of municipal and county offices, eventually serving in the Michigan state legislature.

Crosby married twice. With his second wife, Sarah Jane Wilson (1833–June 1, 1916) of Maine, he had three girls and a youngest boy. The youngest daughter was named Jessie Bell Eaton, born in 1862 in New Baltimore, near their home in Casco.

Jessie Bell Eaton, the maternal grandmother of Oliver Eaton Williamson, was the middle child of Crosby and Sarah Eaton. Jessie had married a successful Wisconsin real estate agent, Oliver Erastus Dunn (August 3, 1869–1938).

While the Eaton namesake contained a state governor and a founder of Harvard University, the Dunn namesake is no less illustrious and fascinating. Oliver Erastus Dunn, the real estate tycoon of Superior, Wisconsin, and the mentor to Oliver Eaton Williamson's father, who had left teaching to join Oliver Dunn's real estate business before his son was born, could trace his American roots back equally far as could the Eatons, but, in this case, via Canada.

The Dunn name can be traced back to Thomas Dunn, who was born in 1540 in Yorkshire, England during the reign of Henry VIII. While his son John Dunn (1561–March 24, 1601) and grandson and namesake Thomas Dunn (December 16, 1586–December 16, 1648) remained in their village of Brandesburton, Yorkshire, a young Thomas Dunn (August 24, 1606–1699) set out as a 14-year-old indentured servant to Sir George Yardley of the Virginia Company from Bristol, England on January 29, 1620. Destined for Jamestown, Virginia on the vessel *Temperance*, they arrived on April 19 in Jamestown. Thirteen years earlier, Captain John Smith had founded Jamestown, and Sir George Yardley was travelling to take possession of 1,000 acres of land upriver from Jamestown to establish a tobacco plantation.

Thomas Dunn and his wife, Ann Burgess (August 24, 1606–1699), had a son, Thomas, in Virginia (1640–1725), who eventually migrated to Massachusetts and established himself in Barnstable. This branch of the Dunn name remained in Massachusetts through a son George (1720–78), who was followed by James Dunn (May 3, 1766–December 29, 1843). James had migrated north in 1795 to Bakersfield, Franklin, Vermont, where he met his future wife, Margaret Fulton (September 20, 1775–June 21, 1866). There, they raised a family of five boys and three girls, including a son, Aaron (July 7, 1800–June 25, 1861).

Life in Bakersfield was challenging in the early 1800s, especially for families with the last name Dunn. The War of 1812 is often remembered, ironically, as the Forgotten War by Americans today. The declaration of war by the United States against Britain was not widely endorsed across the fledgling nation. Many of the New England states were not unsympathetic to Britain, and enjoyed profitable trade relations with Canada. Also, many of those who settled New England and Virginia came over as representatives of English corporations, and were not so offended by the British governance model. When American patriots began to prosecute the war, traitors, and smugglers with increased zeal, there were migrations of loyalists across the Northern border, to wait until the suspension of hostilities. While New York State was at the epicenter of conflict, Vermont, and especially the communities near the border, supplied the British with livestock and also wood for their shipbuilding just north of the border. Families married across the border, and farms often spanned the border with Canada.

Aaron Dunn became a teenager just as the War of 1812 was heating up in the region in which he lived. Following the war, Americans along its northern border quickly resumed the relations that had been discouraged for more than two years. Subsequently, Aaron married a Canadian, Carolina Fader (June 25, 1809–April 6, 1878).

Aaron and Carolina Dunn raised five girls and four boys in Canada before they returned to the United States and settled in Wisconsin. Their third child, Phillip Erastus Dunn (May 1832–October 28, 1907), was born in Gaspereau, Nova Scotia and followed his family to Wisconsin not long after the return of their family. Phillip Erastus Dunn repatriated to the United States with his Canadian wife, Mariah (January 1, 1843–November 27, 1924), whom he had married on August 30, 1863. They had four children, the third being a boy, Oliver Erastus Dunn (August 3, 1869–1938).

Oliver Erastus Dunn and Jessie Eaton Bell embodied the history of two illustrious pioneer names, of which the family was well aware. While Oliver Eaton Williamson was born well after his paternal grandmother passed away, he was too young to remember either his maternal grandmother or his paternal grandfather, and had barely entered grade school at the time when the family lost Oliver Erastus, their legacies remained in the family history.

Oliver Eaton Williamson's upbringing shared no pretense proportional to his family name, however. Scott Williamson had met Sara Lucille Dunn at a small high school in Superior, Wisconsin, where she had risen to the position of principal. Scott Williamson did not continue to teach for long, though. Once he married Sara Lucille, he left teaching to join Sara Lucille's successful family real estate business in Superior. Sara Lucille's father, Oliver Erastus Dunn, was a stalwart in the Superior community in the early part of the twentieth century, and Scott Williamson both followed in his business footsteps, and also exceeded his father-in-law's ambitions for public life. Subsequently, Scott was elected to the Superior City Council and attained the role of Council President.

Sara Lucille Williamson supported her husband in his public and commercial life. When they married and started a family, Sara Lucille resigned from her high school teaching position, as was expected of married women in that era. Nonetheless, she was able to use her familiarity with local education to help her children navigate their grade school years.

Scott and Lucille first had a son, Scott Gilbert Williamson, Jr., born August 31, 1928, just a year before the Great Crash. While their first son did not live past his thirteenth birthday, his brother, Oliver Eaton Williamson was born on September 27, 1932, and two sisters, Aline Lee (September 4, 1933–) and Sarah Louise, born two years after Aline, constituted the Williamson family.

These two boys and two girls attended grade school in Superior. At that time, Superior was a comfortable middle-class town that shipped the iron ore and copper mined in nearby mills in Minnesota and Wisconsin to the ports and manufacturing centers that rim the Great Lakes.

Superior had been a trading port for almost as long as it was settled. The Bois Brule–St. Croix River Portage Trail was part of a trade route that linked Lake Superior to the Mississippi River. Its strategic location was used for trade first by First Nations' tribes and then by French fur traders, the Hudson's Bay Company, and John Jacob Astor's American Fur Company throughout the period from the 1600s to the 1800s. From there, ships could reach the Gulf of Mexico down the Mississippi or the ports of Chicago, Detroit, Toronto, and Montreal, and eventually the Atlantic Ocean through the St Lawrence River and Seaway.

In its heyday between 1890 and 1920, the city was settled by immigrants from the British Isles, Scandinavia, Belgium, and the nations of the slowly unwinding Austro-Hungarian Empire. Superior's population peaked and plateaued at between 35,000 and 40,000 residents in Oliver's parents' and Oliver's youth. In the days of Great Lake ships such as the infamous *Edmund Fitzgerald*, Superior loaded ships with taconite iron ore destined for the mills near Detroit. Its heyday sunset, and Superior's population began to plummet, as was the pattern that afflicted many of the towns and cities which depended strongly on iron ore and steel mills.

When Oliver was a child, though, the Superior public schools were good, the town had a great civic spirit, and children grew up going to high school dances, playing basketball and football, working summer jobs, and enjoying a middle American lifestyle. Oliver thrived in this safe and nurturing environment and established friendships that have lasted him a lifetime. He was a good student who was, at first, determined to become a lawyer until he discovered a strong aptitude for mathematics and science. These hard skills afforded him no comparative advantage in the study of law, a discipline that instead relies on the softer skills of rhetoric, writing, and logic. He instead set his sights first on engineering. His mother encouraged him to study at one of the world's best engineering schools, the Massachusetts Institute of Technology.

Oliver's mother had heard that nearby Ripon University offered an academic plan that allowed engineering students starting there to continue on at MIT. Williamson matriculated first to Ripon College, in Ripon, Wisconsin, about five hour's driving distance southeast of Superior, and near Milwaukee, Oshkosh, and Lake Michigan.

Williamson graduated in May of 1955 just shy of his 23rd birthday, and took a job first as a project engineer for General Electric, and then for the U.S. Government in the nation's capital, Washington, D.C. It was there that he met Dolores Celini. They married, and within a few years of work behind him, Williamson applied to the Ph.D. program at Stanford University's Graduate School of Business. He moved his family to California and began studying business in 1958. At Stanford, he discovered that his hard and soft skills could be exploited to full advantage by studying economics rather than business. There he was taught to challenge conventional wisdom and to stop not where others often do, but rather to pursue his intellectual explorations to their fullest extent. His natural analytic abilities and his training in engineering and in statistics and model-building provided him an excellent foothold that most of his colleagues at Stanford did not have. He quickly discovered that his analytic skills could be best tapped by studying economics. There, he developed an intuition about the scientific method that offered him a unique perspective.

In both science and in economics, simplifying assumptions are made to reduce complex relationships to ones that are easier to grasp and describe. For instance, the laws that govern how gases behave assume that molecules can move without friction. This simplifying assumption must then be relaxed to treat such problems as the turbulence that is generated by moving gases, or the heat generated when a body moves through the gas. Williamson came to realize that the assumption of frictionless transactions so often employed by economists and finance theorists to explain how suppliers and demanders interact within free markets may be overly restrictive and may even obfuscate other important factors, like transactions costs, asymmetric information, or differential power. The resulting failure of the predictions of an over-idealized free market ideal could sometimes be corrected in the private sector. However, the development of public policy solution to these challenges were more problematic.

Williamson honed these intuitions as he diverted his attention from the business curriculum to economics. One of the business classes that he had taken was from Prof. James Howell, who had recognized the need to understand the underpinnings of markets, rather than just to memorize the rules of thumb common in business courses. Howell also recognized Williamson's probing and analytic mind and encouraged the Ph.D. student to take a course from the then visiting professor and future Nobel Memorial Prize winner Kenneth Arrow. Arrow also made a particularly strong contribution to Williamson's intellectual maturation.

Another class that impressed Williamson was given by another influential professor at the business school, Charles Bonini. From Prof. Bonini, Williamson learned about the new and highly cross-disciplinary approach to the Theory of the Firm that was being developed at the Carnegie Institute of Technology. Subsequently Williamson applied for and was offered a three-year fellowship by the Ford Foundation to study there.

In the fall of 1960, the family, which had now expanded with the birth of a son, Scott, and daughter, Tamara, packed up and moved to Pittsburgh, Pennsylvania, to study organizational theory at a novel and incredibly imaginative faculty recently assembled at the Graduate School of Industrial Administration at Carnegie. There, he rubbed shoulders with seven eventual Nobel Memorial Prize winners in a period in which Coase's new paradigm was developed more rapidly at Carnegie than at any other institution in the world.

The free thinking and cross-disciplinary philosophy of the Carnegie Institute of Technology was instrumental in shaping Williamson's evolving intuition in the area of finance. He realized that one could tease out few specific results with the simple wave of a hand that transactions costs act as a barrier to otherwise profitable exchanges. Williamson set out to develop a more systematic approach that relied much more heavily on analytics, and especially on the intuitions he had developed as a student of engineering and sciences. He developed the analog that transactions costs are to markets what frictions are to gases. From there, he teased much more formal results and arguments with regard to the advantages for a firm that could minimize transactions costs by internalizing what it might otherwise contract out.

With this new paradigm at hand, Williamson was able to say a great deal more about the creation of goodwill in firms that are vertically integrated, and he demonstrated the explicit benefits of integration. His explorations culminated in the completion of a Ph.D. thesis in 1963 entitled "The Economics of Discretionary Behavior: Managerial Objectives in a Theory of the Firm." His dissertation won the Ford Foundation dissertation competition and was subsequently published as a book by Prentice Hall. In the fall of that the same year, following his graduation, he was given the opportunity to join the Berkeley Campus of the University of California. His family would be packing their belongings again to move across the country once more.

At Berkeley, Williamson found a fantastic fit. He was trained in a brand new and much richer approach to the reasons for the existence of firms. The Carnegie Institute of Technology, and subsequently Berkeley, became two of the most influential departments in the study of corporate value from a new and decidedly non-neoclassical approach. In creating this new approach, researchers were casting aside the relatively uninteresting industrial organization paradigm that had grown stale at Harvard University. They offered Williamson an alternative approach that was much more intuitive and rich in ramifications and predictions. Williamson had found himself at the academic heart of these freshly motivated departments embarking on a new school of academic and financial thought.

19
The Times and the Theory

In 1937, Ronald Coase, then a young 27-year-old lecturer at the London School of Economics, had posed a provocative puzzle. When should a firm outsource an intermediate factor of production, and when should it produce the good or service in-house? This relatively simple question spawned the first academically rigorous explanation for the modern corporation and provided a theoretical explanation for the valuation of a corporation that is in excess of its book value of assets.

This simple question created both a new understanding of the theory of the firm and also a new subdiscipline, now called Transactions Cost Economics.

Before Coase's innocuous question, neoclassical economics ruled the day. The black box neoclassical production function obscured the mechanism producers use to transform inputs into outputs. Economists called the actual process the *technology* of the firm, and assumed, with little actual exploration, that any two companies with identical *technologies* should be able to produce the same final product at the same price. This paradigm dominated economics for almost a century, and is still taught in the introductory microeconomics classes every finance major takes. Because it was replete with predictions, its cause-and-effect nature meant it lent itself well to inquiry by the scientific method. What it lacked in intuition and insight, it made up in mathematical simplicity and beauty, and in its ability to generate a plethora of data and predictions.

Unfortunately, though, it offered little intuition, except perhaps for its constant redeployment of the simple law of diminishing returns. It still did not explain why companies made profits or why one company is more profitable than another. To the neoclassicist, these *institutional* details were best left to other scholars with greater patience, and who might be more *mathematically challenged.*

But while economists were pontificating about how many angels could dance on the head of a neoclassical pin, financial analysts were trying to understand how corporations create value and the synergies that explain why they might be valued more than the sum of their assets. Ronald Coase lobbed this ball into the air by noting that a firm can take advantage of internal contracting at lower cost than they could if they had to purchase each intermediate factor of production on the open market. Oliver Williamson knocked the ball out of the park with his 1971 paper "The Vertical Integration of Production".

Williamson began with the premise advanced by Ronald Coase that organizations form to take advantage of the coordination of production when to coordinate outside of the firm through market exchanges would be more expensive. Imperfect information can be improved by coordinating within the corporation, and the firm can then capitalize on these savings, according to Coase. This was one of the first departures from the neoclassical model which had, in the 1920s and 1930s, increasingly enamored conventional economics. A tenet of the neoclassical model is that competitive forces direct firms to a point of minimum efficient scale upon which economies of greater scale are balanced with diseconomies, and average costs of production are minimized. This is a world of locally constant returns to scale that suggests each firm is like every other and no firm can earn a surplus over what is precisely required to pay a market return to each factor of production. At this convenient balance point, the mathematics of the neoclassical model simplifies substantially, almost compellingly so.

Of course, such an approach appears simplistic to entrepreneurs who often strive to grow and become more vertically integrated so that it may capitalize on greater internal efficiencies and reduced transactions costs, as observed by Coase.

Coase went on to observe that while a firm operates in an external environment of uncertainty, it has a much greater degree of control over its internal operations. Within the firm, a potentially complicated set of market transactions and contracts are replaced with the direction and commands of a firm's manager. One can appeal to empiricism to validate this claim. Were there no internal advantages to firms, there would be no firms. And were there no advantages to markets, there would be no markets. In the real economy, there must be a division of economic activity which directs perhaps simpler transactions and processes best accomplished by markets to markets, and subsumes more complex processes to the central planning within the firm.

Coase noted a number of reasons that give internal control an advantage. Some employees might prefer to work under the direction of others rather than directly, immediately, and temporarily through the market. Others prefer to manage workers, while some purchasers may prefer to buy from firms who can stand by the assembly of production that constitutes their product. However, the main reason to maintain production within the walls of the firm is to avoid the repeated transactions costs and to avoid the payment of a risk premium inherent with an arm's length market transaction only partially within the firm's control. Some of these risks could be avoided by contracting with insurers or information specialists, but these transactions would impose additional costs on the market participants. Finally, these transactions would have to be repeated often. The greater the frequency, and the greater the uncertainties, the higher are the transactions costs a firm can avoid by bringing operations in-house.

The firm replaces these myriad transactions and uncertainties with internal systems and implicit contracts that can replicate market results at lower cost and with a greater degree of control. Indeed, the firm can exercise even more sophisticated transactions of greater complexity because of management's ability to compel actions by fiat and with little or no negotiation or uncertainty.

Such immediacy of management prerogative runs counter to the voluntary nature of the market, which defies and frustrates the employee–employer arrangements upon which firms rely. Uncertainty is the force that gives rise to the advantage of firms. The greater the uncertainty, and the greater the costs of short-term contracting versus long-term predictability, the greater the raison d'être for the firm.

Coase went further. He noted that mechanisms which frustrate or attempt to control the marketplace, such as sales or value added taxes, market regulations, or price controls, confer upon the firm a further advantage if it can internalize many transactions and avoid layers of intervention.

Williamson's awareness of Coase's approach that defied conventional wisdom was in some sense a credit to his graduate training. With the advent of the neoclassical model from the great minds of such luminaries as Edgeworth, Marshall, and Clark came a paradigm that was almost solely devoted to an understanding of the market price system. This highly mathematical approach, as espoused by schools such as Chicago and the Massachusetts Institute of Technology, was achieving interesting, and sometimes even beautiful, results, and had been garnering the lion's share of awards of the Nobel Memorial Prize for their work. This neoclassical approach was also describing a world of extreme rationality and full information. Yet it said little about the bounded rationality that most of us employ when we make real world decisions. Such an approach may describe the workings of the overall market, but its overly mathematical neoclassical approach was not resolving the question of value creation within the firm. And, without that, it could say little about corporate finance.

Williamson was trained at the Graduate School of Industrial Administration, at the Carnegie Institute of Technology to question *conventional wisdom*. The school which prided itself on multidisciplinary and nuanced approaches to real world business problems. When Coase stated:

> ... to bridge what appears to be a gap in economic theory between the assumption (made for some purposes) that resources are allocated by means of the price mechanism and the assumption (made for other purposes) that allocation is dependent on the entrepreneur-coordinator. We have to explain the basis on which, in practice, this choice between alternatives is effected

Williamson instantly knew what Coase meant, even if few others had digested Coase's insights over the intervening decades. Williamson revived the intuitive strand within industrial organization theory. Meanwhile, Coase bolstered his transaction cost analysis and built further momentum by applying his concept to markets in *The Problem of Social Cost*. His second stab at the problem was an exercise to try to better understand the price system if there existed no contractual or transactions costs. Coase was delving more broadly into the nature of transactions costs just as Williamson was delving deeper into the black box, or Coase's Pandora's Box, as he once put it.

Williamson eventually rued the notion of transaction costs because it soon became the term that was applied to any situation in which some sort of fudge factor was necessary to explain away an inconvenient observation with the wave of a hand. It was equivalent to the dark matter astrophysicists rely upon, without any direct observation, to make their conventional model of the universe work. Yet Williamson believed transactions costs were as real, quantifiable, and justifiable as any other cost of the firm.

Williamson's realization arose from a brush with the world outside of academia. In 1966, he accepted a position as Special Economic Assistant to the Head of the Antitrust Division of the U.S. Department of Justice. There, they asked him to provide an economic analysis of a particular antitrust case with which they were dealing. Schwinn Bicycles was accused of anticompetitive behavior because Schwinn insisted that their franchisees maintain certain exclusive relationships with Schwinn. While many in the Justice Department prejudged Schwinn's behavior as an effort to lessen competition, Williamson's position was that Schwinn was enforcing its provisions simply to reduce contracting costs between it and the franchisees with whom it dealt downstream. In taking these actions, Schwinn was attempting to create a de facto vertically integrated firm that could act more seamlessly up and down the production line from procurement to production to customer.

Williamson believed the Department and the courts viewed vertical integration through the lens of exploitation by such Gilded Age companies as Standard Oil, which tried to monopolize the oil industry from the wellhead, through the transportation networks and then the refineries, to the gas stations and the end consumer. However, while Standard Oil may have done so to extract monopoly profits, directly, or through the trusts they tried to organize to circumvent regulators, Williamson posited a more benign reason for such integration. He asserted that vertical integration creates greater efficiencies by reducing transactions costs, generating economies of scale, and providing a better pricing mechanism between intermediate stages of production. The former vertical integration creates monopoly inefficiencies. Williamson's vertical integration generates efficiencies that we usually attribute to competitive firms.

Following his experience with the Justice Department, Williamson resumed his teaching career at the University of Pennsylvania. There, with a cadre of colleagues and graduate students, Williamson once again immersed himself into a new theory to justify firm efficiencies and profits. Williamson's logic and argument about the virtues of vertical integration to his colleagues at the Department of Justice subsequently resulted in the publication of a 1971 book on vertical integration, entitled *The Vertical Integration of Production: Market Failure Considerations*.[1]

This major work differed from the neoclassical model, which typically assumes arm's length transactions and the exercise of choice to optimize profits or the utility of fully informed and rational agents within a market context. Instead, Williamson focused on contracting among those able to exercise only a bounded rationality within a less extensive set of available information and without the ability to construct complete and complex contracts that can include every contingency.

By framing corporate decision-making within the context of bounded rationality, Williamson departed significantly from the orthodoxy and tautology of neoclassical economics. In the traditional treatment, there is no room for strategy. Agents on each side of a transaction are considered small in comparison to the extent of their market. Hence, they cannot exercise any strategic power. By contrast, Williamson presumed that traders are not atomistic, and that their attempts to exercise bargaining power create an additional advantage to internal contracting. Firms ultimately evolve and adapt to capture these gains from insourcing, especially in the internal production of intermediate goods that are idiosyncratic, or for which strong competitive markets do not exist.

His new paradigm, hinted at by Coase, but fully elucidated by Williamson, gave renewed energy to what was often labelled institutional economics. His results are not more illuminated through mathematics, however, but instead benefit from arguments that more fully describe the inner workings of the neoclassical black box. By refocusing the unit of analysis from the black box of a firm toward the individual decisions and transactions that operate within the firm, the unit of analysis was changed dramatically. Instead of asking the question whether a firm can make a cheaper mousetrap than the next firm, it asks how a firm can use internal contracting, streamlining, and internal transfer pricing to build the cheaper mousetrap.

Through his analysis, Williamson gives fuel to the traditional financial analyst whose instinct is to walk the firm's floor to better understand how it extracts value and increases earnings. This is precisely what Coase found so illuminating when he exercised his fellowship to explore shop floors in Depression-era American firms. Coase's studies did not look for the generic widget at the competitive price, but rather drilled down into an exploration of what makes a particular corporation unique and hence what makes it profitable. Coase, and then Williamson, described the nature of the firm not through sterile equations, but through examples that honed our intuition.

Williamson's transactions cost economics was not immediately embraced by everybody, though. Those who made their careers manipulating the neoclassical model found such a shift disconcerting. And those who demanded the mathematical precision, but worried less about the simplistic assumptions of full rationality and unrealistically extreme optimization, found that a shift toward complex contracts was simply unamenable to the familiar and increasingly complex mathematics teased out of the classical model. These scholars had invested in a complicated and extensive mathematical toolbox that simply lacked the subtlety necessary for this new institutional economic approach. Some scholars found this fork in the road disconcerting. Few finance or economics scholars followed Coase and Williamson down that path.

Other disciplines found his approach most helpful, though. The institutional approach was much more useful in elucidating issues in law or political science. New techniques in game theory and strategic behavior could also bolster the study of transaction cost economics. Even the business literature on mergers and acquisitions benefitted from this broader and more subtle approach. Antitrust considerations aside, in the neoclassical model, there would be little reason to merge unless, for some reason, the market was not sufficiently large to allow each company to achieve the necessary size and economies of scale. But Williamson's transactions cost economics demonstrates that two merged firms, especially when the integration is vertical rather than horizontal, can extract efficiencies in informal internal contracting that are unavailable to the unmerged firms. Such mergers create value, routinely, even despite the benign prediction of much of the neoclassical model.

The value of such mergers, and of the firm, rests with the transactions costs identified by Williamson and Coase. In the absence of such transactions costs, or, alternately, in the limit as transactions costs go to zero, the approach converges to the neoclassical mode.

This extension, which leads to the neoclassical model only in the limit of perfect information and zero transactions costs, was one that was embraced at the institutions where Williamson taught. The University of California at Berkeley, where he taught industrial organization and public policy-related courses from 1963–5, and at the University of Pennsylvania from 1965 on, both inspired and embraced Williamson's more cross-disciplinary and nuanced approach.

As Williamson developed and matured as a scholar, he began increasingly to see the forest through the trees and saw additional avenues for which his transactions costs approach could affect the workings of a corporation. His 1975 book, *Markets and Hierarchies: Analysis and Antitrust Implications*,[2] followed a year later by *Franchise Bidding for Natural Monopoly*, and, in 1979, *Transaction Cost Economics: The Governance of Contractual Relations*,[3] increasingly teased out public policy and corporate governance ramifications of the institutional approach he pioneered.

Williamson's extension and formalization of Coase's characterization was recognized with the awarding of a Nobel Memorial Prize in 2009. In their commendation the committee cited "his analysis of economic governance, especially the boundaries of the firm."[4] Williamson's approach might not be quite as constraining as the award sounds. He was well trained at the Carnegie Institute of Technology to blur boundaries and employ cross-disciplinary approaches to economic and social problems. In Williamson's mind, the approaches to the theory of the firm can lend understanding to public sector and private sector institutions alike. All organizations form to overcome the contracting and enforcement costs of myriad necessary transactions. And regulatory bodies form to respond both to market transactions, to create level playing fields, and to prevent anti-competitive behavior within firms or organizations. Hence, the work of Coase, and the elaborations of Williamson are useful in our understanding of market and non-market interactions alike.

These observations are helpful because they add both nuance and reality to the reasons for and relationship between firms, agencies, regulatory bodies, and the marketplace. Before Williamson's elaborations, an evangelic application of free market principles, based on the perceived beauty of the neoclassical model, often prevailed because there was little formal and scientific voice to the subtleties assumed away by the neoclassical model. His institutional approach also opens up whole new avenues for public policy. If markets cannot capitalize efficiently on all opportunities to increasing returns to scale, then entities that manage firms must act to discipline production in the absence of arm's length markets. This necessity means that corporate governance takes on a greater responsibility as it substitutes for transparent markets.

Through his theory, Williamson created a much richer vocabulary for the value of a firm and the responsibility of its oversight. His theories also shift the focus away from our scrutiny of the market, which long ago reached diminishing returns in our greater understanding, or need to understand, and toward the various mechanisms needed to create corporate value. Coase, and then Williamson, combined to produce insights that created a parallel branch in economic theory which we now label New Institutional Economics. While the traditional branch has discovered much about how markets work and when they fail, but will probably reveal few great new revelations, a whole new field of analysis within the firm is creating rich avenues for corporate value that had gone unexplored.

20
Applications

The insights of Coase and Williamson were transformational in nature. Their fresh insights and new analysis forced us to look at all too familiar problems under an entirely new light. Corporations have been evolving in ways that appear on the surface to differ from the monolithic firms Coase visited during the Great Depression. Henry Ford saw value in vertical integration in his constant effort to increase efficiencies. When he received wooden crates of parts, he sought a way to reuse the wood. From these crates he created Kings-Ford, or Kingsford charcoal briquettes for barbequers. He created his own transportation networks to bring cars to dealers. And he maintained such a tight and exclusive relationship with his new car dealer network that, even though these franchisees were independent business people, they appeared to be the downstream terminus of a vertically integrated conglomerate. His efforts to create an immense vertically integrated enterprise was loved by some and loathed by others. Despite the antitrust regulations that constrained Gilded Age market concentration, by the 1920s and 1930s, it appeared that firms were becoming larger, more integrated, more profitable, and more efficient. Ford began a post-Gilded Age wave that, despite some setbacks, continues to this day. Yet, such vertical integration, and the efficiencies it created, was not universally embraced by regulators.

Such integration reached its heyday in the 1960s, but this was followed by a wave of decentralization, partly at the behest of the U.S. Department of Justice, but also partly because of the neoclassical recognition that a large firm with significant market power can grow too big, and expand beyond the most efficient scale, much like dinosaurs that evolved to be too big for their own weight. More recently, corporate governance has encouraged companies to decentralize, to spin off only peripherally related units, and to focus on their core missions. Before the era of decentralization, their missions were to become bigger. In the era of decentralization, small became beautiful.

However, this shift in focus was not an abandonment of Williamson's principles. A changing labor force demanded more flexibility. Some employees began to view themselves as more independent contractors, with flexible hours, but still under the supervision of the firm. Improvements in information technologies, and especially innovations in computing and the Internet, accelerated the process and has allowed an increasing number of workers to do their jobs from home, especially in a new world of developed nations in which consumer demand for manufactured goods have plateaued while demand for services have ballooned.

In the course of a single century, the workforce has evolved from a situation of more than two-thirds of workers being employed in manufacturing and agriculture to the current position of well less than one third. This evolution of the modern economy means that, while once the majority of workers worked where their machines resided, workers are now afforded much greater independence and flexibility within the corporation, without any rise in transactions costs. Firms are able to decentralize toward more contract-based workers without the rise in transactions costs that once limited growth. This is the most significant promise of the information and Internet age.

Now, commissioned sales employees, temporary workers who work for a temp agency but under the direction of the firm, franchisees under the increasingly restrictive and structured control of the franchiser, or even the companies that spin off from larger firms but remain within the *corporate family*, have taken advantage of new ways to construct formal or informal contracts without the transactions costs which once gave rise to the transactions cost economies.

The prophecies predicted by Coase and Williamson are now well verified, but they are not the contributions for which Coase is best remembered. That honor goes to his *Coase Theorem*, which is simple, but has wide-ranging applications. It states that, in the absence of bargaining or transactions costs, individual agents can resolve disputes or trade property rights to their mutual advantage without the need for any government intervention. The resolution of economic conflicts takes the form of a reassignment of property rights to a chattel or any other right through a transfer of wealth from the owner of the right to another who values it more and is willing to pay accordingly. The outcome is then *Pareto efficient* in that the entity which values the right the most highly ends up with the right.

Coase pointed out, though, that such gains from trade that are so familiar from the economics of free markets is only replicated through private contractual exchange if bargaining and transactions costs are insignificant. He went on to point out that such is rarely the case. In many cases, the idiosyncratic nature of such exchanges imposes informational, contracting, legal, and other costs on a potential exchange. In these cases, courts and government are often invoked to direct the transaction in the Pareto optimal direction.

For instance, consider an example similar to one posed by Coase. A firm operates a paint-shaking machine next to a jeweler who must perform delicate tasks to cut diamonds. Government zoning laws could simply deem that these two activities are incompatible and try to determine which one to prevent. On the other hand, the paint mixer and the jeweler could negotiate amongst themselves. If the jeweler's needs are more valuable and capable of generating greater profit than the operations of the paint mixer, the jeweler can pay the paint mixer not to make paint during certain hours, and still come out ahead. Alternately, if paint making is more valuable than jewelry making, the paint mixer can compensate the jeweler.

It is likely that, in the absence of costs to bring the two parties to an agreeable solution, these entities can forge an agreement that is better tailored to their needs and economic realities than could a government that imposes a solution on both parties. Interestingly, it does not matter who initially has the right. Assume, for instance, that the diamond cutter has the more valuable enterprise. If the diamond cutter also has the initial right to operate without conflict, no exchange is necessary and the optimal outcome is obtained. On the other hand, if the paint mixer has the right to operate, the diamond cutter can then afford to purchase that right from the paint mixer for the value of the mixer's operation, and still net a profit after that purchase. In either case, the property right will end up in the hands of the entity who can most profitably employ it.

Coase offered a similar example, and other examples in his discussion of transactions costs in "The Nature of a Firm." His goal was not to argue that transactions costs are insignificant, but rather to demonstrate the degree to which transactions costs are important determinants in the final economic outcomes.

Coase provided yet another example of clear-headed economic thinking in his 1974 paper, "The Lighthouse in Economics." In that paper, he addressed the role of a public good. Economists had argued that such public goods are best provided for by the government because no private firm would offer a service for which it is difficult or impossible to exclude anybody from enjoying free of charge. Coase relished in defying such conventional wisdom. He showed that lighthouses in Britain, often claimed to be such a public good, were privately provided in the nineteenth century. For that industry, ships were charged for their use once the ships entered port.

Coase never fought the crusade for free markets in quite the same way as some of his Chicago colleagues, though. Instead, he felt his biggest contribution lay in highlighting the importance of transactions costs in both the exchange of property rights and also the inner workings of the corporation. Within the corporation, he saw the manager as one who could efficiently define internal transactions to promote better intra-corporation exchanges and more efficient production. Thus, transactions costs and managerial costs overlap.

21
Life and Legacy of Ronald Coase

Coase made a memorable contribution to our understanding by pointing out starkly just how little we understood, but which managers take for granted. The notion that markets function costlessly, and that firms operate efficiently may be a convenient extreme but it is invariably untrue. Instead, it is clear that information within the firm is costly, and that within the market it is very costly, and the ability to prevent shirking and human opportunism is a challenging one.

Ronald Coase won the 1991 Nobel Memorial Prize "for his discovery and clarification of the significance of transaction costs and property rights for the institutional structure and functioning of the economy."[1] His contributions were especially noted for their ability to span the disciplines of law, organizations, and economics.

For much of his academic career, and until his death, Coase served as the Clifton R. Musser Professor Emeritus of Economics, and Senior Fellow in Law and Economics at the University of Chicago Law School, from 1982 to 2013. He had also been a visiting Distinguished Professor of Law and Economics at the University of Kansas in 1991.

Coase was a Senior Research Fellow at the Hoover Institution at Stanford in 1977. Earlier in his career, he had been a Fellow at the Center for Advanced Study in the Behavioral Sciences at Stanford University, for the academic year 1958/59, a decade after he was a Rockefeller Fellow. He was also a Consulting Director and Academic Advisory Chair for the Contracting and Organizations Research Institute at the University of Missouri-Columbia from 2002 to 2006.

Coase also advised the Ronald Coase Institute from 2000 to 2013, presided over the International Society for New Institutional Economics in 1997, and chaired the Advisory Board of the Center for Research on Contracts and the Structure of Enterprise at the Katz School of Business of the University of Pittsburgh from 1991 to 2002. For the last seven years of his career, he was a fellow at the School of Global studies at Arizona State University. Coase founded both the Coase Center for the Study of the Economy at Zhejiang University in 2012 and the Coase China Society in 2011.

Coase enjoyed the editorship of the *Journal of Law and Economics* from 1964 to 1982. In 1988, he earned honorary doctoral degrees from the University of Cologne, followed a year later by an honorary doctorate at Yale University, Washington University in St Louis in 1991, the University of Dundee in Scotland in 1992, the University of Buckingham, England in 1995 and both Beloit College and the Université de Paris in 1996, and the State University of New York in 2012.

Coase also earned a number of academic honors, including a Distinguished Fellow at the American Economic Association, Honorary Fellow at his alma mater, the London School of Economics, a Fellow at the American Academy of Arts and Sciences, Corresponding Fellow for the British Academy, and a Membre Titulaire at the European Academy. He received the Law and Economics Center Prize at the University of Miami in 1980 and the D. Francis Bustin Prize at the University of Chicago, 1988. He was most recognized for winning the Alfred Nobel Memorial Prize in Economic Sciences in 1991. Coase also won The Economist's Innovation Award in the category of "No Boundaries."

Coase summed up his academic philosophy in the following terms:

> As I see it, progress in understanding the working of the economic system will come from an interplay between theory and empirical work. The theory suggests what empirical work might be fruitful, the subsequent empirical work suggests what modification in the theory or rethinking is needed, which in turn leads to new empirical work. If rightly done, scientific research is a never-ending process, but one that leads to greater understanding at each stage.[2]

His Coase China Society sought to advocate for Coasean economic principles in China. He called his doctrine the "right economics," which is the study of how real economies work. He saw economics as a tool to be used to determine how to improve economic systems. His multidisciplinary sensitivity suggested to him the analogy from biology that the system works much like the human body, from the individual cellular level through the complex organs, in a way that is coordinated and symbiotic at best, or which needs intervention if diseased.

Near the end of his career, Coase was increasingly active in fostering a better understanding of China. He had been interested in China ever since his interest in history as a young child and his fascination with Marco Polo. Coase used his Coase Foundation to organize and then fund the 2008 Chicago Conference on China's Market Transformation and the 2010 Chicago Workshop on the Industrial Structure of Production. At these two gatherings he assembled scholars from China and North America, from various disciplines, and government officials and entrepreneurs to discuss China's transition to a market economy. He followed that up with a book, co-authored with Arizona State University Professor Ning Wang, entitled *How China Became Capitalist*, published jointly by Palgrave Macmillan and the Institute of Economic Affairs.[3]

Coase was active to the very end of his life. At the time of his death in Chicago on September 2, 2013, just shy of his 103rd birthday, he was the oldest living Nobel laureate. Coase remains one of the most cited economists over the course of the past half-century. His contributions informed and enriched not only academia, but also government, and society at large. His ideas were both intuitive and accessible. His intuition endures.

22
Life and Legacy of Oliver Williamson

With the exception of a two-year period, from 1963 to 1965, when he taught at the University of California, Berkeley, Williamson spent the majority of his early career barely a stone's throw away from the Carnegie Institute of Technology. Much of his career was devoted to the Department of Economics at the University of Pennsylvania, where he spent the academic years from 1965–6 to 1983. There he twice chaired the economics department, in 1971–2 and in 1976–7. He eventually earned a joint appointment and worked with colleagues at their School of Public and Urban Policy and with the School of Law.

In 1983, Williamson moved to New Haven, Connecticut, to join the Department of Economics at Yale University. There, he also enjoyed cross-disciplinary work with Yale's School of Organization and Management and their School of Law. Like Coase, Williamson immersed himself in the interface of economics and contracts, and served as the founding editor of the *Journal of the Law, Economics, and Organizations*, the journal that competes most closely with Coase's *Journal of Law and Economics*. He found Yale a complex environment to navigate, though, and, in 1988, moved back to the University of California at Berkeley. Fortunately, this later move did not once again displace an entire family as his five children, Scott, Tamara, Karen, Oliver Jr., and Dean, were all adults when he and his wife returned to Berkeley.

Upon his return to Berkeley, Williamson was able to continue his studies into the institutional approach to economics in an environment that celebrated alternatives to the neoclassical model. With a campus not far from San Francisco Bay, the Williamsons enjoyed a home with a view of sunsets over the Bay. As he enjoyed elsewhere, Williamson received appointments in both the department of Economics within the Haas School of Business, and also with the prestigious Berkeley Law School.

Williamson was brought to Berkeley to cultivate his revolutionary approach to the economics of institutions and also to reinvigorate a public policy curriculum in the business school. There, he benefitted from collaborations with scholars of like mind at Berkeley, and remained close to the equally innovative institutional economists down the California coast at the University of California Los Angeles campus.

Within the University of California system, Berkeley maintains the reputation as the flagship research school and is able to attract top students and Ph.D. candidates from around the world. Williamson very much appreciated the challenge and diversity of thought offered by the cadre of top Ph.D. students regularly recruited by Berkeley.

Oliver Williamson's wife, Dolores, also adapted well to Berkeley life. Always actively engaged in community work, Dolores presided over the local League of Women Voters, thrust herself into the areas of local governance and civics, and helped promote the arts and the relationship between the university and the City of Berkeley. Dolores shared her husband's penchant for engagement and for community.

While at Berkeley, Oliver Williamson could not resist engaging in the sort of governance he had often described in his research. He chaired the Academic Senate for a year at Berkeley in the 1990s, a senate that has a long-standing reputation for activism and engagement.

Although Williamson retired from his academic position in 2004, he still accepts assignments from the university to assist in recruiting and fundraising and he also continues with his research. At present, he is particularly interested in measuring the degree to which information imperfections affect economic outcomes. Of course, in the limit with perfect information and zero transactions costs, the results of the neoclassical model is typically obtained. As both Coase and Williamson pointed out, the degree of information imperfection or transactions cost barriers determines how much results depart from the neoclassical ideal. Williamson developed the term *information impactedness* to gauge the degree to which economic outcomes are sensitive to information and uncertainty. He defines information impactedness as a:

> condition that arises mainly because of uncertainty and opportunism, though bounded rationality is involved as well. It exists when true underlying circumstances relevant to the transaction, or related set of transactions, are known to one or more parties but cannot be costlessly discerned by or displayed for others."[1]

Telegraphing his belief in cross-disciplinary approaches, as he was indoctrinated so thoroughly at the Carnegie Institute of Technology, Williamson made great strides in applying his concepts to a wide variety of different economic and social problems. He delved into credible commitments between firms that also had international relations ramifications in his 1983 paper *Credible Commitments: Using Hostages to Support Exchange.*[2] There he argued that offering incentives to follow through with commitments increases the likelihood of successful trade.

Williamson followed his Credible Commitments paper with a paper that provides a unified theory of three different types of institutions – the market, the hierarchical organization, and a hybrid intermediary form, depending on the nature and cost of transactions. In *Comparative Economic Organization: The Analysis of Discrete Structural Alternatives,*[3] Williamson argued that these three types of organizations differ in the degree to which they can adjust to shocks and also in terms of the coordinating mechanism they employ. Each is also governed by various types of contract law that have been adapted to best utility in these applications. There, he introduces the concept of *forbearance law.* Williamson (1991, p. 274) notes:

> The implicit contract law of internal organization is that of forbearance. Thus, whereas courts routinely grant standing to firms should there be disputes over prices, the damages to be ascribed to delays, failures of quality, and the like, courts will refuse to hear disputes between one internal division and another over identical technical issues. Access to the courts being denied, the parties must resolve their differences internally. Accordingly, hierarchy is its own court of ultimate appeal.

In effect, the hierarchy within an organization can be viewed as an institution that facilitates, and must, at times, adjudicate internal contracts. An institution can also be viewed as an alternative dispute resolution mechanism should there be a contract dispute. This *nexus of contracts* approach is one which Michael Jensen and William Meckling, and Arman Alchian and Harold Demsetz took up, as described later in this volume.

Williamson argued that the firm creates value because of its ability to organize processes in ways that are more efficient than those of the market. He also devoted some effort to the implications of his Transactions Cost Theory on corporate governance and on the limits to size of a firm. In *The Economic Institutions of Capitalism,* Williamson showed that governance and management eventually create diseconomies of scale in their inability to fully accommodate the increasingly complex needs of the organization at it grows.[4]

Williamson also weighed further in on corporate governance and corporate finance in his 1988 article in the *Journal of Finance*, entitled *Corporate Finance and Corporate Governance*[5] and his follow-up 2008 *Journal of Law, Economics, and Organizations* paper entitled "Corporate Boards of Directors: in Principle and in Practice".[6] These articles argue that the debt and equity mix is not merely a capital structure decision but also has ramifications for corporate governance because the capital structure affects both the institutional environment and the way a board governs the organization.

Over his career, Williamson served his discipline through his membership and governance responsibilities on numerous associations, including being the Vice President of the American Economic Association in 2001, the President of the International Society for New Institutional Economics from 1999 to 2001, the President of the American Law and Economics Association from 1997 to 1998, and the President of the Western Economic Association from 1999 to 2000.

Williamson was awarded more than a dozen honorary degrees over the course of his career, including a Docteur Honoris Causa, from the University of Paris-Dauphine in 2012, Honorary Doctor of Economics and Organization, Carnegie-Mellon University in 2011, Honorary Professor at Tsinghua University in 2010, Doctoris Honoris Causa in Economics at Nice University in 2005, Valencia University in 2004, and the University of Chile in 2000, an Honorary Doctorate in Economics and Business Administration at Copenhagen Business School in 2000, Doctoris Honoris Causa, Groupe HEC in Paris and St. Petersburg University, Russia in 1997 and at Turku School of Economics and Business Administration in 1995, Groningen University in 1989, and St Gallen in 1987. He also received an Oeconomiae Doctorem Honoris Causa from the Norwegian School of Economics and Business Administration at their Jubilee Celebration in 1986.

In 2009, Williamson won the Nobel Memorial Prize "for his analysis of economic governance, especially the boundaries of the firm." His contribution:[7]

> (p)rovided a theory of why some economic transactions take place within firms and other similar transactions take place between firms, that is, in the marketplace. The theory informs us about how to handle one of the most basic choices in human organization. When

> should decision power be controlled inside an organization, and when should decisions be left to the market.

In granting the award, the committee was noting the importance of economics and finance beyond the narrow walls of the Ivory Tower and into the board rooms of organizations.

Williamson also received numerous other awards, being made Distinguished Fellow at the American Economic Association in 2007, Distinguished Fellow of the Industrial Organization Society in 2005, Founding Honorary Editor for the *Journal of Law, Economics, and Organization* in 2003, Eminent Scholar of the Fellows of the Academy of International Business, Honorary Editor, *Journal of Economic Behavior and Organization* in 2002, the prestigious John von Neumann Award at the Laszlo Rajk College for Advanced Studies at Budapest University in 1999, the Irwin Award for Scholarly Contributions to Management at the Academy of Management in 1988, and, early in his career, the Alexander Henderson Award for Excellence in Economic Theory at Carnegie-Mellon in 1962.

While Williamson's research reached into the boardrooms and the offices of chief financial officers in major corporations, he was never to abandon his Wisconsin rural roots. His father died in the early 1970s and he purchased the family summer home on Lake Nebagamon in Wisconsin so that the extended family could keep one foot grounded in their Wisconsin sensibilities. This remains a magnet that holds together a Williamson clan that spans generations and it also allows Prof. Williamson a reflective environment in which to continue his work when not in Berkeley.

Section 4
Alchian and Demsetz

Modern finance has become rocket science. Motivated by the twin pillars of optimization and arbitrage, the value of a firm, as represented by its stock price, is buffeted by what theorists term random shocks. Any corporate events, such as an earnings release or a matter that may materially affect its stock price, will move the security discretely either up or down. However, lost in the analogy that treats a stock price much like a ballistic rocket buffeted by invisible atmospheric forces is the very nature of what the firm does – and how it does so.

Such institutional detail was once the bread and butter of the financial analyst's assignment. However, while technical analysts use statistical techniques to determine security and corporate value, there has been renewed interest in opening up the black box of the modern corporation to see what makes it tick. Armen Alchian and Harold Demsetz were instrumental in offering us the tools not only to peer inside the corporate black box, but also to craft more effective managerial tools to tease even more value out of a well-governed and managed corporation.

23
Alchian and Demsetz

As much as some spend a lifetime denying it, our heritage typically creates an indelible imprint on our nature, for better or for worse. Armen Albert Alchian's life was formed in the wake of conflict and genocide. It is perhaps an interesting juxtaposition for a great mind who devoted a career to understanding how organizations can create symmetries and function as cohesive teams.

Armenia is a nation at the intersection of two worlds. A mountainous region in the South Caucasus region of Eurasia, it, and its neighbor Turkey, is at the crossroads of Western Asia and Eastern Europe. It includes Mount Ararat, where the Old Testament states Noah's Ark came to rest. Armenia is a Christian nation, a religion it adopted in the fourth century. However, it has, for centuries, also been the battleground of titanic military forces from elsewhere. As a crossroads, Armenia was often viewed for its strategic location rather than for its own historic identity. It was the buffer upon which battles were fought between others. The Armenian people were often the unfortunate casualties of these battles between titans.

As Turkey became increasingly Muslim, Armenian Christians were subject to discrimination. To insulate themselves, they sought autonomy, but were instead faced with genocide. The Hamadan massacres between 1894 and 1896 resulted in the loss of as many as 300,000 Armenians.[1] World War I resulted in even more Armenian losses as the Turks, in battle with Russia, mistrusted the allegiance of their neighbors to the east.

By the nineteenth century, its territory was torn between two empires, the Ottomans to the west and the Russians to the north. With these increasing tensions and with the discrimination it suffered at the hands of the Russians in the late nineteenth century, Armenians sought refuge. First a few, and then many Armenians found their way to Fresno, California.

In the heart of the San Joaquin Valley and in the wake of the California Gold Rush, Fresno was named for the Spanish word for the ash trees that lined the San Joaquin River. At the tail end of the nineteenth century, it was still a pioneer area, with men significantly outnumbering women. Fresno was also a unique refuge for Armenians escaping persecution. Its climate and geography reminded Armenian refugees of home, but without the threat of death. While they may have escaped death, however, they were unable to escape a perhaps more subtle but equally pervasive discrimination.

It was Fresno where a young couple, Pascal Martin Normart (October 1858–January 8, 1927), his wife, Pearl (November 1860–?) and their three children Ornian (November 1880–?), Angeline (1886–?), and Onnig (January 20, 1886–August 21, 1969), immigrated in 1888. They were among an early wave of a hundred Armenians. Soon after their arrival, they had a fourth child Lily (1889–1976), the first child born in the growing Armenian community of Fresno.[2]

Other members of their family followed. The tripling of the Armenian population in Fresno in the wake of the Hamadan massacre brought a young 15-year-old named Alexander Alchian (1886–?) in 1901. Soon upon settling in Fresno, Alexander met Lily Normart among their close-knit Armenian community of Fresno. The two were married, with Alexander seeking work variously as a musician and then as a jeweler, and they raised two boys, Armen Albert (April 12, 1914–February 19, 2013) and Robert Haig Alchian.

Armen Alchian was a bright and imaginative child, but he was raised in a region of limited opportunities and in a family of modest means. Within the Armenian community that created his de facto extended family, Armen was to become something of a local hero. He attended Fresno High School and excelled in both academics and athletics. In 1932, he started his education at Fresno State College. Following the encouragement of his high school athletic coaches, he transferred to Stanford University in 1934. He obtained his B.A. in 1936 and stayed on to complete his Ph.D. dissertation, "The Effects of Changes in the General Wage Structure" in 1943. In the interim years 1940 and 1941, he had also worked at the National Bureau of Economic Research and Harvard University. In 1942, just prior to graduation, he had already joined the University of Oregon as an instructor.

The Armenian community in Fresno may have suffered some nascent discrimination, but Armenian men were particularly patriotic. They

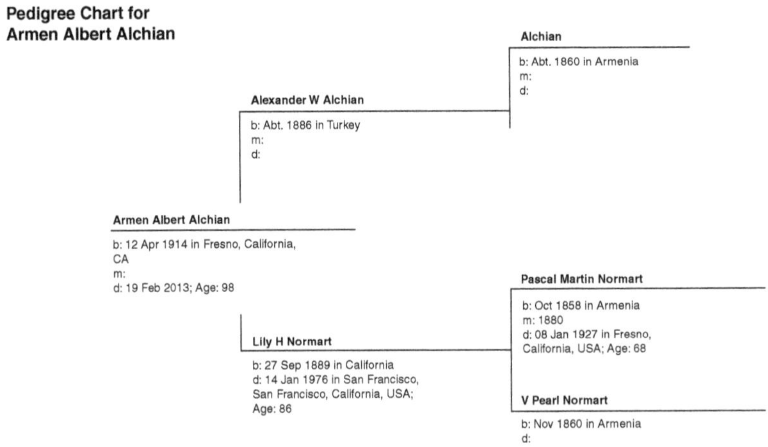

Figure 23.1 The Armen Alchian Family Tree

frequently demonstrated a willingness to contribute to the American war efforts, especially in its determination to defend democracy and human rights. When Armen graduated from Stanford in 1942, he put his talents to perhaps their best possible use – as a statistician in the Army's Air Force.

Following his service, Alchian returned to California to join the faculty of UCLA and the think-tank at the RAND Corporation in nearby Santa Monica. The RAND Corporation (for Research ANd Development) was a Cold War-era institute that grew out of the efforts of World War II. Luminaries and Nobel Memorial Prize winners in finance from William Sharpe to Harry Markowitz, Kenneth Arrow, William Meckling, and others all crossed paths at the RAND Corporation.

RAND had assembled the greatest minds in sciences and social sciences united in their desire to have the United States maintain its military and academic lead. Its mission was "to further and promote scientific, educational, and charitable purposes, all for the public welfare and security of the United States of America." To this day it remains a major think-tank devoted to national security issues.

The Institute was formed as part of the effort during World War II under the leadership of Commanding General of the Army Air Force H. H. "Hap" Arnold. With a budget that was sufficient to meet any need, it wooed the greatest minds in science, mathematics, economics and finance, and strategy in the Cold War era following World War II. While it was associated with the Army during the war, it became a civil institute in the latter half of the 1940s. As a result its scope was then broadened to include social issues such as national economics, finance, health care, and education.

Los Angeles' RAND Institute quickly became a leading institute for finance theory, rivaling Chicago's Cowles Institute. These two major institutes each shared faculty with UCLA and Chicago, respectively, and also shared faculty between the two institutes. This cross-pollination in turn advanced the free market approach of the Chicago School and the more institutional approach of UCLA into a hybrid school of thought that was most influential in the development of theories on the valuation of corporations.

As the RAND Corporation increased in stature and prominence in the late 1940s and early 1950s, so too did the University of California at Los Angeles. Even before this era, UCLA was uniquely prominent, along with the University of Chicago, for its advocacy of free markets, whereas the University of Virginia was a proponent of the argument that the public sector plays an important role in our national economy. These fresh perspectives were alternatives to the classical approaches among the Ivy League institutions. UCLA's perspective was not unlike that of the RAND Corporation – that our institutions ought to provide subtle and nuanced solutions to real economic questions.

These more intuitive approaches were not of the highly mathematical and technical nature promulgated by the Massachusetts Institute of Technology or Harvard University. Alchian was one of the greatest practitioners of such practical and intuitive approaches that had immediate applications, rather than the contrived problems and elaborate, and perhaps elegant, analyses that were growing in vogue in the finance and economics disciplines in the late 1950s and the 1960s.

Alchian became a full professor at UCLA in 1958. Under his influence, there emerged a UCLA school of institutional economics and finance, with Alchian as one of the primary mentors. The school cultivated a number of bright graduate students, including Alchian's thesis advisee, the great mind William F. Sharpe, who subsequently won the Nobel Memorial Prize for his Capital Asset Pricing Model. Sharpe described Alchian as a mentor who "... taught his students to question everything, to always begin an analysis with first principles, to concentrate on essential elements and abstract from secondary ones, and to play devil's advocate with one's own ideas. In his classes, we were able to watch a first-rate mind on a host of fascinating problems.

I have attempted to emulate his approach to research ever since." Sharpe added,

> While personally gentle and traditional, Armen was and is clearly an eccentric economic theorist. He started the course (in graduate microeconomics) by asserting that 95 percent of the material in economics journals was wrong or irrelevant. He then proceeded to discuss the economics of the illegal market for buying babies. At one point, he spent five or six lectures wrestling somewhat unsuccessfully with the meaning of profit. Indeed, most of his classes had the characteristics of a wrestling match. We witnessed a brilliant mind grappling, usually very successfully, with the most difficult concepts in economics in creative and innovative ways. There could be no better training for a fledgling theorist and no higher standard.[3]

Alchian's academic mission was to approach real world problems in unconventional ways. In doing so, he made a brilliant and lasting contribution to the literature. His papers constitute volumes. Many of his works are considered ground-breaking and prized for their intuition, even though they remain mathematically unsophisticated. And, just like Franco Modigliani, he often sought out or nurtured young scholars as co-authors who learned much about intellectual curiosity and ingenuity from him.

24
Harold Demsetz

Harold Demsetz had a legacy that has not been all that unusual for pioneers in finance. His roots can be traced back to the countries of the Austro-Hungarian Empire that produced such great minds as John von Neumann. However, the amazing innovativeness of the Austro-Hungarian Empire was not broadly shared among its residents.

Galicia, once a proud and incredibly ethnically diverse nation of nobles and serfs, had suffered for centuries as a prize in the conquests between other, larger nations. It often offered refuge for those escaping persecution, including the Jews who had once inhabited Germany. By the late nineteenth century, Galicia was under the auspices of the Austro-Hungarian Empire, a vast economic union that was the cradle to some of the greatest intellectual revolutions of the nineteenth and early twentieth centuries.

Galicia was a neglected province that became infamous in the late nineteenth century for its extreme levels of poverty, not only within the Empire, but throughout the continent. Its economy stagnated, and its residents earned only a tenth of the Empire average; there was a very poor level of education, and the Imperialist leaders showed little interest in introducing reforms. Residents suffered famine and disease, especially among the Jews, who also suffered from resentment and anti-Semitism. The resulting misery and migration to safer lands of greater opportunity, often to the United States, was comparable to the economic exodus of the Irish earlier in the nineteenth century.

Jewish Galician suffering affected a family named Blats, whose story ended tragically. Simcha Ben Itzchak Blatt (1836–96), the son of Simcha Itzchak Blatt (1816–76), died at the height of anti-Semitism and poverty. Already, before his father's death, Simcha Ben's son, Moses Avrom Blatt (1858–December 1924), was seeking an opportunity to escape. In

1903, he arrived at Ellis Island with his wife, Pauline Pesha (1862–?), and with a large family in tow.

Moses Blatt's middle daughter, Estella Blatt (September 27, 1892–November 9, 1969), was born at the beginning of the worst of the proverbial Galician poverty. At the age of 11, she had arrived in New York and embarked on a life that, while difficult, created much more opportunity than the situation they had left behind. The large extended family worked in the Jewish clothing factories in the garment region of turn-of-the-century New York City. Younger children were often allowed to go to school, but, from the age of 17 onward, members of the extended family were expected to work to support each other. Both Jews and the members of the broader Hungarian region from which they came placed a great deal of importance in education, but the family

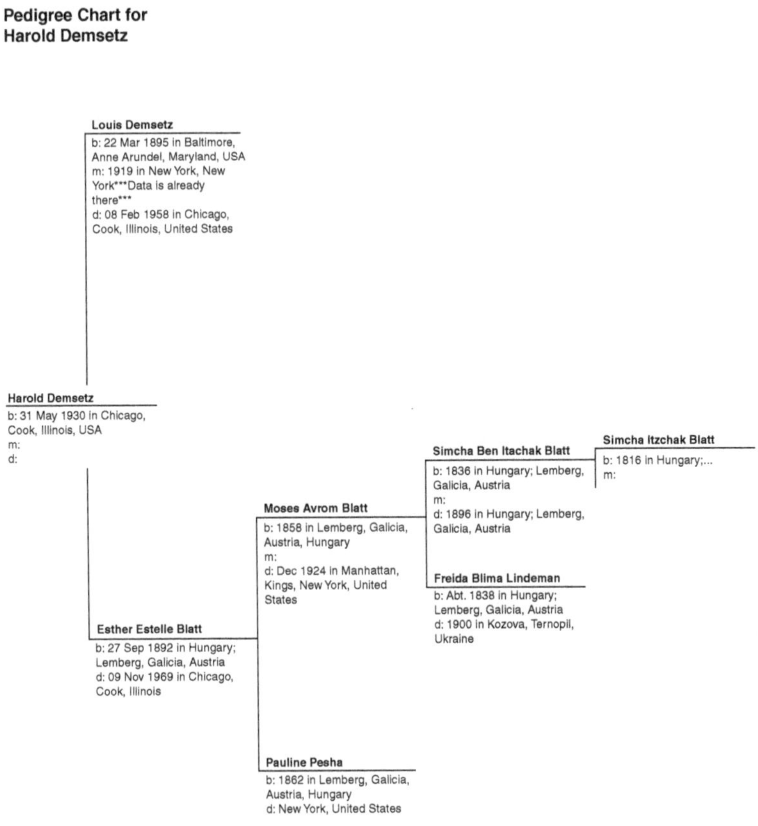

Figure 24.1 The Harold Demsetz Family Tree

poverty among the Jews often made formal education beyond high school unaffordable. The United States often afforded greater educational opportunities than the homelands from which many immigrants travelled, particularly for the Italian and Jewish communities within which Estella lived.

Estella worked first in New York City, and then in America's second city, Chicago. In each of these cities, the immigrant communities always remained acutely aware of their humble beginnings, and of the thin line that separated them from the poverty of their past, and the necessity for hard and steady work to create a better life for their children. Decades before the nation would broadly learn these same principles from the Great Depression, these immigrants were, in some sense, a greatest generation. They took modest jobs (often more than one), and translated hard work, ingenuity, and street cleverness into a working class existence. Their children were the first generation to enjoy these benefits. In some ways, Estella was doubly blessed. She recalled her family's hardship and also inheriting their work ethic.

Estella had two daughters, Edith Gold (1913–?) and Molly Isabella Gold (1919–?) with Abraham Gold (1890–?) but then married Louis Demsetz (1895–1958).

Not unlike the Blatts, Louis's family emigrated from Eastern Europe. His family had arrived from Russia in 1894. He was born in Baltimore, Maryland, 190 miles south of Ellis Island just one year later. Louis made his way to Chicago and New York City, where he worked as an electrician's helper and married Estella. At first, he, his new bride, and her children lived with her parents in New York. While there they had a child of their own, Philip Marcus (November 3, 1920–March 14, 1984). The family subsequently struck out on their own and moved back to Chicago, where Louis gained steady work as an electrician and a janitor. Soon after their arrival in Chicago, they had two more boys, Sidney (May 11, 1924–July 1959), and Harold (May 31, 1930–).

The neighborhood for these three boys in Chicago was made up mostly of renters and of immigrants, who, by Harold's birth, were suffering from the economic onslaught of the Great Depression. Fortunately, Harold excelled in high school, and was afforded the opportunity to be the first in his generation to attend college, so long as it was he studied in some area that would provide him with a good job. By the time he graduated from high school, the Great Depression and World War II were over. As a consequence, he was thrust into college with many other slightly older men whom had served their country in the war and whom were benefiting from the educational benefits of the G.I. Bill.

Harold initially set out to become an engineer at the nearest and most affordable, free, junior college very near his home. He helped support himself by driving a cab and working as an usher at Chicago's opera house. He changed majors often, from engineering to philosophy and forestry, at four different colleges before he finally graduated in 1953, just short of his 23rd birthday, with a degree in economics from the University of Illinois.

Upon graduation, Harold served in the Army just as the Korean War was winding down. His relatively short stint in the Army was followed by his acceptance into the Ph.D. program at Northwestern University. Also, in 1955, he married Rita Coleman (July 23, 1934–).

Rita, too, had parents who had emigrated from Eastern Europe – in this case, Russia. Morris Coleman (1895–?) had arrived with his family from Russia in 1912 when he was just 17 years old. His future wife Rose (1902–?) and her family had arrived that same year, when she was ten years old. Both of the families were escaping the persecution of Jewish, Yiddish-speaking Russians during a great emigration from 1880 to 1920. In Europe throughout this period, organized riots (called pogroms) massacred thousands of European Jews, and destroyed thousands of Jewish businesses. While the most notorious was the *Kristallnacht* of 1938 in Nazi Germany, similar pogroms occurred throughout Western Russia over this period of mass emigration.

When Morris arrived in the United States, and met and married Rose, he began a career first as a superintendent of a Chicago laundry, and eventually a partner in the laundry. Morris and Rose had four daughters together between 1923 and 1934. Rita was their last child.

Harold's family and Rita's family had lived within a block of one another in Chicago. Harold and Rita had known each other as children. Their parents. Louis and Estella Demsetz, and Morris and Rose Coleman, felt it would be good for these two young people be together. Such parental meddling was not a subtle influence for the young adults.

Regardless of the external pressures, Harold and Rita seemed an ideal match. Rita had attended the University of Chicago, and graduated in 1953, and was contemplating her first major career move post-graduation, all the while biding her time working at a publishing house in Chicago. Harold had just returned from the Army, and was working on his MBA when they fell in love and married in 1955. At first they lived in a small apartment on the North Side of Chicago, near Harold's studies at Northwestern. She helped support him through college, and they subsequently had four children together.

Harold progressed well through his studies. To hedge his bets on whether he could complete a Ph.D. program, he also obtained an M.B.A.

from Northwestern's business school. Part of his dissertation ended up as his second publication, a paper on brand distinction, in the prestigious economics journal *Economica*. He also had a paper on monopolistic competition published in the equally prestigious *Journal of Political Economy*, written before he graduated. Even before he graduated with his Ph.D., he had already pending two paper publications in top journals and by 1958 he had also been offered a good entry-level academic job at the University of Michigan. Harold was ready to embark on his career, and moved with his family to Ann Arbor, Michigan.

While Harold had not attended Chicago, his wife's alma mater, he nonetheless subscribed to the Chicago tradition of probing and challenging questioning, and an almost unrelenting pursuit of knowledge. The University of Michigan was unable to capitalize on his rigorous academic intuition for long, though. During his second year at the University in Ann Arbor, he was offered a $400 higher annual salary to join the University of California in Los Angeles. While this potential raise amounted to only about a 6 percent salary increase, but would require his family to move to a city with higher housing costs than its rural competitor, Harold remained ready to decline the offer and stay in Ann Arbor, but only if Michigan would at least match UCLA's offer. Michigan would not, and Harold packed up his car with Rita and a young daughter and they moved west.

Harold quickly found himself back in a big city, and he soon realized that he had been missing urban pleasures. After only three years in Los Angeles, though, he was subsequently attracted back to Chicago to join the prestigious faculty at the University of Chicago. Harold had attended a meeting of the American Economic Association in 1963, held in Chicago. While he was there, the University of Chicago's Reuben Kessel sought him out based on a recommendation from Armen Alchian. Kessel inquired rather bluntly if Demsetz was happy at UCLA. In a distinctly Chicago style, Demsetz responded "make me unhappy."[1] Kessel did, and Demsetz moved his family across the country once again.

Demsetz remained at Chicago for eight years, from 1963 to 1971, until he returned to UCLA for good, but with a retained enthusiasm for what we now call the "Chicago School." During his time Demsetz had the opportunity to work with some of the greatest minds in the foundations of finance and of our understanding of corporate synergies. Of course, the famous free marketeers, Milton Friedman and George Stigler, cast their long shadows. But others, including Richard Posner, Frank Knight, and, in particular, Ronald Coase, also came across his path while Demsetz was in Chicago. Most notable in that era, though, was an intense effort to develop a much more quantitative understanding of the value of a firm. Coase had produced the foundational work on how a firm creates goodwill. And Fischer Black and Myron Scholes had been attracted to Chicago to improve our understanding of how risk affects the value of a firm, a concept that Frank Knight had pioneered in his work almost half a century earlier. Demsetz was in the hotbed of thought on these ponderous issues, and became thoroughly inoculated with rich ideas he would bring back to UCLA.

Actually, Demsetz helped conspire to create the UCLA branch of this new school of thought of corporate finance when Armen Alchian came to visit the University of Chicago for a year. Demsetz and Alchian instantly renewed their academic relationship, and the potential to continue to work with Alchian was influential in one last institutional decision, to return to UCLA in 1971.

This was start of a new era at UCLA.

25
The Times

In the late 1940s, business and finance were emerging out of the shadow of economics. Previous scholars had set the stage for more advanced and quantitative business studies, but few programs in business were prepared to move beyond a relatively simple narrative in business studies. Chicago was the exception in this respect. In the 1950s, Chicago had almost singlehandedly formalized a new quantitative approach to finance that was mathematically rigorous and free market-oriented. Left by the wayside, though, were the important institutional subtleties within the corporate black box.

These nuances were not lost on Alchian and Demsetz. They argued that a firm is a convenient coalition of resource owners who contract to produce together a marketable product and, in turn, enrich each resource owner with net benefits in excess of what they could garner separately. These are the points that Oliver Williamson made in his employment of terms such as impacted information, opportunism, idiosyncrasies, shirking, or small numbers.

Harold Demsetz and Armen Alchian constituted the Los Angeles School that successfully revitalized the nuance and detail of an institutional approach to the study of finance that had been eclipsed by the neoclassical black box in the 1920s. Part of this movement away from institutional detail and toward mathematical formalism had a distinctly American flavor. John Bates Clark (January 26, 1847–March 21, 1938) was a renowned American economist for whom the top prize in economics for American economists is still named. He pioneered the transfer of the theory of the consumer developed by Francis Ysidro Edgeworth (February 8, 1845–February 13, 1926) and Alfred Marshall (July 26, 1842–July 13, 1924) and others to the theory of the firm. Their marginalist revolution, with its attendant adherence to sterile mathematical sophistication over complex human intervention, was in stark contrast to the Institutionalist school of economics. The mathematical approach was compact and compelling, though, and placed economics and finance on a firm footing with the sciences in a post-World War I era that saw a rapid development in and dispersion of scientific methods.

With these new tools at hand, finance and economic theory very quickly transitioned from the tedious analysis of individual industries toward a generic model of the motivation behind the modern corporation. Yet this mathematically sophisticated theoretical approach stood in stark contrast to empirical observations. In 1932, Adolf Berle and Gardiner Means published a book entitled *The Modern Corporation and Private Property*.[1] Had the book first been published when it was republished in 1967, a few decades later, it would have been pronounced as being revolutionary and sacrilegious. Yet in 1932, it merely offered a different look at the corporation from a novel economic and legal lens, as Coase was to do once again five years later.

Berle and Means argued that an important institutional detail was that those who legally own a corporation, the shareholders, are separate from those who manage it. They asserted that the concept of legal personhood for corporations determined the separation of ownership and control of the firm. This separation of ownership and control casts into a new light the notion of property. Traditionally, property owners control the use of property. Rarely is there a separation of this nexus. However, modern corporations routinely operate based on this separation. In effect,

> The property owner who invests in a modern corporation so far surrenders his wealth to those in control of the corporation that he has exchanged the position of independent owner for one in which he may become merely recipient of the wages of capital... [Such owners] have surrendered the right that the corporation should be operated in their sole interest.[2]

In their book, Berle and Means explore the implications of this separation. They postulate that the dichotomy between ownership and control increases as firms grow and the number of shareholders disperses ownership. Meanwhile, professional directors who earn income through directors' fees rather than capital gains of the corporate stock also become separated from the goals of shareholders. The authors stated:

> the owners most emphatically will not be served by a profit seeking controlling group... Where such a separation is complete one group

> of individuals, the security holders and in particular the stockholders, performs the function of risk-takers and suppliers of capital, while a separate group exercises control and ultimate management. In such a case, if profits are to be received only by the security holders, as the traditional logic of property would require, how can they perform both of their traditional economic roles? Are no profits to go to those who exercise control and in whose hands the efficient operation of enterprise ultimately rests?... Furthermore, if all profits are earmarked for the security holder, where is the inducement for those in control to manage the enterprise efficiently? When none of the profits are to be received by them, why should they exert themselves beyond the amount necessary to maintain a reasonably satisfied group of stockholders.[3]

These concerns demand either a better way to organize complex organizations or a better way to unify the goals of shareholders and management. Once the black box of the corporation is flung open, however, other intellectual challenges remain. For instance, Ludwig Heinrich Edler von Mises (September 29, 1881–October 10, 1973) spent a career describing how the external market works, the ways in which it arrives at prices, and the informational content of prices. These same forces are at work within the corporation, where resources must be coordinated, rewards must be offered, and exchanges must be made. Meanwhile, there is an equivalent of the market's "invisible hand" that must guide these various transactions within the firm.

It is this monitor and coordinator of the process that remained misunderstood. The leader of the team earns the surpluses generated from the coordinating function. We often call this individual the entrepreneur. They offer a factor which we can call management, and they earn a reward we call a profit.

The neoclassical model merely characterizes the net result and implications once this coordination process performs with perfect efficiency. Yet, before Armen Alchian and Harold Demsetz concentrated in the coordination problem, the dynamic complexities within the corporation remained obscured. There was scant discussion of how the teams internal to the firm organize themselves to perform functions that, in other contexts, are left to the marketplace. Alchian and Demsetz correct this omission.

26
The Great Idea

Armen Alchian and Harold Demsetz epitomized the Los Angeles School that added flesh to the bare bones neoclassical model. Their work on a new definition of the firm was both their magnum opus and an important contribution to an understanding that has now been integrated into the fabric of finance and corporate value.

Alchian and Demsetz, in their classic 1972 *American Economic Review* article *Production, information costs, and economic organization*,[1] offered a novel definition of the corporation. According to these finance pioneers, a modern firm that exhibit joint production must satisfy a number of stakeholders. The first of these are the various owners of the factors of production that make up the firm's inputs. The manager must contract with these input owners, and has the ability to renegotiate any of these implicit and explicit contracts separately without the necessity of renegotiating other contracts. Finally, the shareholders or owners, often called the residual claimants, have the right to any surpluses, net of costs, generated by the performance of myriad implicit or explicit internal contracts within the corporation.

Under this view of the modern corporation, value is created because the firm can provide the nexus and mechanism to contract between all the internal participants of the firm. This value is capitalized to represent a new net asset (over liabilities), sometimes labelled rather generically as goodwill. As with the firm's physical assets, ownership of this asset can be divided and sold as shares without implications on the internal contracting structure.

This alternative view of the firm as the nexus of many implicit contracts begs some questions that were raised in Milton Friedman's provocative 1970 article[2] in the *New York Times* Magazine in which he asserts, rather enthusiastically, that the only responsibility of a corporation is to create profits, and that it should not seek to promote other social values. Friedman argued that the firm is not an individual and cannot even be viewed as representing the wills of a collection of individual shareholders. Were one to draw a Venn diagram of the various interests of shareholders, their only intersecting value would be the pursuit of profits. Instead, the firm's goal must remain the pursuit of efficiencies within this nexus of contracts so the product can be brought to market at the lowest cost. This is the behavioral assumption of the firm.

This discussion had in fact been initiated by the work of Coase, but Alchian and Demsetz brought a greater clarity to bear on the problem. Corporate value is created because the internal team can produce additional output at lower cost through the coordinating effort of their manager(s). These managers must constantly monitor the effectiveness of the team, reward effort, and prevent the moral hazard problem that occurs if results do not affect behavior. The manager is the motivator, the measurer and monitor, the moral hazard internalizer, and, ultimately, the money maker for the firm.

In particular, Alchian and Demsetz emphasized this monitoring role of management as the team leader. The moral hazard problem of shirking begs the need for monitoring and lies at the crux of the failure of other markets.

Moral hazard is a term that may date back to the 1600s, or at least since the institution of insurance has allowed one party to indemnify the risks and actions of another. Such indemnification sometimes induces the indemnified to take risk they may not otherwise accept. The use of the word *moral* has some obvious implications that the hazard they in turn impose on another might be regarded as fraud or wrongful behavior. However, the term *moral* was once used synonymously with *subjective,* meaning subject to differing interpretations. It was co-opted into the finance literature in the 1960s to describe the various inefficiencies that can result when those who commit acts are not aligned perfectly with those who pay the price of the acts.

For instance, the term became part of the vernacular as a result of the Credit Crisis and then the Global Financial Meltdown that began in 2006. It was argued that banks or insurance companies that were viewed as 'too big to fail' could take big risks, knowing that if the risks pan out, they can make immense profits, and if the risks prove costly, the company can unload those responsibilities onto customers or taxpayers.

More generally, Bengt Holmström proposes the following definition:[3]

> It has long been recognized that a problem of moral hazard may arise when individuals engage in risk sharing under conditions such that their privately taken actions affect the probability distribution of the outcome.

There are a couple of different types of moral hazard. *Ex ante* moral hazard is when a change of behavior affects the outcome of some random event, while *ex post* moral hazard occurs when such an event subsequently affects behavior. An example of *ex ante* moral hazard might occur when someone who obtains insurance subsequently drives faster because of the knowledge they are indemnified for their risk of an accident. *Ex post* moral hazard occurs when one incurs the cost of risk but subsequently burdens an indemnifier with that cost. For instance, if an insurance policy could be purchased after a hazard has already occurred, it would be financially advantageous to avoid premiums and only pay for insurance once the hazard occurs. This is a fear of the provision of a health insurance policy that is not mandatory but for which application cannot be denied because of a pre-existing condition. One has no incentive to purchase the insurance until after they become ill. The greater risks, or the less responsible commitment to diligence results because of the unfortunate incentives insurance creates.

This type of problem can also preoccupy management. If there is a lack of, or an inability to monitor effort, workers may shirk in the belief their compensation is not adequately coordinated with their production or effort. The effect on the corporation valuation arising from this type of moral hazard is further explored later in this volume's description of the work of Jensen and Meckling. For instance, moral hazard occurs when managers do not bear the full brunt of poor decision-making, or when a manager has tenure or other protections and cannot be removed on the grounds of poor performance. For instance, government bureaucracies are sometimes accused of committing to spending that is not adequately tied to the project's success. Sometimes, within complex organizations, it is difficult to determine who or what entity is responsible for a project failure. The problem that Jensen and Meckling addressed in particular, though, is when senior management seem to commit to goals that are inconsistent with the creation of long-term value for the corporation.

In contrast to Jensen and Meckling's problem, Alchian and Demsetz explored the implications of inconsistencies in what is good for the principal, and what is performed by the agent, or worker, at the level of the shop floor.

One might conclude too quickly that Alchian and Demsetz believed all value of the firm is created because of the ability first to coordinate and then to monitor the performance of a team. While Alchian and Demsetz themselves would agree this is a simplistic reading of their research, they do focus on the advantage of coordinating behavior from within an institution rather than through the marketplace, just as Williamson had observed. In essence, the corporation creates value by solving the problem of asymmetric information. Within the corporation, information is superior because it can be shared broadly with both sides of each transaction. However, in broader markets, differences, or asymmetries, in information abound.

Alchian and Demsetz begin by establishing a few tenets. First, they note that managers do not own all their inputs. In particular, while they can own their financial, resource, or physical capital, they do not own their human capital, or labor. Instead, they must form implicit or explicit contracts with their human capitalists who offer incentives for the factor to perform in a manner consistent with corporate profits. Through this lens, the ability to direct human capital through implicit contracts and their constant renegotiation creates the value of the firm. Any cost of contracting within the firm is small relative to the additional value successful goals alignment yields. The ability to prevent shirking and the opportunity to create synergies creates the corporate profits.

Alchian and Demsetz go on to offer a description of the phenomenon of shirking among employees. Typically, all workers in a similar position are paid an equal amount. This compensation scheme may also be negotiated collectively rather than individually, based not on direct measures of productivity, but rather on the relative bargaining strength of each side.

Under this scenario, if all workers earn the same compensation but differ in terms of their effort or productivity, then individual workers may decide to reduce their effort, and hence their individual costs, thereby improving their personal ratio of compensation or reward to effort.

Alchian and Demsetz note that this problem of shirking is worsened if the compensation scheme is rigid, if the match between employer and employee is difficult to renegotiate or terminate, if it is difficult to adjust the implicit contract between the employer and employee, or if productivity is difficult to monitor.

Effective monitoring can help eliminate shirking. However, these scholars recognize that it is often difficult to measure and monitor effort and productivity with regard to human capital. This difficulty is exacerbated as production is moved increasingly from the goods manufacturing sector, with its well-developed methods of productivity measurement, to the service sector, which creates an output that is far more subjective and hence difficult to measure. The production of a widget can be counted in units. But the provision of a service often has both a quantity and a quality dimension.

Beyond the metering problem, productivity measurements on an individual basis are worsened when production occurs in teams. Within the team, it is often difficult to measure individual contributions. Anybody who has worked on a group project in college can attest to the increased likelihood of shirking when all are rewarded with the same grade, regardless of each student's individual contribution.

In some sense, the corporation could, if left poorly managed, suffer from a so-called Tragedy of the Commons, a concept initially articulated in the environmental context by Garrett Hardin.[4] In this context, when a number of entities each attempt to capitalize on a property right without coordination or some sort of allocation mechanism, human nature induces participants to attempt to appropriate the right to their own advantage. Over time, ill-defined rights become diluted and the overall entity becomes devalued. The authority that arises from well-defined property rights is necessary, while monitoring and coordination is essential to ensure goals are aligned and value is created.

Of course, the challenge then is to tailor contracts so that they are not generic but instead reflect the idiosyncratic abilities that can be offered by each of the parties to a contract. At the same time, monitoring and coordination can prevent shirking or counterproductive efforts. If a firm can manage effectively, it will be able to avoid the high transactions costs inherent if the marketplace organizes these functions. In turn, corporate value is created.

Alchian and Demsetz also note that other institutions, such as piece-work, profit-sharing or workers' cooperatives, can also more effectively align effort, productivity, and reward. Workers' cooperatives have the added quality that the workers are able to self-monitor. An individual worker earns the productivity of all workers, and suffers the lack of productivity of any worker. Hence, each worker has an interest in monitoring the effort and productivity of others.

Management is effective when it recognizes these challenges and produces compensation schemes that are sufficiently flexible to address them. Often, however, organized labor is equally adept at increasing the rigidity of such implicit or labor contracts.

The shirking paradigm is a useful construct to view either the ability or the inability of a firm to extract value. However, while Alchian and Demsetz honed our intuition to recognize value creation within the modern firm, their results were not specific enough to guide policy or afford empirical verification. They nonetheless allowed two additional great minds, Michael Jensen and William Meckling, to tease out even more intuitive and useful results that have since been fully incorporated into the corporate finance discussion, to be described more fully latter in this volume.

27
Applications and Extensions

Like many great ideas, Alchian and Demsetz present an argument that seems obvious after the fact: That the ability to coordinate teams creates synergies for which value exceeds the sum of its parts. The philosophy of the Boston Red Sox baseball team and the New England Patriots American Football team is in the promotion of teamwork over individualism, in sharp contrast to the criticism levelled against their arch-rivals, the New York Yankees or New York Jets, respectively, which are sometimes seen as a collection of individual stars who lack team spirit.

The greatest challenge of implementing Alchian and Demsetz's approach, though, is the measurement problem. As processes increase in complexity, it becomes more difficult to ascertain individual effort and contribution. In this respect the innovative genius of Henry Ford is not so much in the introduction of the assembly line, which he had adopted based on the ways in which Chicago meat packers brought carcasses to workers along tracks for *disassembly*, but rather in the breaking up of processes into small elements, each of which is much easier to monitor. If a car is assembled by a team, it is not obvious where any bottlenecks may occur. However, if a car is the sum of its parts, it is possible to add up the time it takes for each of four workers to install four wheels, two workers to install seats, two workers to install a windshield, and so on. Ford intuitively understood that teamwork must be oriented in a way so that individual effort and output can be monitored and motivated. This separability is essential in the process of creating profitable synergies. Each element is acknowledged to perform in his or her self-interest, but incentives are aligned so their self-interest is consistent with the creation of corporate value.

Ronald Coase had initiated the discussion of the role of transactions costs within the firm, as distinct from the costs of management. From his perspective, long-term explicit and implicit contracts within the firm help to reduce these transactions costs. This approach allows management to avoid repeated renegotiations of the implicit employment contract. It also initiated a greater discussion of the employer–employee relationship that represents the majority of an economy's value.

Following the work of Alchian and Demsetz, Jensen and Meckling were acutely interested in this employer–employee relationship. The durability of the employer–employee relationship may have other advantages, beyond the reduced transactions costs described by Coase. For instance, if transactions costs were zero, a given employer and employee could constantly and repeatedly renegotiate their contract. Clearly, the advantage of the firm lies in something simply beyond the minimization of transactions costs of these sorts. Alchian and Demsetz argued that optimal incentives, and solutions to moral hazard problems, represents this greater purpose for the creation of corporate value. In particular, the authors show that the degree to which monitoring is necessary and effective to avoid shirking and the principal–agent problem defines the nature of the firm for various industries.

Alchian and Demsetz noted, in particular, that shirking and monitoring becomes increasingly problematic as a corporation grows larger. Shirking increases as the employee's association with the larger corporation is diluted. And as the complexity increases, monitoring falls prey to informational problems. Finally, while the ability to reduce the cost of shirking may offer an explanation for one of a corporation's efficiencies, it does not offer a complete explanation for the existence of firms.

They assert that the corporate form is superior when the management of opportunism and the minimization of shirking is more difficult within markets than within the firm. The jointness of production and coordination within a firm confers an advantage for such a structure to attain efficiencies and reduce freeriding and shirking, both in the horizontally defined and the vertically integrated firm.

Alchian and Demsetz also demonstrate that the greater understanding and adeptness acquired by workers in respect of firm-specific production capital can also explain why there may be gains in corporate value over time. Institutions that promote longevity attempt to capitalize on growing firm-specific expertise and on the minimization of turnover costs for the firm. Mergers, too, can create value by providing a wider set of committed employees along with a broader set of firm-specific production assets. They can also provide an opportunity to break some long-term contracts that previous incarnations of each company could not easily break, at least without significant cost implications.

These discussions, first initiated by Coase and then Williamson, and elaborated upon by Alchian and Demsetz, began the process of adding formality and significance to Adam Smith's definition of specialization of labor a couple of centuries earlier. The discipline had come full circle.

28
Harold Demsetz Later in Life

Armen Alchian and Harold Demsetz established the Los Angeles School that has been influential ever since. Theirs is a school which shares some similarities with Chicago's emphasis on the free market, Harvard's tradition of institutional studies, and the strategic thrust of both the RAND Corporation and of the Hoover Institution, to which both contributed intellectually.

Alchian and Demsetz both contributed to this new institutional approach at UCLA, but also both worked to foment discussion on market implications of the *New Institutional Economics* at the Hoover Institution, a short 300 miles north of the UCLA campus. The Hoover Institution on War, Revolution and Peace is housed at Stanford University and is one of the country's leading public policy research institutes, combining advanced study in politics and economics with the goal of creating an international marketplace for ideas in a free society. While it is not as focused on strategy and global competitiveness as its RAND sibling, it nonetheless attracts some of the world's top scholars. It embodies the personal and political philosophy of its inspiration, Herbert Hoover (August 10, 1874–October 20, 1964), the nation's 31st president, who stated that:

> This Institution supports the Constitution of the United States, its Bill of Rights and its method of representative government. Both our social and economic systems are based on private enterprise from which springs initiative and ingenuity... Ours is a system where the Federal Government should undertake no governmental, social or economic action, except where local government, or the people, cannot undertake it for themselves... The overall mission of this Institution is, from its records, to recall the voice of experience

> against the making of war, and by the study of these records and their publication, to recall man's endeavors to make and preserve peace, and to sustain for America the safeguards of the American way of life. This Institution is not, and must not be, a mere library. But with these purposes as its goal, the Institution itself must constantly and dynamically point the road to peace, to personal freedom, and to the safeguards of the American system.[1]

Demsetz embraced the Hoover Institution and its ideals of a vibrant private sector, motivated by the decentralized acts of self-interested individuals, and held together by a scaffold of market-determined prices. Within this framework, Demsetz, and his colleague Alchian, sought to further explain how institutions behaved internally in response to this broader external framework. This fascination with what makes a corporation tick from within, and governed by its own financial system, had fascinated Demsetz just as it had the pioneer John Burr Williams almost a half-century earlier.

Demsetz prided himself as an academic, but not necessarily as a Nobel-level researcher. When he began graduate school, he expected that one day he would enjoy a teacher's life of nine months in the classroom and three months of "fun, travel, and relaxation."[2] Instead, he found himself immersed in ground-breaking research, at UCLA, at the Hoover Institution and as Senior Analyst of the Center for Naval Analyses, and then, eventually, as the Arthur Andersen Alumni Chair at UCLA.

Demsetz enjoyed a distinguished academic career by focusing on the ways agents in institutions respond to incentives. He felt he had little to add to market incentive mechanisms, but he recognized that agents internal to corporations do not have similar cues. In his analyses, he viewed game theory as offering some advantages. A discipline pioneered by John von Neumann, a chemical engineer and mathematician, like John Burr Williams, but also a nuclear physicist, co-founder of the computer language and algorithms, and early originator of game theory, this is based on the actions and reactions of entities that acknowledge their strategic interdependencies. In the early years of Demsetz's career, through the 1950s, game theory and industrial organization theory were developing freshly and rapidly. Demsetz thoroughly enjoyed this marketplace of new ideas, and was never hesitant about espousing his own take on these new problems. He would later attribute much of his success to this intellectual courage.

Demsetz was not isolated in his pioneering work, though. While at Northwestern University, he had the opportunity to work with the colleagues such as Charles Mills Tiebout (October 12, 1924–January 16, 1968), who died relatively young but not before he demonstrated that institutions can develop mechanisms to discourage free riders from benefitting without paying for the contributions of others. While Tiebout described competition among political jurisdictions when residents can choose by *voting with their feet,* Demsetz also worked at Chicago with Ronald Coase, who similarly showed that private institutions, too, can mimic free market exchanges and allocations even in the absence of a price system. These were invaluable insights for Demsetz, and his colleague Alchian, to show that corporations, too, can respond internally in ways that mimic the results obtained within the price system, but in the absence of formal markets.

While at Chicago, Demsetz was also influenced by the founder of the free market Chicago School, Frank Hyneman Knight (November 7, 1885–April 15, 1972), the author of *Risk, Uncertainty, and Profit,* and also Nobel Memorial Prize laureates Milton Friedman, James Buchanan, and George Stigler (January 17, 1911–December 1, 1991). Stigler, the 1982 Nobel Memorial Prize in Economics winner, in particular, was influential through his sponsorship of the industrial organization workshop at Chicago. It was partly as a result of the inspirational and stimulating atmosphere found there that Demsetz developed the ideas of many of his most important works, including *Why Regulate Utilities?, Toward a Theory of Property Rights, Information and Efficiency: Another Viewpoint,* and *The Cost of Transacting.* These works inspired Armen Alchian to collaborate with him when Alchian came to visit Chicago for a year. Together, they began *Production, Information Costs, and Economic Organization,* which they completed together when Alchian returned to UCLA and Demsetz soon followed.

The fortunate reuniting of Alchian and Demsetz was not based simply on shared professional philosophies, though. Demsetz appreciated theory and the opportunity it creates for a wide range of new ideas. UCLA's prominent great minds were housed in a school of economics, and had access to many theoretically minded graduate Ph.D. students. On the other hand, while Demsetz certainly enjoyed the many academic luminaries and eventual Nobel Memorial Prize winners he had the opportunity to work with early in his career at Chicago, these great minds were housed within the business school and hence did not have the broad access to students who wished to delve into more theoretical issues than issues of pragmatic importance to business. In a business school, economics is only a small part of the curriculum, along with accounting, management, finance, and perhaps even marketing. The graduate students in business had no more experience with economic theories, and perhaps even less interest, than a senior undergraduate student in economics. At Chicago, the most serious Ph.D. students interested in theory were supervised typically by the economics department, outside the business school. By moving to UCLA, Demsetz could, ironically enough, given Chicago's stellar academic reputation, be exposed to students of higher average quality because, at UCLA, Demsetz could work directly with economics students who possessed greater quantitative skills. Demsetz was concerned that his education and skills would depreciate if he were not afforded the opportunity to be challenged by, and supervise, top economics students.

Another attraction of UCLA was purely financial. Demsetz and a number of his Chicago colleagues had collectively invested in the purchase of bonds with a leverage ratio of 19 to 1 at a time when they were confident that prudent monetary policy would surely increase the price of these bonds. However, economists can often tell you what will occur, or when it will occur, but they are not particularly good at predicting both. Demsetz and his colleagues were constantly having to write checks to feed their margin calls, ever hopeful that their economic intuition would eventually prevail. It never did, Demsetz lost his savings, and he was enticed by an attractive offer to move to UCLA, first for a year, and eventually for the rest of his career.

There remains a legitimate and prevailing theme in Demsetz's work. His contributions push the boundaries of corporate finance and economics into the realms of business, law, and even ethics and morals. His work divines internal and broader institutions that can confine our actions toward the greater good of the organization. However, he believes that inducements to behave in a collectively optimal way are best done within free systems rather than through coercive ones. While freedom and free markets are often taken for granted and are little pondered by those who grew up, and whose ancestors were raised, in free societies, immigrants from Eastern Europe, and the sons and daughters of those immigrants, are often acutely aware of and appreciate the relative advantages of free market systems that lack the coercive elements of centrally planned economies. Demsetz recollected Friedrich von Hayek's (May 8, 1889–March 23, 1992) statement in his *The Constitution of Liberty*:

> We are concerned... with the condition of men in which coercion of some by others is reduced as much as is possible in society. This state we shall describe... as a state of liberty or freedom. ... Coercion should be carefully distinguished from the conditions or terms on

> which our fellow men are willing to render us services or benefits... (It cannot) be called "coercion" if a producer... refuses to supply me with what I want except at his price.[3]

Coercion occurs when individuals are forced to act in ways beyond which they would volunteer to render their services. In effect, coercion is the antithesis of freedom, being instead the exercise of differential power. The corporation resolves this dilemma by defining a series of acts performed without extensive transactions costs or debates over a potential coercive element of each request. Instead, the employee performs a series of acts in the full knowledge that she could, at any time, withdraw her entire portfolio of services. At its essence, Alchian and Demsetz argued that the cost savings of the streamlining of these transactions confers a benefit on the corporation that is capitalized in its share price.

29
The Later Years of Armen Alchian

Alchian, too, harbored similar passions for the intellectual and market freedom the Hoover Institution espoused, and concerns about differential power. His family had also escaped a harsher life in Eastern Europe where there was an intense monopolization of power, and where the populace subsequently revolted to wrest power, only to replace it with another form of coercion. Alchian and Demsetz were kindred spirits in their regard for the often painful power of coercion.

In a speech given at the University of Chicago Law School Dedicatory Conference on November 18, 1957, Alchian spoke in a heartfelt manner about the power to affect the actions of others. He advocated that such power is exercised morally when it does not resort to threats of violence, and ethically when it can be exercises free of the coercion of bribery or persuasion that, while perhaps compelling at times, still offers choice without threat of harm.

While Alchian recognized the natural coercive, but nonetheless voluntary, nature of the free market, he did not hold harmless the modern corporation of inappropriate exercise of power, though. He remained impassioned in opposition to the exercise of ruthless monopoly power, and, by implication, the effort to extract gain advantage not through innovation but through the creation of market power. He recognizes that this monopoly power may sometimes be exercised for seemingly altruistic reasons than may still have a less-than-altruistic aspect. For instance, a union may monopolize the supply of labor so that it can raise the wages of its members. However, it may also limit the choice of workers who are not permitted to join the closed shop. In this case, by raising the wages of some, others are deprived of opportunities and hence earn lower wages as a consequence of fewer opportunities.

Alchian notes that other entities also have garnered such power. If utilities had the power to deny energy to companies unless companies shared in their profits, they too could extract unfair advantage through monopolistic coercion. Regulators guard against such behavior by ensuring that utilities must offer the same terms to all similarly situated clients. Alchian argued that unions are not so constrained, and can exercise tools such as strikes or work stoppages differentially to extract advantages on behalf of its members.

Alchian not only remained a giant at the University of California Los Angeles. He was also viewed as a pioneer and co-founder of the New Institutional Economics revival, of which UCLA was at the center. While Alchian was viewed as a generous advisor and educator of graduate and undergraduate students alike, his research record and productivity placed him in the highest echelon of scholars in the social sciences. He applied his unique and cutting intuition to a variety of problems within the general areas of corporate value and business organizational analysis, market efficiency, and even personal finance and choice. In recognition of his achievements, he was named a Distinguished Fellow by the American Economic Association in 1996. His varied contributions at this time were collected together in two volumes that constituted *The Collected Works of Armen A. Alchian,* published by the Liberty Fund in 1996. Another earlier collection by the Liberty Fund in 1977, titled *Economic Forces at Work,* documented his collection of papers, including many of his most important ideas about shirking and on information efficiencies.

Alchian also prepared a textbook, *University Economics,* co-authored with William R. Allen, which was issued in six editions, and was adopted by many professors for the instruction of both graduate and undergraduate students The text was even adopted for an intensive summer program at the University of Rochester to teach economics to law professors. His text emphasizes the role and importance of property rights, an approach that is well appreciated in the legal discipline. He repeated this effort for decades and influenced many hundreds of law professors. Alchian himself taught most of these sessions. Through this initiative, Alchian was celebrated as one of the founders of the study of Law and Economics. As these workshops spread also to members of the judiciary, he recruited other great minds. Like Paul Samuelson, Milton Friedman, and Harold Demsetz to the cause. This is one of the most distinguished cadre of workshop professors ever assembled. Collectively, they were most influential in a field charged with regulating and overseeing markets and corporations.

Alchian's prevailing theme over his illustrious academic career was the nature of *the economic man,* or *homo economicus.* He argued that the self-interested rationality assumed by the field since Adam Smith was a consequence rather than assumption. Much like Darwin's notion of the survival of the fittest, efficient and rational institutions eventually prevail over those guided by other objectives. He remains best remembered, though, for his collaboration with Harold Demsetz in the ways in which firms can create corporate value by solving incentive problems and internalizing on some of the externalities that arise when there exist incentive incompatibilities. Their work spawned an extensive literature on shirking, monitoring, moral hazard, and the efficiencies that can be garnered through long term contracting.

Alchian presided over the Western Economic Association, was named a Fellow of the American Academy of Arts and Sciences in 1978, and a member of the Mt. Pelerin Society. The Armen A. Alchian Chair in Economic Theory at UCLA was named for him. Alchian was also named Distinguished Fellow of the American Economic Association in 1996. He received an honorary doctorate degree from Universidad Francisco Marroquín in 2010.

When Alchian died, his passing was marked by a wide range of tributes. Over the course of his career he influenced many great minds, including some Nobel Memorial Prize winners. Alchian was broadly respected both at UCLA, where he had spent the vast majority of his career, and across an entire discipline to which he devoted over fifty years of his life. Most students in his department studied under him because he taught the required price theory course. His classrooms were lively and Socratic in nature. He eschewed the traditional lecture method. Students knew they had to be prepared when they entered his classroom, very much as if the class were an introduction to contracts in law school. Yet his students did learn, and they learned from the best.

One of Alchian's unique qualities lay in his style of exposition, both in his academic papers and in the classroom. He expressed real world challenges using the rhetoric of an educated and modern Renaissance man. He was learned, and he expressed himself as such, but without arrogance. He also included sophisticated wit in his expositions.

Many great minds expressed gratitude to Professor Alchian. For instance, Nobel Memorial Prize winner William F. Sharpe, most associated with the Capital Asset Pricing Model, stated:

> Armen Alchian, a professor of economics, was my role model at UCLA. He taught his students to question everything; to always begin an analysis with first principles; to concentrate on essential elements and abstract from secondary ones; and to play devil's advocate

> with one's own ideas. In his classes we were able to watch a first-rate mind work on a host of fascinating problems. I have attempted to emulate his approach to research ever since. When I returned to pursue the PhD degree, I took a field in microeconomics with Armen and he also served as chairman of my dissertation committee.[1]

Others advocated for Alchian to receive a Nobel Memorial Prize for his seminal and varied contributions. His textbook co-author, William Allen, described to the Nobel Memorial Prize committee that:

> Economics is a broad discipline in methodology, as the Committee is fully aware, ranging from detailed historical, institutional, legalistic description to totally abstract, arcane theory. All such approaches, techniques, and emphases are appropriate. But there is much specialization among the members of the fraternity. And, increasingly, the profession has dealt in rigorous, elegant manipulation, even when the work is purportedly empirical – and even when the substantive results hardly warranted such virtuoso flair. Professor Alchian is a splendid technician, and he has contributed significantly and conspicuously to general "theory." But, in contrast to many, he has always appreciated that the final payoff of Economics is elucidation of the real workings and phenomena of the world. I know of no one at any time who has had a finer sense of how to use economic analytics to explain the world. Sometimes the explanation requires involved, complex analysis, and Professor Alchian does not fear to use the tools which are required; what is uncommon is his lack of fear in using the MINIMUM tools which are required. In large part, his peculiar genius (the word is used advisedly) is to make extraordinarily effective use of elemental, and often elementary, techniques of analysis. And a host of people – many of whom are now in strategic positions in universities, in government, in the legal system, in the world of business and finance – have enormously benefited from the tutelage of Professor Alchian... I present Armen Alchian as a giant – a giant who, because of his lack of pretension, is easily overlooked by laymen and even by some supposed professionals – who has greatly honored his profession and uniquely contributed to its usefulness. He would grace the distinguished fraternity of Nobel Laureates.[2]

Many of Alchian's colleagues had gone on to win Nobel Memorial Prizes. These include James Buchanan, Ronald Coase, Oliver Williamson, and others who also explored the same sort of questions that may not be the most glamorous or mathematically beautiful but which make a positive difference in the area of the creation of corporate value. The Nobel Committee often rewards scholars not merely for the stature and importance they have established within their disciplines. Rather, the Prize recognizes contributions that make a difference to all of our lives, and also to our broader understanding. If such is the test, the quality, the quantity, and the breadth of Armen Alchian's contributions are at least proportional to the other great minds we document who have been acknowledged by the Nobel Committee.

Alchian is regarded as one of the most influential and intuitive theorists to have ever contributed to the field of corporate value. He, working with a number of collaborators, formed our understanding of concepts that are now both widely regarded and broadly accepted. He was the product of a style of scholarship borne out of the challenges of the Great Depression and the Second World War. Scholars immersed in this school of thought used mathematics sparingly as a tool, and kept their focus on the intuition that plays such an important role in framing and addressing real world problems.

Perhaps his service in the Army Air Forces during World War II honed his dedication to the exploration of problems of practical significance. It was in service to his country that he made observations which developed into important concepts in the creation of corporate value, but which also were sufficiently accessible to allow for extensive application and made significant differences in corporations within the broader business world.

For instance, he introduced concepts such as the learning curve, shirking, monitoring, incentive compatibility, and moral hazard which have remained important, or have indeed assumed a greater significance as the world experienced a series of events such as the Enron financial scandal, the Sarbanes–Oxley corporate responsibility statutes, and the Credit Crisis that gave rise to the Global Financial Meltdown. Like Coase, Alchian expressed his ideas through rhetoric and intellectual persuasion rather than mathematical sophistication. As a consequence, his concepts remain both accessible and timeless.

When Alchian passed away peacefully in bed early in the morning of February 19, 2013 in his Los Angeles, California home, he was 98 years old. While he is remembered by the finance community for his deep finance intuition and valuable insights, he is remembered by his colleagues for his humanity, his play, and his joy of life. They recall how, in his spare time, Alchian enjoyed early morning golf outings before work. He also enjoyed his family. He was survived by his wife of 73 years, Pauline, daughter children, Arline Hoel, who is married to Carlton Hoel, and son Allen Alchian, who is married to Ann. When he died, he was also survived by six grandchildren and three great grandchildren.

Section 5
Jensen and Meckling

No corporation can exist without clearly defined property rights. Ronald Coase and Oliver Williamson described why this should be the case. Funds cannot be raised, nor corporate shares sold unless the value of a corporation can be determined. But no corporation can sustain itself without certain advantages over other organizational forms beyond their ability to raise equity and exchange the equity they create. Collaborators Michael Cole Jensen and William Henry Meckling demonstrated some of the reasons why corporations can create value in excess of their constituent components. They show that the way a corporation is organized depends crucially on the types of implicit contracts it develops within and its ability to solve problems in the gap between what the corporation needs and what those employed by the corporation prefer to provide. In describing this fundamental tension, the great minds Jensen and Meckling established a lens upon which we can view the corporation and its agents that has ramifications for the very efficiency of corporations and the functioning of global financial markets.

Before discussing their contribution to economic thought I begin with a brief discussion of their respective ancestries.

30
The Early Years of Michael Cole Jensen

The advantage of corporations have only been discovered over the last couple of centuries and described and appreciated over the past couple of generations. While John Burr Williams may have explained how a corporation might be valued based on expected future cash flows, and Ronald Coase taught us the importance of property rights and transactions costs, some new thinking was necessary to more fully explain why corporations have advantages, and some disadvantages, over alternative market-based institutions. The majority of those in any field apply conventional wisdom, or perhaps elaborate on this wisdom at its edges. Great minds often reject conventional wisdom and replace it with new and often revolutionary ideas. It is an interesting academic question how these great minds develop novel intuitions. Perhaps the new thinking for Michael Cole Jensen epitomizes a heritage of pioneers who originally settled a new country and who came from the old to the new, attracted by an economic engine like the world has never seen before.

Michael Cole Jensen carries this dual heritage proudly through his namesakes Cole and Jensen.

The Cole family can be traced to the original founders of a new America. James Cole (July 25, 1600–October 1688) was first Cole to make it to a new America. The son of William Cole of Highgate, London, England, James left England and landed in Saco, Maine in 1632. The following year, he arrived at the Plymouth Colony in Massachusetts in 1633, along with his wife, Mary Tibbes (June 15, 1598–March 7, 1660), whom he had married in England eight years earlier, on May 8, 1625.

Some came to the new colony seeking religious freedom. Many came as indentured servants, which required them to save to repay those that commissioned them to come. Once their debt was repaid, they were declared freemen. James Cole was soon of that minority of settlers who

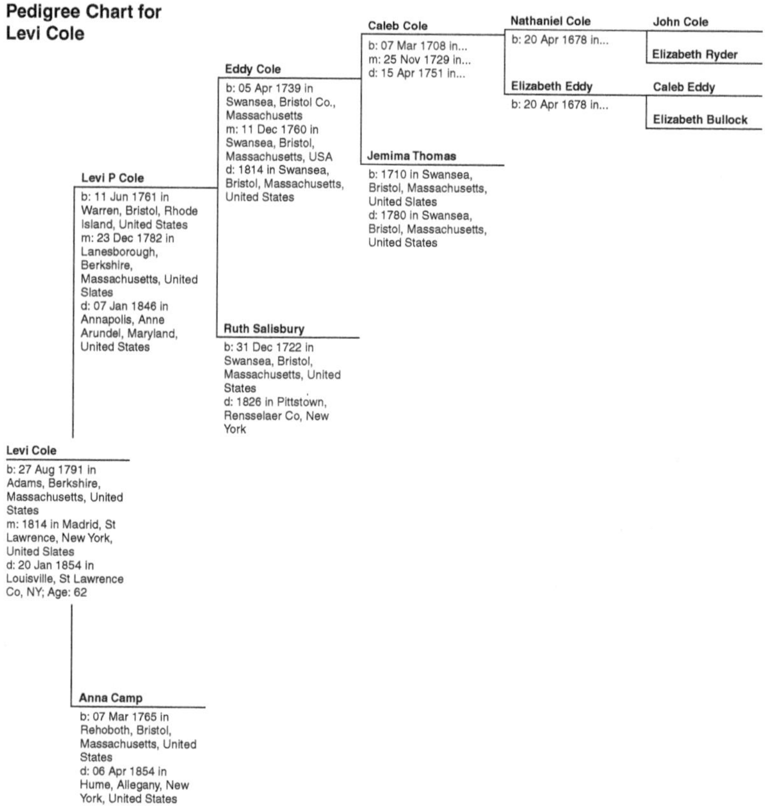

Figure 30.1 The Early Cole Family

ran their own businesses and worked for themselves. When James Cole arrived with his family, he settled an area that is still known as Cole's Hill, fought in the Pequot Indian War in 1637, and acted variously as a constable and surveyor for his town. While his trade may have been that of a shoemaker, his avocation was an innkeeper. This was not uncontroversial for a new puritan order that nonetheless appreciated discrete opportunities to imbibe. The municipality even provided for regular maintenance of the public house, otherwise known as the "pub" or the "ordinary", to ensure the drinking houses remained well maintained. At various times he came into conflict with the authorities, being sanctioned for selling beer on a Sunday, selling liquor to Indians, and on one occasion, in 1637, being fined ten shillings for "selling less than a Winchester quart, but not in ignorance."[1]

James's role as publican was later assumed by his son, James Cole Junior, who also continued the occasional brushes with the authorities. One of his customers, John Sprague, was fined for "highly misdemean(ing) himself" by riding his mare into the parlor.[2]

While James Cole Senior's firstborn may have followed in his father's footsteps, the fourth Cole, the third son of James, and the first Cole to be born in the New World, was named John Cole.

John Cole (November 21, 1637–June 7, 1677) was born in Plymouth, Massachusetts. Young John departed from the family legacy and found his legitimacy in farming. He migrated forty miles southwest to found the settlement of Swansea, Massachusetts, where he was granted land to start a farm and raise his family. On November 21, 1667, he married Elizabeth Ryder (September 6, 1647–September 3, 1685), who had been born in Yarmouth, Massachusetts. Elizabeth was also a first-generation colonist. Her father, Samuel Ryder, a surveyor of highways, had brought his wife, Anne Gamlett, from Northampton, England in 1639. Elizabeth was born eight years later.

John and Elizabeth Cole raised two boys, John Jr. (1672–February 19, 1740) and Nathaniel (1674–June 20, 1743), and a middle daughter, Elizabeth (1675–November 1705). The family farmed 26 acres of land granted to them by the Town of Duxbury in Massachusetts.

John died while his children were still in their infancy. When this occurred the Town of Swansea ordered, through the decision of their court, that the small estate should be left to the widow so the profits from the land could help raise her children until they become of age. The court afforded that some land may need to be sold, should the family be unable to support themselves, and provided that the balance be disposed by the two sons.

In 1700, in Swansea, Nathaniel Cole expanded his extended Cole family by marrying Elizabeth Eddy, the daughter of Caleb Eddy and Elizabeth Bullock of Plymouth, Massachusetts. They had four children together. The mother, Elizabeth, died while giving birth to their second son, Caleb Cole (March 7, 1708–April 15, 1751), who had been named for his maternal grandfather. By then, Caleb was a third generation colonist. All of Caleb's grandparents had been born in the New World to the first settlers of the Massachusetts colonies.

Caleb Cole married Sarah Jemima Thomas (1710–October 19, 1787) on November 25 1729. They had five boys and three girls together at their farm in Swansea, Massachusetts. Their fourth child, and their second son, was named Eddy for his grandmother's family. Eddy Cole (April 5, 1739–1814) represented the last generation to remain in the

Swansea area, within a long day's ride of the place their ancestors first settled.

Eddy Cole married Ruth Salisbury (December 31, 1722–1826) on December 11, 1760 in Swansea and they began their family in nearby Bristol, Rhode Island. There, they gave birth to Levi P. Cole (June 11, 1761–January 7, 1846), named for Eddy's younger brother, precisely six months after their marriage. Their first son was followed with Mary and Patience.

Levi became a military man at an early age. On September 1, 1779, at the age of 18, he travelled north to Boston to enlist aboard the ships under the command of Commodore Abraham Whipple of the Continental Navy. He started as a gunner before being promoted to the position of ship's corporal. He was captured during the defense of Charleston, South Carolina, but spent much of the Revolutionary War as a prisoner. When he was eventually released, he returned home to Rhode Island, where he continued to serve in the volunteer militia.[3]

Following his return from the Revolutionary War, on December 23, 1782, Levi married Anna Camp (March 7, 1765–April 6, 1854), by oath to James Barker, Justice of the Peace, in Adams, Massachusetts. Soon after their marriage, Anne gave birth to a boy, Zaben (May 16, 1784–March 12, 1874).

During this period of his life Levi was footloose. They migrated west from Rhode Island to Adams, Massachusetts, the Mohawk Valley towns of Canajoharie and Otsego, New York, just west of Albany, and then back to Adams, where Levi and Anna gave birth to their third son and last child, Levi Junior (August 27, 1791–January 20, 1854).

Within a year of the birth of their final child, the father Levi became estranged from his wife, whom she labelled a "quarrelsome ugly man."[4] By this time their second son Eddy had already been given to his grandparents to raise. After not seeing her husband for a dozen years, Anna Camp Cole married the Reverend John Watkins, a former Navy Chaplain, in 1804, who would help raise her children in the area of Albany, New York.

In 1825, well after the death of her second husband on July 29, 1812, Anna Camp discovered her husband Levi was alive and living in Washington, D.C. By then, he too had remarried. When he subsequently died on January 7, 1846 in Annapolis, Maryland, he left two wives who were left to contest his wartime pension.

Levi Sr.'s youngest son Levi Cole, Michael Jensen Cole's great great great grandfather, set out on his own to the fertile St Lawrence Valley farmland bordering the Saint Lawrence River in New York. There, he was a founder of the new town of Louisville,[5] and in 1814 he met and married Phoebe Baxter (December 6, 1971–October 25, 1884).

Phoebe's father and mother, Asa and Submit, had come to St Lawrence County to farm an island in the St Lawrence River. In the years between the Revolutionary War and the War of 1812, the narrow band of land between Canada and the United States was often in dispute. During the War of 1812, the British considered this land part of their Kingdom, and its landowners British subjects. As a consequence, Asa was drafted into the British Army. In demonstration of his loyalties to the United States, he deserted. But, when he returned from hiding in Vermont before the

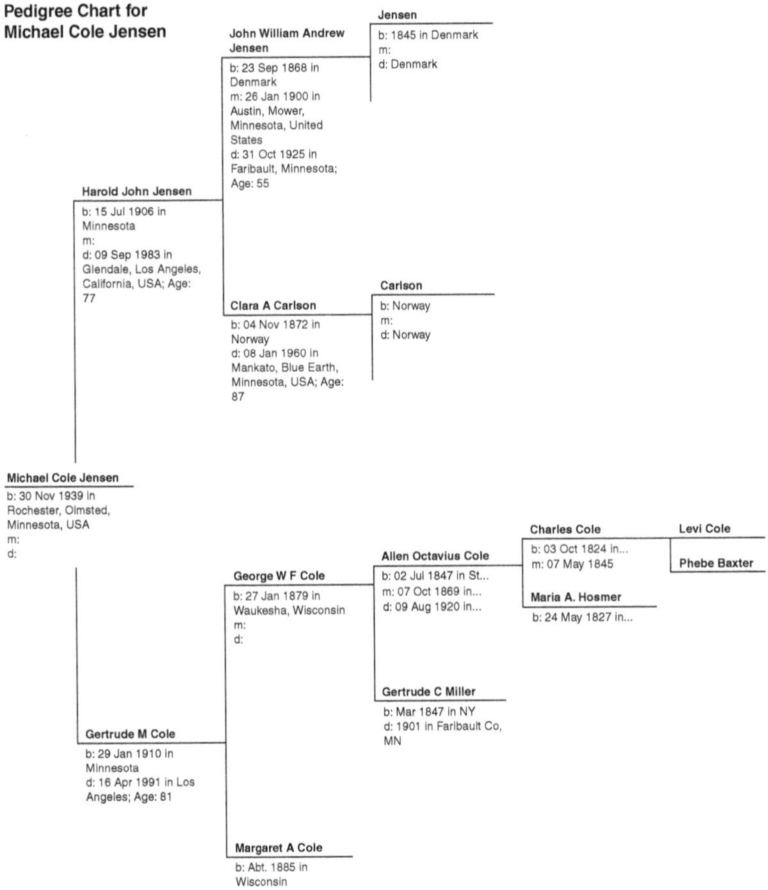

Figure 30.2 The Family Tree for Michael Jensen Cole

end of the war, he was arrested and confined to a Cornwall, Ontario jail from April to August of 1814, while he awaited trial in Kingston, Ontario. On his way to trial, he escaped. He surrendered upon the completion of the war. By then, the British had no jurisdiction over his island, and he remained there as a farmer for several years until the island was purchased by Judge Ogden, the namesake for the nearby New York town of Ogdensburg.

Levi had married Asa's second daughter, Phoebe near the end of the War of 1812. Many of the settlers in that region, and perhaps even Levi's father, Levi Senior, had migrated up to the area from the Mohawk Valley of Central New York State, where two of Levi's siblings were born. Many were Loyalists seeking comfort by locating nearer to Canada. There were abundant trade links and bonds of friendship between this region at the intersection of Lower Canada and Upstate New York, even during the War of 1812. For self-protection, though, Louisville formed its own militia. Nonetheless, it escaped the invasions and battles that many nearby towns experienced in the two years from 1812 to 1814.

While living in Louisville Levi Junior and Phoebe had five boys and five girls. Their third son, Charles, was born on October 3, 1824 and he went on to marry a local Louisville woman, Maria Hosmer (May 24, 1827–June 22, 1886). That couple had nine boys, and five girls. All but the last two children were born in Saint Lawrence County, but, by the 1870s, the family had made their way west for abundant and rich farmland, to Red Mound, Vernon County, Wisconsin, in the late 1860s, just before the birth of their last two children.

The Cole family worked the farm with the help of their male children. Shortly after the family had moved to the Midwest farming frontier, on October 7, 1869, in Viroqua, Wisconsin, Charles' and Maria's eldest child Allen Octavis Cole (July 2, 1847–August 9, 1920) met and married a young women, Gertrude C Miller (March 1847–1901), whose family had also moved to Wisconsin from New York. Allen Cole began as a farm laborer but he eventually purchased his own family farm in Sterling, Wisconsin. The young family had four daughters and three sons in Wisconsin, including their youngest child, George Cole, born on January 27, 1879.

George was raised a farmhand and went on to marry Margaret Neville, five years his junior. George and Margaret, the maternal grandparents of Michael Cole Jensen, moved one state over and continued to farm, in Faribault, Minnesota up to the beginning of the twentieth century. In 1901, George's father, Allen, lost his wife, and he left his farm to move in with his son and daughter in law, George and Margaret. He found employment as a telephone operator. George also left the farm to work as a rural mail carrier.

Having very largely put farming behind them, the Coles did not need the ready labor supply that was required for a family farm. George and Margaret had three children, Gertrude (January 29, 1910–April 16, 1991), named after her grandmother, George Michael (January 14, 1912–October 16, 1987), and Clifford (1919).

Michael Cole Jensen's mother Gertrude, grew up in a middle-class Midwest home before meeting and marrying Harold John Jensen. Harold was born in Minnesota on July 15, 1906, the son of a journeyman printer. His father, John William Andrew Jensen, had been born in Denmark on September 23, 1868 and he had arrived in the United States in 1890. He made his way to the Scandinavian communities of Minnesota, and had married Clara A. Carlson on January 26, 1900, at the age of 31. He had come to America endowed with a trade, which he passed on to his eldest son, the fourth of Clara and John's seven children.

Harold's father John died on October 31, 1925 when Harold was just 19 years of age. Already by then, he had learned the printing trade, and was also reporting for his newspaper employer.

A good career already established, Harold met and married Gertrude Cole. They had a son, Michael Cole Jensen (November 30, 1939) and a daughter, Judith (born June 12, 1942).

Young Michael Cole Jensen grew up in Rochester, Minnesota during and in the aftermath of World War II. His formative years in public school were a curious combination of a national belief in its manifest destiny and an acute awareness of one other looming superpower at the height of the Cold War. Minnesota was relatively protected, though. It was a curious combination of liberal social thought allied to a faith in markets and a strong work ethic. He was also born the son of a first-generation American and of an American family that came in the original wave of colonial settlers.

When Jensen was ready for college, he did not venture far from home. He attended Macalester College, little more than an hour north of Rochester, and received his A. B. there in 1962. His grades and his clear aptitude for mathematics allowed him to continue his studies in finance by taking the University of Chicago's Master's in Business Administration, which he received in 1964. It was at Chicago that Jensen was exposed to an approach that had a profound effect on his intellectual development. He continued his studies at Chicago and earned a Ph.D. in economics, finance, and accounting in 1968.

In the year before he completed his Ph.D., he was offered and accepted an assistant professorship in finance by Dean William Meckling at the University of Rochester. He was promoted there to Associate Professor in 1971, Professor in 1979, and the endowed LaClare Professor of Finance of the William E. Simon Graduate School of Business Administration in 1984. He remained in the institution until 1988, where he also served as the director of their Managerial Economics Research Center, which he had founded in 1977 with the strong encouragement of Meckling.

31
The Early Years of William Henry Meckling

Some children are born to destiny. To demonstrate anything but brilliance shortly following birth with a family name like Bernoulli would be unimaginable. An academic pedigree opens doors for some that are closed for most others. Their family wealth and position assures them the best education at the most elite schools. From there, they enjoy academic careers at other elite schools that cater to the finest students. Few can overcome the challenge of lack of pedigree but succeed nonetheless. William Henry Meckling is one such exception.

William Meckling was born on September 20, 1921, in the heart of America's Iron Belt and coalfields. One of two boys, his parents, William Henry Meckling and Katherine Elizabeth Barth, also raised four girls.

The Meckling family was firmly planted in Westmoreland County, adjacent to Allegheny County, where Pittsburgh is located. Westmoreland coalfields are well remembered for the labor strikes and strife, worker–management conflicts and hazardous coal mine working conditions that gave birth to the United States union movement. The land is hilly, and supports farming and the coal and ore extraction that made Pittsburgh an iron-producing powerhouse in the Gilded Age.

The Mecklings had only adopted their family name relatively recently. William's grandfather, Harry Frank Mechling, had changed the spelling of his name to include the consonant "k" as an adult, probably in an attempt at Anglicization. Before that time the Mechling family had maintained the French pronunciation of their name ever since their ancestor, Theobald Dewalt Mechling (1695, April 17–1765), had left his homeland in Palatinate, Germany in 1728 to make his way to the land and resource-rich area of Pennsylvania that was populated by hard-working puritan Lutherans of Dutch and German decent.

Not long after he arrived, Theobald met and married Anna Elizabeth Lauer (1710–September 3, 1804), who was born and raised and lived her entire life in Northampton County, Pennsylvania. The couple had five boys and a girl to help run the family farm. Their fourth son was Phillip Mechling, born in 1749, still more than a generation before their nation fought for independence from Britain.

Although the son of an immigrant, Phillip Mechling willingly fought in the Revolutionary War. He was an ensign in the First Company of the Second Battalion on behalf of the Northampton County Militia under the command of Captain Joseph Kochens. A few years earlier, on June 11, 1770, he had married a young local woman, Katherine Wetzel, at the Northampton Zion Lutheran Church. Following his service in the war, he supported his family as a tanner of leather. He died on November 11, 1817, after raising six sons and two daughters of the American Revolution, including Phillip Jones Mechling.

Phillip Jonas Mechling was born in 1774, just before his father went to war. At the age of 21, he married his wife, Catherine Elizabeth Coder (1777–January 4, 1864), and raised four boys and two girls on their plantation in Hempfield Township. They were a family of faith, with one of the boys, Jonas J. Mechling, going on to become a Lutheran reverend. They raised five boys and two girls, all but two who were born, lived their lives, and died in Westmoreland County.

Their third boy, Philip Jonas Mechling, Jr., was born on December 31, 1800, on the last day of the first year of a new century. Philip had married Sarah Ann Durlin, (June 22, 1812–December 12, 1895), a woman 12 years his junior, on September 27, 1832, at the First Lutheran Church in Greensburg, Westmoreland County. They raised five boys and two girls together, including their youngest son, Harry Frank Mechling, who was born in 1854.

On August 20, 1874 Harry was married to Mary Biddle by Rev. Spargrove at the Murrysville Presbyterian Church. For the first few years of their marriage, Harry was employed as a brakeman for the Pennsylvania Railroad, and soon after he was promoted to a conductor. The family had left farming behind and no longer needed the large family to support the land. The couple had two girls together, Gertrude and Margaret, and they adopted a boy, William Howard Meckling, born on February 28, 1892.

Before William Howard married, he enlisted in the U.S. Army. His first engagement was as part of the party attempting to chase down the Mexican Revolutionary General Pancho Villa. Villa had been roaming Northern Mexico and some western United States territories, seizing

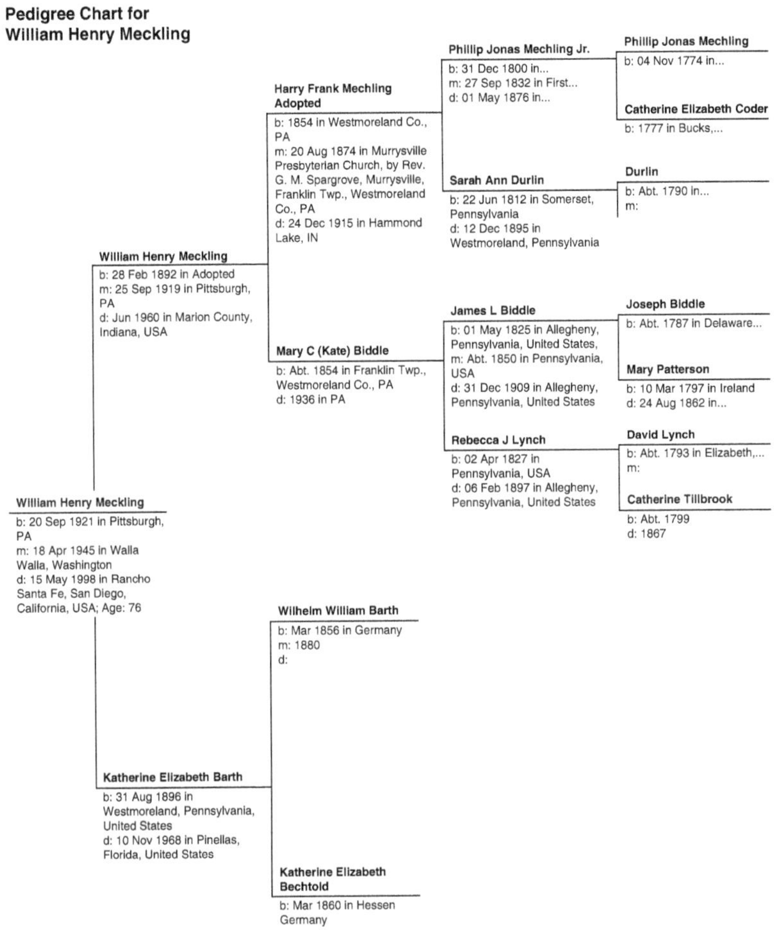

Figure 31.1 The William Meckling Family Tree

land and valuables, and printing money to support his own military colonies. After a raid on Columbus, New Mexico in 1916, U.S. Army General John Pershing pursued him for nine months, until the United States entered World War I. Upon commencement of the war, William went on to active combat duty.

Following the end of hostilities in 1918, William returned to Pennsylvania and married Katherine Elizabeth Barth (August 31, 1896–November 10, 1968), the daughter of German immigrants Wilhelm Barth and Katherine Elizabeth Bechtold. Wilhelm's family had arrived and settled in Westmoreland County when he was six years old, in 1880, and Katherine arrived 13 years later, when she was 18 years old.

Following the war and their wedding, on September 25, 1919, William took a job as an electrical salesman in Dayton, Ohio. They settled into an apartment at 22 West Second Street, but soon returned to Pittsburgh for the birth of their first daughter, Katherine, in 1920, and then their first son, William Henry Meckling, on September 20, 1921.

Before the Meckling children were grown, the family moved back to Westmoreland, Pennsylvania, and eventually settled into a single family home at 5948 E. 60th Street in Indianapolis, Indiana. By then, the family had expanded. William had three younger sisters, Marilyn, Frances, and Janet, and a younger brother Ralph.

The family was not well off, by any measures, and had not enjoyed the legacy of college education. William had demonstrated academic promise, but the family could not afford to send William to a top school. One of their region's most affordable alternatives was a Presbyterian school named Westminster College in New Wilmington, Pennsylvania, less than an hour's drive north of his extended family's locale and William's childhood home during the Great Depression before his family had settled in Indianapolis.

William entered Westminster in the fall of 1938, just as Europe was marching quickly toward war, and in a period in which the United States was resisting entry into the hostilities across the Atlantic Ocean. The United States subsequently entered the war in late 1941, immediately following the Japanese bombing of Pearl Harbor, just a few months before William graduated. William was able to defer conscription because of his attendance at college.

Meanwhile, he availed himself to campus life, which included his membership to the Westminster chapter of Kappa Phi Lambda, the nation's first KPL fraternity. However, upon graduation, Meckling could defer service no longer. He entered the Army's Air Corps as an enlisted soldier. At the conclusion of the war, he left the Army with the rank of sergeant.

During his service in the Army, William Meckling met Rebecca Frances Ely. The pair had both been based in Walla Walla, Washington at the 357th Army Air Force Base.

William Meckling had married up. The Ely family were pioneers and stalwarts of their towns of Ainsworth and Marion, Nebraska, where Rebecca's grandfather, William Brown Ely, had been the town doctor.

Born in Connecticut to New England parents William H Ely and Mary P White, William Brown Ely (March 5, 1842–May 1, 1921) was born and raised in Connecticut. He left to go to school to study to be a teacher. Upon completion of his studies, he took a job at a boarding school in Canandaigua, New York, and married there in 1865.

By 1871, William Brown Ely had married again, to Mary Francis Potter, from nearby Marion, New York. Mary Francis came from a very well-established family in Marion. Her father, Alden Potter (April 30, 1819–September 11, 1889), a farmer, had been one of the town's founders. The Potter name can be traced back to Nathaniel Potter, who arrived in Rhode Island from Sussex, England in 1638. Potter ancestors fought in the War of Independence more than a century after they arrived. On Mary's mother's side of her family, the McLouths came from Scotland in the mid-1700s and fought on the American side in the Revolutionary War. Her grandfather, and William Brown's great-grandfather, was also a doctor, John McLouth (December 16, 1795–January 18, 1887). He had settled his family in nearby Wayne County, New York.

Rather late in life William Brown Ely made his way to the University of Michigan to embark on the study of medicine. By the time he graduated at the age of 36, he was already the father of two children. Upon graduation, William supported his wife Mary Francis Potter (July 6, 1844–November 7, 1926), and the two sons, Alden Potter and William McClouth Ely, with a new medical practice in Francis Potter's hometown of Marion. William Brown Ely eventually moved the medical practice to Nebraska not long after it established statehood. There he led a distinguished life, serving for a time as the president of the Nebraska State Medical Society.[1]

William McLouth Ely, the youngest son of William and Mary, had begun his education in public school in Penfield, New York, and then the nearby Marion Collegiate Institute.[2] He went on to complete high school in Ainsworth, Nebraska when his father moved the medical practice to Nebraska. But, rather than follow in his father's footsteps, he went on to study law at nearby University of Nebraska. He graduated with his law degree in 1900 and went on to become a highly respected lawyer to a number of banks in Marion, Nebraska. He also served the community as a prominent Republican, and eventually became a judge.

William McLouth Ely married Grace Maude Chesnut (May 8, 1881–November 18, 1970) of Denver, Colorado, with whom he had two children, Samuel C. and Rebecca Francis Ely, who was born on January 30, 1923. Rebecca grew up privileged in Marion, but, as a young woman near the end of World War II, decided to support her nation.

Rebecca Ely and William Meckling met each other while each was in service to their country during the latter years of World War II.

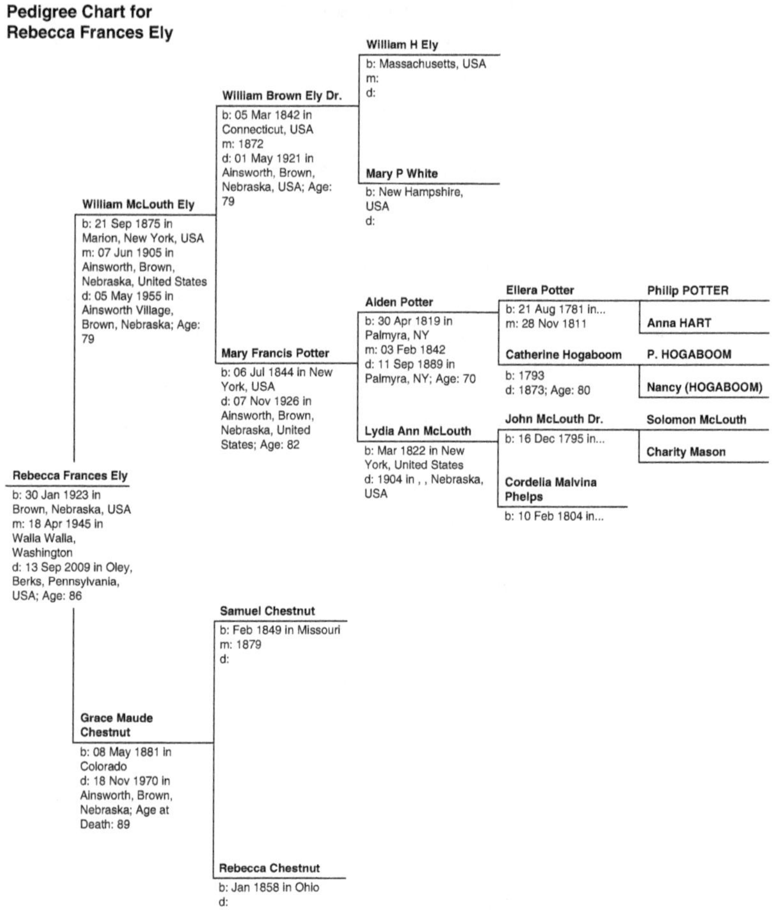

Figure 31.2 The Ely Family Tree

They married at the war's conclusion and relocated to the hometown of Rebecca's mother, Denver, Colorado. There, William pursued his Master's in Business Administration at the University of Denver. He graduated from the program in 1947, continued on with additional postgraduate business studies, and subsequently taught for a couple of years at the University in Denver.

In 1949, Meckling enrolled in the prestigious University of Chicago to continue his graduate studies. He remained there for three years, but did not complete a Ph.D. These years were just when the University of Chicago was attracting numerous future Nobel Prize winners to its

Cowles Foundation and was revolutionizing the study of finance. For young Meckling, this was a most formative and exciting time to study finance and business.

Following his graduate work at the University of Chicago, Meckling returned home to teach at Butler University in Indianapolis. He then moved his family to Rochester, New York to shepherd a small fledgling undergraduate and evening business program.

Under Meckling's astute leadership, the business school garnered a national reputation. At the same time, he was pondering a novel research agenda that would eventually place him in the highest echelon of corporate finance thought. All the while, he was honing his higher education administration skills.

With Meckling's studies at Chicago and his experience at Butler both behind him, he exhibited an impatience and wanted to get on with life. He was a first-generation college graduate, and was married to a woman whose ancestors included professionals such as judges and doctors. He was intellectually cunning and intuitive, and made up for his more humble upbringing with cleverness, hard work and extraordinary entrepreneurship. He was married to an equally entrepreneurial partner who left him to manage his business school as she managed her antique business.

Meckling's academic entrepreneurship began at an early stage in his career. When he found himself at the RAND Institute in California, he had the opportunity to meet Armen Alchian, who had been hired by John Williams at RAND to create a social sciences division at the think-tank. RAND was firmly planted in the sciences and well-funded from defense dollars, but it also differed from traditional schools such as the nearby Stanford University in that it prized and encouraged entrepreneurship among its participants. One of the early proponents of such entrepreneurship at RAND, Reuben Kessel, met Meckling and recognized his entrepreneurial qualities. Meckling and Alchian immediately struck up a friendship and mutual respect. As Alchian noted quite humorously, perhaps their affinity arose because of their presumed shared Middle Eastern heritages. Alchian quipped that, for him, it was Genghis Khan, and for Meckling, Attila the Hun.[3]

Their assigned task was to attract more of the technically sophisticated engineers from RAND and from UCLA to the economic analysis division for which RAND was already becoming well known. The engineering expertise of their recruitees would be invaluable in the study of the economics of defense and aerospace spending. However, they quickly realized they had an incentive problem. Engineers and scientists exhibited the same sort of self-interest that economists try to describe in their models. Meckling was tasked with creating the incentives and the institutions that could attract the expertise and get the work done.

Meckling understood both incentives and synergies, and thrived at RAND. As was common with many from humble beginnings who lived their formative years in the depths of the Great Depression, he took the resources he was given, assembled those he would need, and tried to create something that was greater than the sum of its parts. He brought these skills with him to Rochester to build a top notch business school.

Meckling demonstrated his academic entrepreneurship in an academic culture for which entrepreneurship is not the norm. In an introduction to a talk Meckling was once about to give, Armen Alchian introduced him as "a most unusual man – one who has never managed a business, who has no advanced degree, and who has never been on a university staff as a teacher or administrator, but who, nevertheless, has just been appointed dean of the Graduate School of Management at the University of Rochester."[4] Alchian went on to describe that Meckling was hired because he did not suffer fools gladly, and holds himself to the same standard he holds others.

These qualities explain much of Meckling's administrative successes. They are also a testament to his cunning intuition of the nature of value creation in an organization, including a modern corporation.

32
The Times

The period following Coase's 1937 "The Nature of the Firm" was one marked by the increasing ascendency of a reinvented American corporate model. The glamour of the Gilded Age was left in tatters following the excesses of the Roaring Twenties and the challenges of the Great Depression. World War II required a rebuilding of industrial capacity, and the 1950s saw dramatic growth and the creation of the modern military-industrial complex. In these heady days of post-World War II expansion, there was scant interest in Coase's observations, and the institutional approach to economics and finance was eclipsed by the increasingly quantitative thrust of finance.

Coase would certainly not claim he offered a model of the modern corporation that demonstrated precisely from where the advantages of these growing and increasingly complex organizations arose. The lack of specificity of institutional approaches to the corporation also made Coase's assertions difficult to prove except through anecdote. Clearly, much more sophistication and greater institutional understanding would be required if the full ramifications and subtleties of Coase's observations were to be realized.

However, explorations into the nature of value within the corporation was receiving little attention at this time. Instead, during the 1960s, there was a dramatic growth in more empirical and market oriented measures of corporate value within finance, first from Harry Markowitz's (August 24, 1927–) Modern Portfolio Theory and then from work of William Sharpe and others on the analysis of share prices. The results these Nobel Prize winning scholars generated clearly demonstrated that corporations created value well in excess of their accounting, or book, value. Few seemed interested, at first, in the precise internal mechanisms for the creation of such corporate value.

By the end of the decade, Oliver Williamson was making a great contribution in our understanding of *New Institutional Economics*. His exploration began with his interest in explaining why additional vertical integration of a modern corporation may create value and enhance efficiency. This conclusion was in sharp contrast with the traditional belief that vertical integration encourages monopolization and discourages efficiency. From Williamson's treatment of vertical integration came much more formal avenues for the creation of value to which Coase had alluded. He did so in a methodological manner that allowed for greater detail and, potentially, for empirical validation. He also inspired others to more fully explore the precise advantages well-run organizations generated.

Williamson saw the primary avenue for the creation of corporate value as being its ability to define implicit contracts within the firm at much lower cost and with a much greater degree of mutual accountability than could be found in the contracts of the marketplace. Market-based contracts were either very limited, represented by a bill of sale and the exchange of a good or service for cash, or costly, complex, expensive, and unwieldy. All but the simplest contracts often required lawyers. Even small changes in terms sometimes required extensive renegotiation, and more lawyers. And a failure to perform may require the intervention of the court system.

To mitigate this complexity, goods or services in the marketplace were instead commoditized so that they could be contracted with greater facility. Such commodification was a tradeoff, though. Greater simplicity in contracting resulted, and economies of scale in production of these commodities could be generated. But, customization was hampered. Just as Henry Ford once quipped, you can have your Model T in any color you want, so long as it's black.

Corporations that could benefit from an intermediate factor of production that was more precisely tailored to its unique needs could do so by producing such factors in-house. Williamson saw the corporation as the entity that could capitalize on this ability to implicitly contract internally for more of its needs. He initiated a discussion on the nature of implicit contracts, and, in doing so, he, along with Coase at the University of Chicago, each helped to form the discipline of law and economics. Both collaborated with the law faculty at their schools, and, while they may have added much greater formality and specificity to the law literature, their treatments still lacked the degree of specificity required by those empiricists anxious to test their theories.

Coase, and especially Williamson, had provided sufficient fodder for the discussion to continue, though, and both were instrumental in renewing interest in an institutional approach that may be amenable to quantification.

Neither Coase nor Williamson felt particularly obliged to specify the precise nature of corporate synergies, though. Williamson had hinted at the route by which such an extension might arise. He noted that one of the corporation's greatest advantages is in its ability to formulate implicit contracts within its organization that provides the incentives for the agents of the corporation, its employees and its divisions, to respond to the needs of the corporation while, of course, agents respond to their own aspirations and internal needs.

This alignment of what is optimal for the corporation, the principal, and what its agents might instead prefer, became one of the most enduring and valuable contributions to our understanding of the creation of corporate value in a generation. Michael Jensen and William Meckling provided the necessary foundation for such a formalization.

Their partnership began a couple of years after Dean Meckling hired Professor Jensen to the Simon School of Business at the University of Rochester. They became collaborators as they attempted to develop a course on the economics of complex organizations such as the modern corporation. Their students found the traditional topics of pricing within the firm rather dry, so Jensen and Meckling began to search for a more interesting and novel approach to the question of corporate valuation.

Another member of the business faculty at Rochester was Karl Brunner, a macroeconomist who had moved to the United States from Switzerland. Europe had a long and established history of analysis of institutional questions, in contrast to the highly mathematical approach that had become de rigueur in the United States. The three conceived the idea of presenting a paper to a conference in Switzerland, and Jensen and Meckling began to ponder a paper of broad strokes along the lines of the great mind Milton Friedman's seminal article in the *New York Times* Magazine, cited earlier, that the social responsibility of corporations is to create profits, and not to promote other, more human values.[1] Jensen and Meckling wanted to come up with a topic that would provoke a similar controversy and spirited discussion and highlight some differences of approach within economics and finance.

As Jensen and Meckling pondered the profits of a corporation, they concluded that while a firm may have the goal of maximizing profits, they rarely manage to do so in practice. By blowing open the black box and questioning the practicality of the assumption of profit maximization, they managed to create the controversy they sought, on both sides of the Atlantic Ocean.

Their approach was to describe the conflicts between interests in the corporations – the bondholders and the stockholders, and also between the principals for whom the corporation earns profits and the agents they hire to produce the products that generate the profits.

As they began to search the literature in preparation of their presentation, they discovered first that they knew little about such an exploration in finance, and that was there very little existing literature in this area, with the exception of the seminal work of Coase and the more recent contributions by Williamson.

Jensen and Meckling honed their ideas into a paper, and submitted it for publication to a good journal, but not a top journal in the field. They received the fate that is often meted out to those with new ideas that defy conventional wisdom or standard approaches. Just as the great mind William Sharpe had taken years to publish his paper on the Capital Asset Pricing Model which would subsequently earn him a Nobel Memorial Prize, and only succeeded once the journal came under new leadership,[2] referees at the *Bell Journal of Economics* rebuked Jensen and Meckling for their impudence in actually submitting a paper that departed so radically from conventional understanding.

Fortunately, the great minds Eugene Fama and Robert Merton were sharing co-editor duties with Jensen at the *Journal of Financial Economics*. Fama had visited Belgium while there was still the buzz in Europe about the controversy Jensen and Meckling had generated. He had read their preliminary working paper and convinced his colleague Robert Merton that the *Journal of Financial Economics* ought to publish the work of Jensen and Meckling.

Having suddenly experienced some success with their new subject matter, Jensen and Meckling decided to share their paper with their University of Rochester colleagues. They were confident that they had home court advantage there, and, of course, Meckling was the dean and the School's fearless leader. Yet the presentation did not go well there either, despite their home court advantage. In an interview he gave years later, Jensen reported that the faculty were furious, almost hateful, at their audacity in presenting such a topic. Jensen and Meckling retreated to the safety of Meckling's office after the presentation, Meckling put his feet up on his desk, lit up a cigar, and pronounced, "Well Mike, we sure didn't sell that one!"[3]

Not to be deterred, a few years later Jensen tried once again to present the paper at a finance workshop at the University of Chicago. In the audience on that occasions were the great minds Fisher Black, Merton Miller, and Eugene Fama. Jensen felt he might be a little better received this time around, especially since Merton Miller and Eugene Fama had both supervised his thesis and had agreed to publish the Jensen and Meckling paper in their journal. Jensen started out by referring to Miller and Fama's well-known textbook, *The Theory of Finance,* and also often referred to as *the White Bible* because of its stature in the literature and its white covers.[4] Jensen had given his presentation the whimsical subtitle of "Why Chapter 4 of the White Bible is All Wrong" – a reference to the chapter in *The Theory of Finance* in which Miller outlined his conclusions, from his work with Modigliani, that capital structure does not matter. Jensen clearly had a peculiar method of softening up his audience. He went on to assert to his audience that a corporate capital structure indeed affects its corporate organizational structure and has important implications on both corporate decision making and productivity. A couple of decades later, he joined Miller at Miller's birthday party. After so many intervening years, Miller finally admitted that there may have been just a grain of contribution to the literature in Jensen and Meckling's paper.

Jensen and Meckling stuck to their position, despite the resistance. They filled the void of our understanding of precisely what corporate managers may be maximizing. They trusted the evidence produced following the period of rapid industrial growth in the 1960s that upwards of half of the value of mergers, acquisitions, and corporate expansions had not been effectively capitalized into the stock price. Jensen and Meckling believed that executives were maximizing something other than value – perhaps revenue as proxies for the size of the enterprise they ran, or perhaps bonuses or other rewards for successfully navigating mergers. Left unchecked, though, this divergence between what is good for the principal and what is pursued by its agents may destroy corporate value. Jensen and Meckling introduced to the corporate finance literature a better understanding of the need to align incentives across the corporation to create the greatest value for the corporation.

33
The Theory

Jensen and Meckling had a great insight that was destined to become one of the most enduring, intuitive, and useful concepts in corporate management. Their analysis of agency costs and its effect on corporate value has become a classic and one of the most cited articles in finance of all time. The paper, *Theory of the Firm: Managerial Behavior, Agency Costs and Ownership Structure,*[1] introduced the term "agency theory" to corporate finance – a concept that has been widely applied and adapted ever since.

Their simple framework of "agency theory" is the analysis of the mutual incentives and disincentives in the interaction between principals and agents, most often management and employees, but also perhaps the board of directors and the chief executive officer, and other relationships when one (the principal) charges another (the agent) to do what is in the interest of the principal. More formally, an agency relationship is one in which an entity (the principal) delegates to an agent the principal's decision-making power to be exercised to further the best interest of the principal.

The most common avenue of this relationship is between an employer and an employee. In general, there is, at best, an imperfect alignment between the incentives of the two parties. The principal prefers maximal effort at minimal cost, while the agent may prefer minimal effort for maximal compensation. These conflicting goals require institutions to align the incentives they offer to the agent with the objectives of the principal. This challenge within the corporation had been articulated as far back as in 1776 in Adam Smith's *The Wealth of Nations*:

> The directors of such companies, however, being the managers rather of other people's money than of their own, it cannot well

> be expected, that they should watch over it with the same anxious vigilance with which the partners in a private copartnery frequently watch over their own. Like the stewards of a rich man, they are apt to consider attention to small matters as not for their master's honour, and very easily give themselves a dispensation from having it. Negligence and profusion, therefore, must always prevail, more or less, in the management of the affairs of such a company.[2]

This tension remained relatively unanalyzed until the great mind Stephen Ross renewed interest in the subject at the 1972 annual meeting of the American Economic Association. He presented a paper entitled *The Economic Theory of Agency: The Principal's Problem.*[3] This relatively brief six-page contribution framed the basic tension between the interests of the principal and those of the agent. The following year, Barry Mitnik, a political scientist, presented a paper to a meeting of political scientists entitled "Fiduciary Rationality and Public Policy: The Theory of Agency and Some Consequences."[4] In this he described the tension in more detail from both the principal's and the agent's perspectives and applied it to a number of circumstances.

When such differing incentives occur, principals and agents negotiate various mechanisms to avoid the dysfunction caused by the tension. These various mechanisms may include increased monitoring, and incentives, such as bonuses and contingent pay, to lessen these incentive incompatibility effects.

However, Mitnick noted that these solutions also impose costs on the principal and the agent. Such solutions are worthwhile only if they are less costly than the dysfunction they strive to correct.

These two efforts to form a foundation of analysis were followed by the contribution of Jensen and Meckling. These authors explore in much greater detail the problems outlined by Ross and Mitnick. They elaborated, in particular, on not only the cost of monitoring agents' actions but also the costs of contracting against malfeasance, and the prevention of certain practices, such as double-dealing or forbidding work with competitors upon separation through non-compete clauses in their employment contracts. Jensen and Meckling asserted that sophisticated corporations can resolve these conflicts to preserve corporate value. Instead, they "Investigate the incentives faced by each of the parties and the elements entering into the determination of the equilibrium contractual form characterizing the relationship between the manager (i.e., agent) of the firm and the outside equity and debt holders (i.e., principals)."[5]

Jensen and Meckling focused especially on the relationship between shareholders and management, with the board of directors being the conduit between the two.

To analyze this relationship, Jensen and Meckling took a particularly quantitative finance approach. They compared the performance of two poles of the firm structure spectrum – one in which the manager owns the firm, and the other in which external shareholders control some equity.

Under the first framework, there is no dysfunction between owners and managers when they are one and the same. In that case, the owner-manager maximizes firm welfare because all returns accrue to the owner/manager. Such an owner-manager makes decisions that equate their after-tax marginal benefit to their after-tax marginal cost.

Once an owner-manager sells a stake of the corporation to outside equity holders, though, the owner-manager will receive only a portion of corporate earnings but must still manage and incur all of the costs of the firm. The manager's incentive to be entrepreneurial, in proportion to the manager's equity ownership, is hence reduced. At the same time, the costs borne by external shareholders to monitor the manager increases as its ownership share is increased. Both these losses create inefficiencies for the corporation, and reduced corporate value, if left unabated.

Their theory offers a number of empirically verifiable claims. From a corporate valuation perspective, it implies that the financial structure of a firm will affect firm earnings, despite the prediction of the most superficial interpretation of the Modigliani–Miller Theorem. This implication is independent of whether or not the firm is competitive or monopolistic.

Jensen and Meckling's theory also suggests why a manager's efforts may nonetheless promote economic efficiency, if more broadly defined. The theory explains why equity financing, in both common and preferred stock, nonetheless remains an efficient form of capital, despite the principal–agent dichotomy. Finally, it explains the advantage of debt financing, even in the absence of any tax advantages.

Because debt and equity holders differ with regard to their stake in the corporation and in their ability to direct corporate decisions, the principal–agent dichotomy impinges upon them differentially. Hence, corporate and capital structure does matter, from a theoretical perspective.

Jensen and Meckling's theory also telegraphed the era of Sarbanes–Oxley, a reporting regulation that began in the United States in the aftermath of the Enron scandal and corporate meltdown, and now enshrined on both sides of the Atlantic Ocean. Accountability of management to the success and propriety of corporations is increasingly demanded by regulators and equity holders alike.

Of course, a solution to the principal–agent problem is not the sole purpose of the modern corporation. Williamson and Coase, followed by Alchian and Demsetz, argued that the implicit contract between managers and workers creates many of the advantages of the corporate form. However, it was clear that Jensen and Meckling's hypothesis was at least an important component of the method in which corporations create value, and also offered a successful explanation of some common observations.

For instance, the limited liability aspect of corporations is also an important aspect of the corporate structure. It allows passive investors to risk no more than their outlay for the purchase of shares of the firm. Were their liability not limited to their investment, they would have as much as, and perhaps more, liability for the poor decisions of the firm as have the managers and directors who are much more involved in the firm's strategies and tactics. This risk would be sufficient to deter many investors and would, therefore, cause financial markets to fail.

Jensen and Meckling did not argue that such a release of risk does not negate risk, though. They merely point out that limited liability merely displaces risk. In the alternate, if each shareholder has jointly and severable liability, the entire wealth of shareholders could be tapped to pay outstanding liabilities in a corporate bankruptcy. The implications of such a provision would be impossibly complex. Each shareholder would have to monitor the risk of the firm, and would also have to monitor the wealth of all other shareholders. These potentially debilitating monitoring costs are prevented by limited liability. Instead, debt holders understand that shareholders' liability extends only to their investment, and any additional liabilities are absorbed mostly by debt holders. This aggregate risk is then capitalized in the risk premium required for the firm to successfully raise debt capital. Hence, any agency problems are capitalized into the risk premium bondholders absorb. The organizational structure indeed does affect capital pricing and hence the capital structure.

Modigliani and Miller actually anticipated aspects of Jensen and Meckling's argument. Recall their conclusion that, neglecting tax preferences on interest payments and bankruptcy risk, the capital structure of a firm should not affect its valuation. They later augmented this result by noting that debt rather than equity financing may confer a corporate valuation advantage. Debt interest payments are tax deductible for the corporation, but dividends paid to those who provide equity are double taxed – first when earned by the corporation, and then when distributed to the shareholder. Thus, the firm might be financed optimally by incurring debt rather than raising new equity. They qualify this extreme prediction, though, because it defies empirical evidence. They note:

> It may be useful to remind readers once again that the existence of a tax advantage for debt financing – even the larger advantage of the corrected version – does not necessarily mean that corporations should at all times seek to use the maximum possible amount of debt in their capital structures. For one thing, other forms of financing, notably retained earnings, may in some circumstances be cheaper still when the tax status of investors under the personal income tax is taken into account. More important, there are, as we pointed out, limitations imposed by lenders (see pp. 292–93), as well as many other dimensions (and kinds of costs) in real-world problems of financial strategy which are not fully comprehended within the framework of static equilibrium models, either our own or those of the traditional variety. These additional considerations, which are typically grouped under the rubric of "the need for preserving flexibility," will normally imply the maintenance by the corporation of a substantial reserve of untapped borrowing power. The tax advantage of debt may well tend to lower the optimal size of that reserve, but it is hard to believe that advantages of the size contemplated under our model could justify any substantial reduction, let alone their complete elimination.[6]

Modigliani and Miller acknowledged that capital structure is influenced by more than just the optimization of the weighted average cost of capital (WACC). They predict other dynamics not yet revealed within the then prevailing black box model of the corporation. Jensen and Meckling took up that challenge of optimal corporate and capital structure, even though their results are primarily remembered for the tool they employed in their analysis – the principal–agent problem. In fact, they viewed their paper as integrating the results of Coase and Williamson, Modigliani and Miller, and agency theory into a model that more successfully explains the myriad corporate structures we see commonly employed. Their new definition of the firm was rich in provocative implications, from better risk sharing to increased accountability, the importance of compensations schemes that align reward with success, and the differential role of debt and equity in not only the capital structure, but also the managerial corporate structure of the firm. In doing so, they added even greater nuance and implications on the Alchian and Demsetz treatment of the firm as a synergistic team.

Jensen and Meckling left to others the mechanisms used to mitigate the principal–agent problem. There is now a large and growing literature about the optimal design of employment contracts, for instance. While Jensen and Meckling argued that the firm is a nexus of contracts, like the framework defined by Williamson, they start from an optimal contract between the shareholder principals and the manager agents, and explore the implications of this optimality. While they left to others to explore how to achieve this optimality, there would not have spawned such a vast literature had they not first framed the problem in a way that permits further exploration and validation.

34
Applications and Extensions

A few years after the publication of their seminal paper, Michael Jensen combined with the great mind Eugene Fama to further explore the hidden costs of the separation of ownership and management. In their paper "Separation of Ownership and Control," Fama and Jensen further specified the nature of the decision process. They described four different steps in the decision process:

1. The solicitation and ranking of various corporate projects.
2. The selection of the projects that offer a return above the firm's weighted average cost of capital.
3. The implementation of the projects selected; and
4. The monitoring of the incentives and their results on each project.

Fama and Jensen formulated a working hypothesis that if managers do not secure the bulk of the wealth they create, those who bear the greater risk (the residual claimants, often the shareholders) will attempt to assert greater influence on those who exercise day-to-day control over project implementation.

They then tested their hypothesis on four different types of organizations of the type that they, building on the work of Coase and Williamson, would argue benefit from the implicit contracting within a firm. They considered four different types of organizations: publicly traded corporations, large partnerships, financial mutual corporations, and non-profit corporations.

In the case of publicly traded corporations, the extent of direct stockholder control is essentially limited to their ability to sell their stock, and hence presents the classic application of the principal–agent dichotomy.

By contrast, the partners of a large professional partnership are both the managers and the residual claimants on the earnings that managers can generate. For these organizations, the sharing of liability among partners ensures there is significant joint monitoring of decisions that affect all partners. In this case, there is no isolated principal–agent problem, but there is a process of monitoring that often as extensive as might be found in a shareholder-owned organization.

Similarly, a financial mutual is designed to be run on behalf of its customers, which could be either policyholders in the case of an insurance company or depositors or fund holders in a mutual bank or fund, respectively. These stakeholders can move their business elsewhere should managers fail to run the organization on their behalf. However, the directors charged with representing their interest are often less motivated on behalf of the customers because the directors' fate is less closely aligned with that of the customer-owners.

Finally, non-profit organizations are often funded by charitable donors who have no ability to withdraw their capital should the corporation act in ways inconsistent with their wishes. Because they do not expect a financial return, there is a reduction in some of the problems inherent in the principal–agent dichotomy. However, such donors often seek assurances that management will maintain strategies consistent with donors' wishes.

An obvious extension and common application of the principal–agent problem is to tailor management compensation to be consistent with long-term corporate performance. Michael Jensen and Kevin Murphy explored the effectiveness of these mechanisms in their 1990 paper entitled *CEO Incentives – It's Not How Much You Pay, But How.*[1] The authors collected the compensation rates for more than 2,500 chief executive officers from over 700 companies during the Great Depression and 1,400 publicly traded companies over 15 years from 1974 onward. They also tabulated the ownership of stock in their companies by the chief executive officers of most of the U.S. Fortune 500 firms in 1988. They made some discoveries that defy conventional wisdom:

1. Changes in executive compensation are rarely directly correlated with corporate performance.
2. Inflation-adjusted compensation remained essentially unchanged between the depths of the Great Depression and 1988.
3. CEO salaries follow remarkably similar variations to their hourly workers with respect to corporate earnings, even though officers were less likely to take real compensation cuts when compared to their hourly workers.

4. CEO share ownership has actually fallen, by an order of magnitude, by 1988 compared to their Depression-era counterparts.

Jensen and Murphy concluded that there is room for much more effective and pronounced pay for performance policies that encourage reward and penalize failure even further. They also concluded that firings for poor performance is not employed often enough. They argue that stock ownership, as a percentage, rather than as a cash equivalent, and rewards for outstanding performance should be used much more extensively.

These authors also noted that the employment of stock options afforded managers both an advantage in deferred taxes paid and in securing a share of upside risk, but that these incentives do not punish sufficiently for downside risk, and nor do they allow managers to capitalize on distributed earnings in the form of dividends. In a later article, Murphy and Brian Hall wrote in 2003 in "The Trouble with Stock Options"[2] that the granting of options is too dilute to be effective. In the ten-year period from 1992, the value of options grew from $11 billion to $71 billion, but it had peaked at $119 billion in 2000. The mechanism began to be employed to attract motivated employees and defer taxes rather than to resolve the shareholder/manager principal–agent problem. They were also used to allow companies to compensate in a way that did not appear directly on financial statements, even though the exercise price was often below the fair market price.

The authors conclude that such a diffuse use of stock options is an inefficient resolution to the principal–agent dichotomy. Rather, they recommend that restricted stock be used instead of options. They noted that the problem with options is that they encourage overly risky behavior if employees own options for which the exercise price is below the prevailing stock price. Risky strategies by managers could raise the stock price above the exercise price, if successful, but would impose no symmetric penalty on managers if unsuccessful.

While the principal–agent problem may have generated much interest among economists, managers and practitioners well understand the notion of specialization that Adam Smith pioneered in 1776. In turn, Smith was enamored with the unique ability for the market to organize itself in a manner more efficient than what could then, or now, be obtained by central government planners. There remains more work to be done to transfer the understanding generated by Jensen and Meckling to practice in the board room and the shop floor.

Smith alluded to the important role of information that arises because skilled workers have intimate knowledge of the production process and potential efficiencies. These informational advantages gave rise to Jensen and Meckling's principal–agent approach, and of much of what has been novel in economics and finance ever since. Financial efficiencies rest crucially on information, both at the market level and in the internal operations of a corporation. It is this information that creates value. It is the extent and range of informational advantages that helps explain and define the boundaries of the corporation. Vertical integration often helps to enhance information and better coordinate production. However, managing and exchanging relevant information becomes increasingly difficult if a firm grows too big. These diseconomies then limit the size of the corporation.

35
Life and Legacy

The Agency Theory developed by Jensen and Meckling transformed how we view the corporation. Its basic conclusion is that the whole is greater than the sum of its parts. Corporations create value simply by doing what other organizations cannot do through arm's length market transactions.

Meckling left a number of other legacies. While he never completed his own Ph.D., his contributions induced others to bestow honorary doctorates upon him for his insights. His Alma Mater, Westminster College, awarded him an honorary Doctor of Science degree in 1978 and the Francisco Marroquin University of Guatemala also awarded him an honorary doctorate in 1980.

His greatest legacies, beyond his theoretical contributions, involved putting theory to practice. Meckling discovered he had a knack for teasing synergies out of schools. He became the second dean of the College of Business Administration at Rochester University. Under his leadership, the school evolved into the Simon Graduate School of Management.

While at Rochester, Meckling established the Center for Research in Government Policy and Business, which has since been named the Bradley Policy Research Center. His belief in the application of a scientific approach to the study of business was also extended to the government studies sector.

Perhaps Meckling's greatest talent lay in the recognition and nurturing of the talent around him. As a dean, he recognized that faculty are most productive when their research agendas mesh. At their worst, academics are islands. At their best, the insights they can generate through honest debate. The ensuing discussion can be transformational. Meckling made a career out of attracting and nurturing others in the best interests of the institution.

During his career, Meckling served on the faculties of the University of Denver, Butler University in Indiana, and the University of California at Los Angeles. Following his retirement from the Rochester deanship, he joined UCLA, where he associated himself once again with the prestigious RAND Corporation. In 1983 Meckling retired from the deanship and the James E. Gleason Distinguished Research Scholar position at Rochester. He and his wife Rebecca retired to a home in Rancho Santa Fe, California, where he continued work on an informal basis at UCLA and at the RAND Corporation. During his first period at RAND, he was one of the first advocates of the economic advantages of possible space-based technologies. The economics of space had piqued Meckling's academic interest. From his earlier work at RAND, the Corporation had played an important role in the creation of NASA, and analyses of the benefits the space race may confer. Upon his retirement from Rochester, Meckling was pleased to return to RAND to continue the work he began there from 1958 to 1962. He was once again able to combine his economic and organizational skills to enhance defense planning.

He also served on the prestigious National Science Board, which directs the National Science Foundation. He was also a member of the board of directors of Superba Cravats, a textiles company, and The Tax Foundation, a Washington think-tank that has been researching tax issues and public policy since 1937.

Meckling always maintained a strong interest in public policy issues, and he tried to bring sound economic analysis to policy studies. For instance, in the 1960s, he assisted New York Governor Nelson Rockefeller and its Council of New York State Economic Advisors in education policy. This era revolutionized the public higher education infrastructure in New York over the late 1960s through the 1970s.

One of the most interesting examples of Meckling's eclectic devotion was in his work on behalf of the Gates Commission. In 1968, presidential candidate Richard Nixon campaigned on a promise to discontinue the draft, which had conscripted young American men into the Vietnam War.

Meckling himself had been drafted into World War II and had pondered the indiscriminate waste of human capital that can occur when a draft is pursued rather than the development of an all-volunteer force. During the escalation of the Vietnam War, Meckling had already been appointed dean at Rochester, in 1962, immediately after his stint in defense policy studies at the RAND Corporation. In 1967, a young Columbia economist named Martin Anderson joined Nixon's campaign, hoping that he might be able to persuade Nixon to end the draft. Anderson crafted Nixon's anti-draft message, and, when he was appointed as a presidential advisor upon Nixon's election, he helped assemble the Gates Commission on an All-Volunteer Force. This Commission included the three economists, Milton Friedman, Alan Greenspan, and W. Allen Wallis, a student, two civil rights leaders, and some businessmen and university leaders. It was chaired by Thomas Gates, who was formerly President Eisenhower's Secretary of Defense.

On the commission the economists and two others were both opposed the draft, five members were in favor, and five commissioners remained on the fence in 1969. Meckling had been appointed to be the executive director of the commission. He had assumed that the commission would be firmly against the draft, so he was ill-prepared for the deadlock. To help resolve the issue, he hired some historians and some economists who could estimate what the supply of enlistees would be in the absence of conscription. He used his analytic skills to foment a cohesive academic policy analysis that eventually persuaded Nixon to follow through with his promise to end conscription, not for the interests of those who may not want to serve, but rather in the interest of creating a highly professional military.

Meckling died in California on May 15, 1998, at the age of 76 and was buried in a military graveyard. His wife, Frances, died 11 years later, on September 13, 2009, in Oley, Pennsylvania, in the town of their oldest daughter Nancy, and her husband Bruce Littlefield. William and Rebecca were also survived by their oldest son William, and by their sons Bruce, Scott, and Greg.

Mechling and Jensen were separated by 3,000 miles following their seminal work together. Jensen was recruited to the Harvard Business School in 1985 and worked at Harvard University for much of his career. At Harvard, he retired as the Emeritus Jesse Isidor Straus Professor of Business Administration.

In his academic life Jensen was awarded multiple honorary degrees. In 1991, he receive the Docteur Honoris Causa by the Université Catholique de Louvain in Louvaine-la-Neuve, Belgium. In the academic year 2000/2001, he was awarded two honorary degrees; the first from the University of Bern in Switzerland and the second an honorary Doctor of Laws degree from the William E. Simon School of Business Administration, at the University of Rochester, the school that had been founded by his collaborator William Meckling.

Jensen also visited a number of other academic institutions. He spent the academic year 2001/2002 at the Tuck School of Business at Dartmouth College, and was named a Fellow of the European Corporate Governance

Institute. While at Harvard, he continued to find other outlets for his academic talents. He participated in the Monitor Company, acting as their managing director for Organizational Strategy Practice.

Over the course of his career, Michael Jensen wrote more than fifty academic papers, a number of books, including *Foundations of Organizational Strategy* and *Theory of the Firm: Governance, Residual Claims, and Organizational Forms*. He also published articles and editorials in the popular press in various subjects in finance, business, and economics, and edited two books for the academic press, *Studies in the Theory of Capital Markets* in 1972, and, with Clifford Smith, Jr., *Modern Theory of Corporate Finance* in 1984.

Like Coase, who was the founding editor of *The Journal of Law and Economics,* and Williamson, who had founded *The Journal of Law, Economics, and Organization,* in 1973 Jensen founded *The Journal of Financial Economics,* which is now widely regarded as one of the top journals in its field.

This new breed of finance academics who offered a refreshing alternative to the mechanical neoclassical approach often demonstrated a willingness to explore diverse and non-traditional approaches to otherwise familiar problems. For instance, while at Harvard, Jensen served on the *Mind Brain Behavior Initiative,* a cross-disciplinary assembly of researchers interested in generating a better understanding of the reasons why humans sometimes make counterproductive decisions.

Perhaps Jensen is most widely known for founding and chairing the Social Science Electronic Publishing Company. In 1994, barely a few years after the founding of the Internet, this service created broad access to the preliminary works of scholars as they prepared their papers and concepts for traditional journals. This network has grown to be the preeminent working paper publication system in finance and economics.

Beyond the honorary degrees, Jensen received numerous accolades. In 1979, he and Meckling received the inaugural Leo Melamed Prize for outstanding scholarship by faculty at the University of Chicago's business school for their seminal *Theory of the Firm: Managerial Behavior, Agency Costs, and Ownership Structure*. This seminal work remains one of the most cited of all finance papers in its field. That same year, he and Meckling were also awarded the Graham and Dodd Scroll Award by the Financial Analysts Federation for their paper *Can the Corporation Survive?* In 1984, he was awarded the Joseph Coolidge Shaw, S.J. Medal by Boston College, and, five years later, he received the McKinsey Award for his paper *Eclipse of the Public Corporation.* In 1990, the Eastern Finance Association named him Scholar of the Year and *Fortune Magazine* listed him as one of the Year's 25 Most Fascinating Business People. In 1996, Jensen was elected to the American Academy of Arts and Sciences.

Jensen received the Lifetime Achievement Award for Contributions to Research in the Field of Financial Intermediation from the Financial Intermediation Society and was bestowed with the Drexel U. LeBow College of Business Distinguished Scholar Award for his work in corporate governance.

Jensen had been asked to consult with numerous foundations, corporations and agencies, and to testify in court and to Congress. He has also presided over the American Finance Association and the Western Economic Association International.

More recently, Jensen has been interested in the issue of leadership. He has authored *The Ontological Laws of Human Nature, A Positive Theory of the Normative Virtues, Being A Leader and the Effective Exercise of Leadership: An Ontological Approach, and,* for the more general business press, *The Three Foundations of a Great Personal Life, Great Leadership and a Great Company: Integrity, Authenticity, and Committed to Something Bigger than Oneself.*

Jensen remains on the faculty of the Harvard Business School as a Professor Emeritus.

Section 6
What We Have Learned

This fifth volume in a series of discussions about the great minds in the history and theory of finance has addressed what creates corporate value and how it is measured. While some of the topics included here are also espoused in all introductory courses in corporate finance, the great minds described here go beyond what we learn in finance courses.

We delved into the lives, times, and contributions of those how have busted open the black box of the corporation's operations and have delved into the ways in which corporations create value. The work of these financial theorists created the basis for what we now know as corporate finance and the *New Institutional Economics*. I finish with a summary of the combined contributions of nine scholars who collectively defined corporate value.

36
Combined Contributions

For more than a century and a half, financial analysts relied upon a story Adam Smith told that explained how corporations create value. In his explanation of how a pin manufacturer uses the specialization of labor to create a corporate synergy, he explained why the value of a corporation exceeds the value of the productive assets it has assembled to do so. The difference between these two sums is what we often call *intangible assets*.

Of course, the market value of these assets capitalize on the surpluses they can create in isolation. The corporation earns its value of combining and coordinating these assets in a unique way. Lost in Adam Smith's compelling narrative, however, is precisely how this value is created and measured. This oversight perpetuated until the late 1930s. Then, in just one year, in 1937, Ronald Harold Coase produced a seminal paper that described the nature of value creation within the firm, while John Burr Williams paid to have his manuscript published which showed how to measure corporate value through discounted cash flow analysis rather than through the more conventional accounting of physical asset value.

Both these expositions failed to receive the audiences they deserved. When the two expositions were published, major global nations were in the depths of the Great Depression, an appreciation of corporate value was of remote interest. The financial manager and economist John Maynard Keynes was the equivalent of an academic rock star for his descriptions of why markets fail and what we ought to do about it. Few, including Keynes, were interested in the exploration of corporate value.

While these works by Coase and Williams remained in relative obscurity for two decades, some took note. John Burr Williams provided an argument for the irrelevancy of corporate capital structure that Franco Modigliani and Merton Miller took up in greater detail. Williams might be better appreciated today had he not died the year before Merton Miller received the Nobel Memorial Prize in Economic Sciences for the extension he proffered with Franco Modigliani. (Modigliani had previously received a Nobel Memorial Prize for his work on the Life Cycle Model of finance, and Nobel Memorial Prizes in a single category are not given to the same recipient twice, nor to those who have died before the Prize is announced.)

And, with the publication of another influential and often-cited 1960 paper by Ronald Coase, there was renewed interest in the importance of our understanding of the inner workings of a corporation and Ronald Coase's account of the ability of a corporation to organize production in ways that the free market cannot.

In the 1960s Oliver Williamson revived interest in the nature of the firm Coase had initiated earlier, and likewise contributed both to corporate finance and corporate law in fascinating and instructive ways. Firms can manage resources in ways that reduce or avoid the transactions costs that hinder arm's-length market transactions. They can also better tailor the intermediate factors of production than can a market provider that must necessarily produce a more generic product for a broader set of buyers.

These contributions did not go unnoticed. Williamson won the 1991 Nobel Prize for his contributions. Coase had won the Prize just a year earlier. For two years in a row, the Nobel Memorial Prize committee recognized nothing but the contributions to our understanding of transactions costs within the neoclassical black box and the modern corporation.

However, while these two approaches were instructive, and while they provided a degree of guidance to corporate leaders, directors, and managers to further enhance value creation, their descriptions were not sufficiently detailed and analytic to fully describe how we might quantify the goodwill that can be created by a modern production process. Two improvements to their analyses helped provide the foundation for a literature that has grown dramatically since that time.

One addition was from Armen Alchian and Harold Demsetz. These two great minds, in their seminal paper *Production, Information Costs, and Economic Organization*, further validated the intuition of Coase and Williamson and opened for discussion the notion of information advantages. The value of information had begun to be modelled and appreciated among financial theorists around the same time. However, informational advantages within the corporate black box had not been described previously. In offering a description of this corporate synergy,

Alchian and Demsetz formed the foundation for a new body of literature that has had a considerable influence on the development of the theory of corporate finance.

Their concept was simple. The neoclassical model states that a rational firm will continue to hire resources until the price it has to pay rises to the increase in revenue provided by the resource. This result assumes the principal that hires the resource is fully informed and able to assess its productivity. In addition, the neoclassical model does not analyze the nuances of the change in this identity over time. The static and less nuanced nature of this relationship may well make sense if the resource is a piece of physical capital such as a machine, or is some other factor for which productivity remains constant, regardless of compensation. Indeed, the neoclassical model does not differentiate between different factors of production.

However, the most widely employed form of capital is human capital. This capital is hardly static in its performance, and one unit of capital likely performs differently than another. In particular, Alchian and Demsetz observe that the very nature of the factor payment scheme may affect performance.

Alchian and Demsetz, in particular, address the issue of shirking. If all units of human capital in a production stage are compensated identically, but some units provide more effort and productivity than another, the more productive unit may contemplate providing less effort, since it produces effort at a cost. The nature of such shirking arises primarily because the compensation scheme is not designed to be correlated directly with productivity.

Alchian and Demsetz illustrate a number of examples of typical compensation schemes that run afoul of the principle that compensation is proportional to productivity. These problematic compensation schemes often arise when compensation is viewed as a component negotiated on behalf of an entire class of employees, rather than being determined individually and related to productivity that can be effectively monitored.

Shirking problems can be viewed as a principal–agent problem – the manager can be viewed as a principal and the employee is its agent. For a given wage negotiated between the principal and agent, or the manager and the workers as a class, the principal has the incentive to maximize the amount of effort and product produced, while the agent has the incentive to provide the minimum amount of effort for a given fixed level of compensation.

This problem is worsened if the wage is increasingly rigid. Other rigidities, such as an inability to fire an employee at minimum cost, or the inability for an employee to find alternative employment, likely exacerbates this principal–agent problem.

Michael Jensen and William Meckling built on these earlier insights by showing how the owners of corporate capital, called the principals, employ agents, the executive officers, managers, workers, and contractors of the corporation, to create corporate value. Jensen and Meckling point out that the interests between the principal and the agent are rarely perfectly aligned at other levels of the corporation, especially in governance and the executive ranks. These scholars show how incentive incompatibilities can reduce corporate value, how well-designed implicit or explicit contracts for factors of production, especially human capital, can tease out greater efficiency and value for the corporation, and how the nature of these contracts, problems, and solutions can even dictate the optimal structure of a corporation.

The efforts of these great minds spawned significant literatures of their own in each of these respective areas. The terms they described, such as the agency problem, moral hazard, transactions costs, incentive incompatibilities, the irrelevance of capital structure and the importance of corporate structure, are now much better understood and receive much more attention, both within the Ivory Tower and among practitioners alike. There remains a significant amount yet to be done, though. Often the same managers who are most affected by compensation incentives are those who recommend to compensation committees their compensation packages. Also, there can be no perfect compensation scheme. Yet, any imperfection in incentives will eventually be exploited, often with perverse results. The finance industry must look no further than the factors that led to the Global Financial Meltdown to see how incentive incompatibilities can result in devastating economic consequences.

37
Conclusions

In a span of 35 years, the field of corporate finance finally found a firm footing. Before 1937, when within a year John Burr Williams and Ronald Coase each showed how corporate value is greater than the sum of its assets, the corporation was viewed as something of a mystery. Financial analysts understood that value was created, but few could really articulate precisely how.

Meanwhile, the field of accounting had been spending centuries adding things up. They could add up the value of a corporation's assets, and they offered a formula for how these assets may depreciate over time. The difference here is known as book value, and, if depreciation occurs at the same rate as the market price of these assets deteriorates, the calculation of book value represents a reasonable estimate of the liquidation value of a firm.

Financial analysts still use book value today, but its importance has been eclipsed by other, much more useful measures. The problem with book value is that it really doesn't represent the value of a corporation that remains a going and profitable concern. Hence, beyond a convenient number that might backstop the value of a firm in a reasonable worst-case scenario, this measure does not remain very useful.

Instead, a measure of the value of a firm over and above book value is far more useful. The difference between the actual market value and book value, known as the intangible value, represents a corporation's ability to create value. To provide for this more meaningful result, though, requires both an accurate valuation of a corporation's ability to generate net earnings, and an understanding of how it does so. John Burr Williams calculated the former, and Ronald Harold Coase gave us the first glimpse of the latter.

Williams's measure of the price of a firm as the discounted present value of future expected net earnings still remains the primary and most frequently employed method to calculate the fundamental value of a firm. It provides a reasonable and straightforward to calculate stock price for a going concern. Coase, and those who followed him, gave us a much clearer understanding of how this value is created within the black box of a corporation. This revolution in corporate valuation, from 1937, through the elaborations of Ronald Coase's model of a firm's economization of transactions costs by Oliver Eaton Williamson, and then through the functioning of internal markets within the firm by Michael Jensen and William Meckling, and Armen Alchian and Harold Demsetz, created a paradigm that has proven to be rich in the creation of value of corporate finance as a discipline.

In doing so, these great minds revived an approach, called the New Institutional Economics, that is much more helpful in understanding the corporation than the black box and mathematically oriented neoclassical model it replaced. Partly because of their efforts, there has been a burgeoning of corporate finance, the value-creation aspect of much of finance, and often the first finance course a student will take. We teach these fundamentals to students because, without corporate value, there is no real economy to be managed. Without the ability to measure corporate value, financial markets cannot be formed. And, without financial markets, there is no ability to mobilize the funds necessary to create the next corporation or expand the scope of a current corporation.

While the field of corporate finance also now encompasses the law, tax consequences, and economics of mergers and acquisitions, bankruptcies, governance, and alternative forms of corporate organization, none of these extensions would have been possible without the contribution of the great minds included in this volume.

Nor would there be a finance industry that increasingly represents the creation of value in its own right. By 2006 in the United States, one in every three dollars of profit was generated by the finance industry. Not only can corporations create profit, but profits can be made in the valuation and financial intermediation of the investments in modern corporations. Indeed, this form of asset accumulation represents the future, the hopes, and the dreams of a large part of the world's middle class, in their retirement savings and pension earnings.

Because an understanding of the ways of corporate finance can make such a difference to humanity is of such paramount importance to the very future of our economy, many of the great minds described here have won Nobel Memorial Prizes for their work. Increasingly, the committee that determines the Nobel Memorial Prize in Economic Sciences looks to contributions not of the arcane nature of the highly theoretical and mathematical, but instead of those who truly contribute to our understanding in ways that can improve the lot of humanity. Certainly, its attention to those who have demonstrated how a corporation can create value reflect this ideal. And, without them, corporate finance would be little more than a few relatively meaningless calculations in a book of accounts.

Glossary

Agency Theory – A theory of financial incentives developed partly by Michael Jensen and William Meckling that demonstrates the agent hired by a principal may not act in ways fully aligned with the principal's goals.

Agent – One who acts on behalf of a principal, usually for compensation, a resource payment, or some other quid pro quo.

Arbitrage – The process by which financial assets will flow toward or from a security that is undervalued or overvalued, respectively, compared to its intrinsic value.

Book Value – The value of an asset carried on a balance sheet. Usually, it is based on the original asset value less calculated depreciation. Alternately, it can be calculated as total assets less any intangible assets.

Capital Asset Pricing Model – A method used to calculate the expected value of a security consistent with its risk, compared to the risk of the overall market.

Capital Structure – The combination of equity and debt financing employed by a corporation to expand.

Compensation Scheme – Payments for an agent to act on behalf of, and presumably in the best interests of a principal.

Conventional Wisdom – Theories and hypotheses that are generally accepted as true, whether valid or not. The term was coined by John Kenneth Galbraith to denote widely accepted theories that may nonetheless be inaccurate.

Corporate finance – The collection of corporate financial and capital arrangements that facilitates the production of goods and services and the generation of earnings.

Corporate Structure – The governance and managerial arrangement that facilitates the production of goods and services and the generation of earnings.

Debt/Equity Ratio – The ratio of outstanding corporate debt to equity in the overall capital structure of a corporation.

Discount Rate – The rate by which future earnings or costs are translated to the relevant present value. Often, this discount rate is determined by the weighted average cost of capital of the corporation.

Discounted Cash Flow Model – A method to calculate corporate value based on its future net cash flows, discounted to the present value.

Discounted Dividend Model – A method to calculate corporate value based on its future dividend payments, discounted to the present value.

Diseconomies of Scale – A region of production that results in marginal costs for an increase in production that are higher than the average costs of production.

This is the region of production for the firm for which expansion results in reduced efficiency.

Dividend – A distribution of earnings from the corporation's retained earnings to its stockholders and owners.

Economies of Scale – A region of production that provides lower marginal costs for an increase in production than the average costs of production. This is the region of production for the firm for which expansion results in greater efficiency.

Efficient Market Hypothesis – A theory of finance that determines how arbitrage will drive the market price of an asset toward its intrinsic value.

Fundamentals Analysis – The analysis of a corporation's intrinsic value based on the difference of assets and liabilities. The asset can include tangible assets, but may also include the intangible asset of the corporation's ability to create future net earnings.

Goodwill – The value of a corporation as a going concern, based on its brand, customer base and relations, the value of its patents and technologies, and proprietary processes. It is an intangible asset.

Implicit Contract – A quid pro quo arrangement between two entities that defines mutual expectations beyond those formally described in a contract.

Incentive Alignment – The creation of a compensation scheme that induces an agent to act in the best interests of the principal.

Incentive Incompatibility – A gap or difference in what is best for the principal and the incentive that directs the actions of an agent.

Intangible Asset – A non-physical asset that provides long term benefits and ability to generate future earnings for the corporation.

Intrinsic Value – The value of an asset based on its ability to create net earnings.

Internal Rate of Return – An imputed effective return on investment of a firm that can be compared to its weighted average cost of capital to determine if the firm creates additional value over the cost of its financial investment.

Moral Hazard – The perverse effect of an incentive that induces an agent to not act in the best interests of a principal. For instance, an insurance policy may induce an agent to take on greater than optimal risk.

Neoclassical Model – A mathematical model of the economy and production that assumes all actors are fully rational and informed and concludes that market determined transactions are efficient.

New Institutional Economics – An alternative to the neoclassical model that explains important phenomena within corporations or organizations which defy the assumptions of the neoclassical model.

Nexus of Contracts – The set of explicit and implicit arrangements a firm employs at its various stages of production of goods and services within the firm.

Option Pricing Theory – A theory developed by Fisher Black and Myron Scholes that permits one to price an option derived from an underlying asset. The option value is a measure of the probability the option will be exercised and, if exercised, the difference in the value of the financial asset and the exercise price of the option.

Principal – An entity that employs agents to act on its behalf.

Retained Earnings – Past and present earnings, net of costs that a corporation has retained for future investment and has not distributed to its owners or shareholders.

Shirking – A less than optimal effort provided by an agent because of the nature of the compensation scheme or managerial monitoring.

Tangible Asset – An asset that earns a quantifiable return. These asset can include inventory, machinery, real estate assets, and other assets that offer a predictable return.

Time Value of Money – The value placed on a present stock of wealth, income, or costs, compared to a future amount.

Transactions Costs – The various fees, costs, or obstacles that arise in the facilitation of trade or a transaction.

Vertical Integration – The inclusion in a corporation's production process of upstream suppliers to the production process and/or downstream markets of the corporate product.

Weighted Average Cost of Capital – An average cost of the various types of debt and equity financing employed or employable by a firm, and adjusted for their various tax treatments.

Notes

1 Introduction

1. Thomas Philippon, "The Cost of the U.S. Finance Industry: A Puzzle?", http://www.newyorkfed.org/research/conference/2011/NYAMP/Fed_Philippon_v1.pdf, accessed May 25, 2014.
2. Adam Smith, *An Inquiry into the Nature and Causes of the Wealth of Nations*, London: W. Strahan and T. Cadell, Publishers, 1776.
3. Frank H. Knight, *Risk, Uncertainty, and Profit*, New York: Hart, Schaffner, and Marx; Houghton, Mifflin Co., 1921.
4. John Maynard Keynes, *The General Theory of Employment, Interest and Money*, London and New York: Harcourt, Brace and Company, 1936. First Published by Macmillan and Cambridge University Press, for the Royal Economic Society in 1936.
5. Ronald H. Coase, "The Problem of Social Cost", *Journal of Law and Economics*, Vol. 3, 1960, pp. 1–44.

3 The Early Life of John Burr Williams

1. Milton Lomask, *Aaron Burr*, Volume 1, New York, 1979, 1983.
2. Thomas Fleming, *Duel: Alexander Hamilton, Aaron Burr, and the Future of America*, New York: Basic Books, 1999.
3. G. Reid MacKay, *Cyclopedia of Insurance in the United States*, vol. 73, New York: R. B., Caverly, Publisher, 1919, pp. 604.
4. https://en.wikipedia.org/wiki/Ivar_Kreuger#End_of_the_Kreuger_empire_and_death, accessed March 29, 2014.
5. John Burr Williams, *Fifty Years of Investment Analysis: A Retrospective*, Charlottesville, VA: The Financial Analysts Research Foundation, 1979.

4 The Times

1. Joe Carlen, "How Benjamin Graham Revolutionized Shareholder Activism," *Bloomberg View*, May 17, 2013, http://www.bloombergview.com/articles/2013-05-17/how-benjamin-graham-revolutionized-shareholder-activism, accessed March 31, 2014.
2. Benjamin Graham and Jason Zweig, *The Intelligent Investor*, 4th edn, HarperCollins, 2003, pp. 18.
3. Keynes, *The General Theory of Employment, Interest and Money*, chapter 12.
4. Ibid.
5. Alice Schroeder, *The Snowball: Warren Buffett and the Business of Life*, New York: Bantam Books, 2008.

6. Ben Graham, "Book Review of The Theory of Investment Value by John Burr Williams, Harvard University Press, Cambridge, 1938", *Journal of Political Economy*, vol. 47, No. 2, Apr. 1939, pp. 276–7.

5 The Theory – A New Finance Paradigm

1. John Burr Williams, *The Theory of Investment Value*, Cambridge, MA: Harvard University Press, 1938, as found in reprint by The Fraser Press, 1977, pp. 72–3.
2. Ibid. at 73.

6 Legacy and Later Life

1. Jack L. Treynor and Fischer Black (1976) "Corporate Investment Decisions", in Stewart C. Myers (ed.), *Modern Developments in Financial Management*, New York: Praeger, pp. 310–27.
2. John Burr Williams, "The Path to Equilibrium," *The Quarterly Journal of Economics*, Vol. 81, No. 2, May, 1967, pp. 241–55.
3. John Burr Williams, *Interest, Growth & Inflation*, Fraser Publishing Co., December 20, 1998.

7 The Early Years of Franco Modigliani

1. http://articles.latimes.com/1987-07-25/local/me-1049_1_sephardic-jews, retrieved March 17, 2014.
2. https://en.wikipedia.org/wiki/Amedeo_Modigliani#Family_and_early_life, retrieved March 17, 2014.
3. https://en.wikipedia.org/wiki/Amedeo_Modigliani#Family_and_early_life, retrieved March 17, 2014.
4. Modigliani, p. 6.
5. Modigliani, p. 7.
6. Modigliani, p. 11.
7. Franco Modigliani, "Liquidity Preference and the Theory of Interest and Money," *Econometrica*, vol. 12, no. 1, January 1944.
8. William A. Barnett and Robert Solow, "An Interview with Franco Modigliani," *Macroeconomic Dynamics*, Vol. 4, 2000, pp. 222–56.
9. Modigliani, p. 68.

8 The Early Years of Merton Miller

1. http://en.wikipedia.org/wiki/Ethical_movement, retrieved March 2, 2014.

9 The Times

1. Williams, *The Theory of Investment Value*, pp. 72–3.
2. Ibid. at 73.

10 The Great Idea

1. Andrew Carnegie, *The Gospel of Wealth and Other Timely Essays*, New York: The Century Co., 1901.
2. F. Modigliani and M. Miller, "The Cost of Capital, Corporation Finance and the Theory of Investment," *American Economic Review*, vol. 48, no. 3. 261–97.
3. Merton H. Miller, *Financial Innovations and Market Volatility*, New York: Wiley.
4. F. Modigliani and M. Miller, "The Cost of Capital, Corporation Finance and the Theory of Investment," p. 271, footnote 13.
5. F. Modigliani and M. Miller, "Corporate Income Taxes and the Cost of Capital: a Correction", *American Economic Review* 53 (3), 1963, pp. 433–43.

12 The Prize

1. Kenneth J. Arrow, T. Harris, and J. Marschak, "Optimal Inventory Policy," *Econometrica*, 1951.
2. Modigliani, 2001, p. 110.

13 The Later Years of Merton Miller

1. http://www.nobelprize.org/nobel_prizes/economic-sciences/laureates/1990/press.html, accessed May 31, 2014.
2. Merton Miller, *Merton Miller on Derivatives*, New York: Wiley, 1997.
3. http://www-news.uchicago.edu/releases/00/000603.miller.shtml, accessed May 31, 2014.
4. http://www-news.uchicago.edu/releases/00/000603.miller.shtml, accessed May 31, 2014.

14 The Later Years of Franco Modigliani

1. Francesco Giavazzi, "Professor Franco Modigliani: Nobel Memorial Prizewinning economist and author of the 'life-cycle theory of spending'," *The Independent*, September 29, 2003, http://www.independent.co.uk/news/obituaries/professor-franco-modigliani-548827.html, accessed December 14, 2010.
2. *Economist*, October 4, 2003.
3. Louis Uchitelle, "Franco Modigliani, Nobel-Winning Economist, Dies at 85," *New York Times*, September 26, 2003, http://www.nytimes.com/2003/09/26/business/franco-modigliani-nobel-winning-economist-dies-at-85.html, accessed December 14, 2010.

15 The Early Life of Ronald Harold Coase

1. Abdullahi, Ali Arazeem and Bashir Salawu, "Ibn Khaldun: A Forgotten Sociologist?", *South African Review of Sociology* 43(3), 2012, pp. 24–40.
2. Adam Smith, *An Inquiry into the Nature and Causes of the Wealth of Nations*, London: W. Strahan and T. Cadell, Publishers, 1776., Book 1, Chapter 1.

3. http://www.surnamedb.com/Surname/Coase#ixzz2vDd0JhoZ, accessed March 6, 2014.
4. Ronald Coase, "The Nature of the Firm," *Economica*, 4(16), pp. 386–405.

16 The Times and the Theory

1. Ronald H. Coase, "The Problem of Social Cost," *Journal of Law and Economics*, 3, 1960, pp. 1–44.
2. Coase, "The Nature of the Firm," p. 338.
3. D.H. Robertson, *The Control of Industry*, New York: Harcourt, Brace and Company, 1923, p. 85.
4. Coase, "The Nature of the Firm," p. 388.

17 Life and Legacy

1. Garrett Harden, "The Tragedy of the Commons," *Science* 162, 1968, pp. 1243–8.
2. R.H. Coase, "Durability and Monopoly," *Journal of Law and Economics*, vol. 15, no. 1, 1972, pp. 143–9.
3. R.H. Coase, "The Lighthouse in Economics," *Journal of Law and Economics*, 17, 1974, pp. 357–76.
4. http://www.nobelprize.org/nobel_prizes/economic-sciences/laureates/1991/coase-facts.html, accessed May 17, 2014.
5. Ronald Coase, "The Institutional Structure of Production." *American Economic Review* 82(4), 1992, pp. 713–19.

18 The Early Life of Oliver Eaton Williamson

1. http://en.wikipedia.org/wiki/Theophilus_Eaton, accessed March 9, 2014.
2. C.W. Bardeen, *History, Genealogical and Biographical, of the Eaton Families*, 1911, pp. 367.
3. http://archive.org/stream/reportofannualre06eato/reportofannualre06eato_djvu.txt, March 9, 2014.

19 The Times and the Theory

1. Oliver Williamson, "The Vertical Integration of Production: Market Failure Considerations", *The American Economic Review*, Vol. 61, No. 2, Papers and Proceedings of the Eighty-Third Annual Meeting of the American Economic Association, May, 1971, pp. 112–23.
2. Oliver Williamson, *Markets and Hierarchies: Analysis and Antitrust Implications*, New York: Free Press, 1975.
3. Oliver Williamson, "Transaction-Cost Economics: The Governance of Contractual Relations," *Journal of Law and Economics*, 22(2), 1979, pp. 233–61.
4. http://www.nobelprize.org/nobel_prizes/economic-sciences/laureates/2009/williamson-facts.html, accessed May 17, 2014.

21 Life and Legacy of Ronald Coase

1. http://www.nobelprize.org/nobel_prizes/economic-sciences/laureates/1991/coase-facts.html, accessed May 30, 2014.
2. Ronald Coase, "The Conduct of Economics: The Example of Fisher Body and General Motors," *Journal of Economics & Management Strategy*, vol. 15, no. 2, 2006, pp. 255–78.
3. Coase, Ronald, and Ning Wang, *How China Became Capitalist*, New York: Palgrave Macmillan, 2013.

22 Life and Legacy of Oliver Williamson

1. Williamson, *Markets and Hierarchies*, p. 31.
2. Oliver Williamson, "Credible Commitments: Using Hostages to Support Exchange," *American Economic Review*, 1983, pp. 519–40.
3. Oliver Williamson, "Comparative Economic Organization: the Analysis of Discrete Structural Alternatives," *Administrative Science Quarterly*, vol. 36, no. 2, 1991, pp. 269–96.
4. Oliver Williamson, *The Economic Institutions of Capitalism*, New York: Free Press, 1985.
5. Oliver Williamson, "Corporate Finance and Corporate Governance," *The Journal of Finance*, vol. 43, no. 3, 1988, pp. 567–91.
6. Oliver Williamson, "Corporate Boards of Directors: in Principle and in Practice," *Journal of Law, Economics, and Organization*, vol. 24, no. 2, 2008, pp. 247–72.
7. http://www.nobelprize.org/nobel_prizes/economic-sciences/laureates/2009/williamson-facts.html, accessed May 30, 2014.

23 Alchian and Demsetz

1. http://en.wikipedia.org/wiki/Armenia, retrieved March 12, 2014.
2. http://www.legacy.com/obituaries/latimes/obituary.aspx?pid=163245781, retrieved March 12, 2014.
3. John L. Lott, *Uncertainty and Economic Evolution: Essays in Honour of Armen Alchian*, London: Routledge Press, 2005.

24 Harold Demsetz

1. Harold Demsetz, *Ownership Control and the Firm*, vol. 1, Basil Blackwell, Cambridge, MA, 1988, p. 8.

25 The Times

1. A.A. Berle and G. C. Means, *The Modern Corporation and Private Property*, London: Macmillan Publishers, 1932.
2. Ibid. at 355.
3. Ibid. at 301.

26 The Great Idea

1. Armen Alchian and Harold Demsetz, "Production, Information Costs, and Economic Organization," *American Economic Review,* vol. 62, December, 1972, pp. 777–95.
2. Milton Friedman, "The Social Responsibility of Business is to Increase its Profits," *The New York Times Magazine*, September 13, 1970.
3. B. Holmström, "Moral Hazard and Observability," *Bell Journal of Economics*, 1979, pp. 74–91; G. Hardin "The Tragedy of the Commons," *Science*, vol. 162, no. 3859, pp. 1243–8.
4. Hardin, "The Tragedy of the Commons."

28 Harold Demsetz Later in Life

1. http://www.hoover.org/about/mission-statement, accessed March 30, 2014.
2. Harold Demsetz, *Ownership, Control, and the Firm: the Organization of Economic Activity*, vol. 1, Cambridge, MA: Basil Blackwell, 1988, p. 6.
3. Ibid., pp. 282–3.

29 The Later Years of Armen Alchian

1. http://www.nobelprize.org/nobel_prizes/economic-sciences/laureates/1990/sharpe-bio.html, accessed May 24, 2014.
2. http://truthonthemarket.com/2010/10/08/nobel-speculation-time/, accessed May 24, 2014.

30 The Early Years of Michael Cole Jensen

1. Robert Charles Anderson, *The Great Migration Begins, Immigrants to New England, 1620–1633*, vol. 1, A–F, New England Historical Genealogical Society, January 1, 1966, p. 495.
2. Ibid. at 496.
3. http://familytreemaker.genealogy.com/users/d/e/n/Tim-(1985), The Economic Institutions of Capitalism, new York: Free Press.Dennison/WEBSITE-0001/UHP-0957.html, retrieved February 24, 2014.
4. http://continentalnavy.com/archives/2011/rev-mr-john-watkins-chaplain/, retrieved February 24, 2014.
5. http://history.rays-place.com/ny/lewisville-ny.htm, retrieved February 25, 2014.

31 The Early Years of William Henry Meckling

1. http://dgmweb.net/FGS/E/ElyWilliamBrown-_-MaryFrancesPotter.html, retrieved February 28, 2014.
2. http://www.usgennet.org/usa/ne/topic/resources/OLLibrary/Nebraskana/pages/nbka0102.htm, retrieved February 28, 2014.

3. Armen Alchian, "Reminiscences of Errors – A Tribute in Honor of Dean William H. Meckling on his Retirement," *The Collected Works of Armen Alchian*, vol. II, Indianapolis: Liberty Fund, 1976.
4. Armen Alchian, "Reminiscences of Errors – A Tribute in Honor of Dean William H. Meckling on his Retirement," *The Collected Works of Armen Alchian*, vol. II, Liberty Fund, Indianapolis, 1976.

32 The Times

1. Milton Friedman, "The Social Responsibility of Business is to Increase its Profits," *The New York Times Magazine*, September 13, 1970.
2. William F. Sharpe, "Capital Asset Prices: a Theory of Market Equilibrium Under Conditions of Risk*," *The journal of finance*, vol. 19, no. 3, 1964, pp. 425–42.
3. Ralph Walking, "An Interview with Michael C. Jensen," *Pioneers in Finance Series in the Journal of Applied Finance*, Issue 2, 2010, p. 3.
4. Eugene F. Fama and Merton H. Miller, *The Theory of Finance*, New York: Holt, Rinehart and Winston, 1972.

33 The Theory

1. Michael C. Jensen and William Meckling, "Theory of the Firm: Managerial Behavior, Agency Costs and Ownership Structure," *Journal of Financial Economics*, vol. 3, 1976, pp. 305–60.
2. Adam Smith, *The Wealth of Nations*, 1776, Cannan Edition, New York: Modern Library, 1937.
3. Stephen Ross, "The Economic Theory of Agency: The Principal's Problem," *American Economic Review,* vol. 63, no. 2, 1973, pp. 134–9.
4. B.M. Mitnick, "Fiduciary Rationality and Public Policy: the Theory of Agency and Some Consequences," Paper presented at the 1973 Annual Meeting of the American Political Science Association. Proceedings of the APSA, 1973.
5. Jensen and Meckling, "Theory of the Firm," pp. 7.
6. Modigliani and Miller, "Corporate Income Taxes and the Cost of Capital," p. 442.

34 Applications and Extensions

1. Michael Jensen and Kevin Murphy, "CEO Incentives: It's Not How Much You Pay," in Foundations of Organizational Strategy, Harvard University Press, 1998; *Harvard Business Review*, no. 3, May–June 1990.
2. Brian Hall and Kevin Murphy, "The Trouble with Stock Options," NBER Working Paper 9784, June 2003.

Index

GPSR Compliance
The European Union's (EU) General Product Safety Regulation (GPSR) is a set of rules that requires consumer products to be safe and our obligations to ensure this.

If you have any concerns about our products, you can contact us on

ProductSafety@springernature.com

In case Publisher is established outside the EU, the EU authorized representative is:

Springer Nature Customer Service Center GmbH
Europaplatz 3
69115 Heidelberg, Germany

www.ingramcontent.com/pod-product-compliance
Lightning Source LLC
Chambersburg PA
CBHW060750150926
51501CB00004B/142
* 9 7 8 1 1 3 7 3 4 1 2 7 3 *